GW00702253

APHASIA THERAPY: HISTORICAL AND CONTEMPORARY ISSUES

Lawrence Erlbaum Associates Ltd., Publishers
27 Palmeira Mansions
Church Road,
Hove,
East Sussex BN3 2FA, U.K.

British Library Cataloguing in Publication Data

Howard, David
  Aphasia therapy: historical and
  contemporary issues.
  1. Aphasia—Treatment
  I. Title II. Hatfield, Frances M.
  616.85′5206   RC425
  ISBN 0-86377-063-0
  ISBN 0-86377-066-5 Pbk

Typeset by Spire Print Services Ltd., Salisbury
Printed by A. Wheaton & Co. Ltd., Exeter.

APHASIA THERAPY: HISTORICAL AND CONTEMPORARY ISSUES

David Howard
*Psychology Department, University College, London
and
Speech Therapy Department, Regional Neurological Unit,
Homerton Hospital, Hackney, London*

and

Frances M. Hatfield
*MRC Applied Psychology Unit, Chaucer Road, Cambridge
and formerly
Speech Therapy Department, Addenbrooke's Hospital, Cambridge*

LAWRENCE ERLBAUM ASSOCIATES, PUBLISHERS
Hove and London (UK)   Hillsdale (USA)

List of Figures

Contents

Preface

Our views have always been developed from ideas and concepts gleaned from our teachers, collaborators, colleagues and friends; to that extent we do not claim any great originality in the content of this book. We are grateful to all those who have discussed these issues with us, wittingly or unwittingly. In particular we would like to thank Edna Butfield, Brian Butterworth, Margaret Elvin, Sue Franklin, Eirian Jones, J-L Signoret, and Oliver Zangwill. Some, more long suffering, friends read and commented on sections of the manuscript at various stages of production; we wish to thank John Morton, Sally Byng, Ruth Lesser, John Marshall, and Karalyn Patterson.

We are grateful to the librarians, at a number of libraries, who have helped us to get hold of literature, which was sometimes obscure and hard to find; we thank particularly the librarians at the Royal Society of Medicine, and the University Library in Cambridge. We also thank John Fletcher for typing the manuscript into the word processor. And we are very grateful to the many friends who have tolerated our enthusiasms for crocodile grease and Vichy water, and those who have explained to us the effects of leeches or bread poultices.

Finally we want to express our debt to the aphasic patients whom we have known and treated. They have taught us more than they may know. We hope that this book will, to some extent, repay that debt.

D. H.
F. M. H.
October 1986

Frances Hatfield died while this book was in the process of production. In 33 years working as an aphasia therapist, she had travelled to many countries in Europe and North America, teaching and learning about aphasia therapy. She had unrivalled knowledge of the nineteenth century and earlier literature in aphasia treatment. Without her extraordinary range and depth of knowledge, this book would not have been possible. Frances Hatfield deeply believed in international friendship and co-operation; she would be very pleased if this book broadened knowledge of aphasia treatment in other countries and at other times.

D. H.
January 1987

Introduction

When a person becomes **aphasic** after some kind of damage to the brain, communication becomes a problem. It is a problem not only for the aphasic person, but also for their family, friends, employers, and work colleagues. The obvious way to deal with this problem is by re-education; by some means or other to help the aphasic person to relearn, or regain access to their language. Without doubt, for many centuries, friends and family have rallied round to attempt this process of rehabilitation; ultimately, aphasia is a problem that *demands* a response.

More recently the re-education of aphasic people has become a professional concern. In the nineteenth century it was mostly doctors, particularly neurologists, who were involved. At that point few patients would survive a stroke or severe head injury for any length of time; as a result the number of aphasic patients was limited. The two World Wars were the impetus for dramatic changes in aphasia treatment. With improved military medical services, and particularly the development of front line casualty clearing stations, astonishing numbers of young men with serious brain injuries survived, many of whom were to some extent aphasic. The large scale development of neuropsychological rehabilitation services for brain damaged soldiers, in Germany during and after the First World War, and in the Soviet Union and the United States after the Second World War, laid the foundations for the establishment of treatment services for civilians who became aphasic.

There are probably more aphasic people alive today than ever before. Increasing survival rates after cerebrovascular accidents and severe head injuries mean that there are more people with language disabilities who might benefit from aphasia therapy.

There are almost certainly more aphasia therapists practising today than ever before. In the years since the Second World War there has been an extraordinary expansion in the provision of therapy services. In practice, therapists are drawn from a wide variety of disciplines: in different countries, and in different ways, neurologists, psychologists, linguists, psychiatrists, speech therapists, and other groups have been involved in attempts to provide language rehabilitation for people with acquired

1

aphasia. We will, in this book, use the term "aphasia therapist" to describe anyone, irrespective of their professional background, who is involved in the treatment of people with acquired aphasia. In Europe and North America aphasia therapy services are now sufficiently well-developed to provide more-or-less systematic rehabilitation for a substantial (but unknown) proportion of aphasic people.

Not only is there extraordinary variety in the professions involved in aphasia treatment, but also in the content of treatment and the way it is delivered. This book is not primarily concerned with the management issues involved in aphasia therapy: for example, whether treatment should be intensive or spaced; whether it should begin soon after onset, or delayed until some later point; whether patients should be treated at home or in clinics; whether treatment needs to be face-to-face or whether telephones provide a viable substitute; whether patients should be treated in groups or individually. Nor is this book concerned with the non-linguistic and psycho-therapeutic aspects of aphasia therapy. Thus we exclude issues like the experience of loss of language; learning to cope with being disabled; the effects of a language disability on relationships within a family or home; the sexual and physical disabilities that often accompany aphasia; and the difficulties for aphasic people in returning to employment. All of these are, of course, vital issues for almost all practising aphasia therapists; this book is deliberately confined to an examination of the *content* of treatment. It is an examination of the kinds of procedures that different therapists have adopted with the aim of improving the ability of aphasic patients to communicate.

With the expansion of numbers of therapists, there has been a corresponding increase in the range of approaches to aphasia therapy. Reading the aphasia literature can be a bewildering experience: one author will explain, with great conviction, that *this* is the correct treatment for a particular sort of patient. Another author, with equally persuasive conviction, will state that a different kind of treatment is correct. This book is intended to make sense of these contradictions: we identify the principal approaches to treatment that have been used in the past, and are in use today. In a book of this size we obviously cannot describe in detail all the individual techniques that have been used in treatment. Instead we examine the general nature of the approach of different therapists (or *schools* of therapists): the theories of the nature of aphasia and the treatment process that motivates the particular therapy techniques that they advocate. In Kuhn's (1962) terms we are trying to identify the different theoretical *paradigms* that make sense of the different approaches.

The first part of the book describes the approaches to treatment up until the Second World War. To divide past approaches to treatment from the development of modern schools, we have taken the year 1947. We chose this date because it was the year of the original publication of A. R. Luria's *Traumatic Aphasia* in Russian. In this Luria develops an approach that we believe to be the first truly modern aphasia therapy.

We devote the first part of the book to earlier approaches. Some readers may consider treatment of aphasia based on crocodile grease, venesection, or Spanish Flies to be historical curiosities of no interest to hard-headed modern exponents of scientifically-based aphasia therapy. This view is, we think, mistaken. First, understanding the history of therapy allows us to see much more clearly from where our modern approaches have developed. An outside appreciation of the theories of the past can help us to examine our more contemporary theories from a critical and more detached viewpoint. We must realise that "facts" that we now take to be self-evident truths were not self-evident to people in the past and probably will not be self-evident to people in the future. In a few hundred years' time, our modern approaches will probably appear quite as quaint and silly as the treatment of aphasia with lotions of crocodile grease and antelope milk in Pharaonic Egypt.

Secondly, understanding the past history of aphasia therapy may free us from the need to repeat old debates on different approaches to treatment, and the need to re-invent old treatment techniques. In this book we document in a little detail two examples of recapitulation of earlier approaches. Stimulation approaches to treatment were first developed before and during the First World War by Froment and Monod in France; essentially the same approach was (independently) re-invented by Wepman and Schuell in the United States after the Second World War. The use of singing and rhythmical abilities, which are relatively well-preserved for many patients, in treatment forms the basis of Melodic Intonation Therapy developed in the United States in the 1970s; but the use of closely-related treatments can be traced back as far as the beginning of the nineteenth century. Knowledge of our history can free us from the need to recapitulate it.

Thirdly, we wish to dispel an increasing ignorance of the history of aphasia therapy. We are constantly astonished by how parochial aphasia therapists have become. A recent article from the United States purporting to be a history of aphasia therapy manages to cite almost no non-American therapists, and claims that before 1900 treatment did not, for practical purposes, exist (Shewan, 1986). While we do not pretend to write a comprehensive history of aphasia therapy, we hope to demonstrate just how misleading and narrow this American viewpoint is. We aim to discuss the full range of conceptions of aphasia, and the approaches to treatment that have been adopted. If we ignore the breadth of our inheritance, we impoverish only ourselves and our generation.

In our survey of contemporary approaches to treatment we describe eight different schools. Each of these is a group of therapists who hold certain common assumptions about the process of therapy, and the nature of aphasia. Our delineation of different schools will inevitably be controversial; therapists within a school will hold both common assumptions, and yet differ at the more detailed level in techniques that they advocate. We try, therefore, both to emphasise the common assumptions that unite a school, and to mention any important differences between the various therapists using the approach. Our coverage of different schools is deliberately uneven; information about some schools—for example the stimulation and neo-classical approaches—is already easily and widely available in English. We have therefore opted to give rather more space to other approaches that are mainly described in languages other than English; or where the approach is still in its earlier stages of development, but nevertheless offers a perspective that, to us, appears to be important. We have tried to be comprehensive: our aim is to identify *all* the significant trends in aphasia re-education that have shaped current views of therapy.

Some readers may feel that we fail to do justice to their particular favourite approaches to treatment. We have been forced throughout to rely on the published works describing different treatment methods and, wherever possible, conversations with therapists who adopt these approaches. But published works will not reflect accurately the overall popularity of different approaches. We suspect, for example, that the didactic and stimulation schools still have many adherents, who choose not to write about their therapy. At all periods, the therapists who have published books and papers describing their treatment approaches will be a very small and biased sample of the whole community of working aphasia therapists.

In the final section we briefly review evidence on the effectiveness of aphasia therapy. The bitter debate of the last 10 years on this issue has done nothing to improve the process of treatment or the lot of the aphasic patient. Much of the evidence is drawn from clinical trials of aphasia therapy. These, we will argue, are based on a fundamental misunderstanding of the uses and assumptions of clinical trials. For more than a century we have had available unchallenged demonstrations that treatment *can* be beneficial for some aphasic patients. The fundamental problem remains that of identifying the specific techniques that will be effective treatment for particular problems with particular patients—or at least particular groups of patients. Clinical trials of therapy are not appropriate for answering this question.

Instead we argue that the effects of treatment should be assessed using approaches that do not make the (invalid) assumptions inherent in clinical trials. We briefly examine the methodology for studying the effects of treatment in single subjects, or using within-subject designs with small numbers of patients, and then review the better studies that have employed these approaches. As Coltheart (1983) points out, studies of treatment in aphasia that achieve methodological adequacy are extraordinarily rare; developments in the 1980s suggest that this may be beginning to change. Serious attempts are now being made to evaluate specific and motivated treatment methods with particular patients.

Many therapists remain extraordinarily reticent about the specific content of the treatment methods they use. One of the main reasons for this reticence lies, we feel, in the problem of relating theory to practice. Theoretically-motivated work from a variety of viewpoints has provided detailed analyses of the deficits underlying some aphasic patients' difficulties. Compared with these sophisticated analyses, many therapists' treatment techniques that are used in day-to-day practice *appear* too simple; they do not feel as if they do justice to the complexity of the problem. We suggest that this is because there is no explicit *metatheory* available that explicitly relates a deficit analysis to the *process* of treatment. The problem can, we believe, be broken down into a series of steps; it is a prerequisite for the development of specific and motivated therapy methods that the decisions taken at each of these steps should be conscious and explicit. Only if we know exactly *how* a particular treatment task is meant to affect *what* ability and *why* it does so, can therapy progress. The results of treatment can support or refute hypothetical answers to these questions; but, until these hypotheses are put to empirical test, we will have no means to improve our treatments.

Aphasia therapy employs an extraordinary number of technical terms of different kinds. This is because it has drawn ideas and vocabulary from medicine (especially neurology), psychology, and linguistics. The topic of aphasia has even been centrally involved in the major philosophical issues of the relationship between mind and brain. To make this text accessible to readers from related disciplines who are not professional aphasiologists, we have added a glossary where we provide a short definition or description of some technical terms. The first time that a word that is mentioned in the glossary appears in the text, it is printed in bold type.

Throughout the book we have referred to aphasic people as "patients." As vocabulary usually indicates a particular ideological perspective, we want to explain why we have used the term. The term "patient" is often taken to imply that the person is passive and is subject to a disease; this disease, which is somehow apart from the person, is then managed by professionals (usually doctors). Aphasia is not a technical problem that can be managed in this way. Language, and its use, penetrates to the heart of our personalities, our self-image; aphasia therapy, if it is to be successful, needs to involve the aphasic patient as an active, involved, and even controlling participant in the re-education process. So, by describing aphasics as "patients," we do not seek to imply that they can or should be passive in treatment; we use the term, however, to recognise that the aphasia is a consequence of physical brain damage, which is a medical problem.

This book is intended to be a comprehensive survey of approaches to treatment in aphasia. We do not, however, pretend to be neutral; this would neither be possible nor interesting. We describe different approaches and their rationales; where we think that these are ill-founded or illogical, we say so. There is no shortage of treatment methods to apply with aphasic patients; but there is a serious shortage of techniques with a well-thought out rationale and proven effectiveness. Our own preferences (and prejudices) will become obvious to the reader. At heart our thesis is that approaches to treatment should be evaluated on two different levels: first, the empirical demonstration that their methods are effective; and secondly, on the theoretical coherence of the ideas that provide the rationale for the approach. As Zangwill wrote shortly after the Second World War:

> No method of treatment is better than the principles on which it is based, and the search for principles should concern us no less than the immediate clinical situation. (Zangwill, 1947, p. 7)

Section 1
Aphasia Therapies of the Past

SOME THEORIES AND THERAPEUTICS BEFORE
THE NINETEENTH CENTURY

There is little general agreement even now in the 1980s on the most effective, the most logical, or even the most enjoyable way of undertaking the re-education of aphasic patients. The methods used depend ultimately on a conception of the nature of the impairment in aphasia and of the character of the therapeutic process. We will briefly trace the history of aphasia therapy through the centuries, both because it can clarify the relationship between theory and therapy and because many of our current methods are not as new as we may have thought. This will lead on to a critical survey of the main contemporary schools the next section.

The view that systematic language re-education can achieve little beyond morale boosting for patients with damage to certain areas of the brain is still held by a surprising number of neurologists in several countries (e.g., Hopkins, 1984). This position is not original; an early example of extreme pessimism is that of the ancient Egyptian surgeon-author of the Edwin Smith papyrus of around 2800 BC, who wrote ("Case 20"):

> Thou shouldst say concerning him: One having a wound in his temple, penetrating to the bone, (and) perforating his temporal bone; while he discharges blood from both his nostrils, he suffers with stiffness in his neck, (and) he is speechless. An ailment not to be treated. (Breasted translation, 1930, p. 286)

The last sentence would seem to mean that no treatment was offered at all, but the reader is relieved in reading on to find some prescription of palliatives: "Now when thou findest that man speechless, his relief shall be sitting; soften his head with grease, (and) pour milk into both his ears." (The grease, one is told, came from the fat of animals: gazelle fat and the grease of the serpent, the crocodile, and the hippopotamus.) The description and recommendations for Case 22 (p. 290), where there is 'a smash in his temple" (with fragments of bone visible in the interior of the ear), are very similar. In an ancient gloss some 500 years later the surgeon explains the archaic Egyptian word for speechless: "As for 'he is speechless,' it means that he is silent in sadness, without speaking . . . (p. 296)."

The author reveals some understanding of the brain's function, including the realisation that it controls movements of the body; he also mentions the importance of observing which side of the body has been injured. Breasted suggests that this shows "an astonishingly early discernment of localisation of function in the brain (Breasted, op.cit, p. xv)"; however, it is not clear that the Egyptian surgeon, Imhotep, understood this significance of his observations for modern readers. He was probably only an acute observer of his patient's condition.

At all times, past and indeed present, treatment of the consequences of brain damage has depended on the medical, surgical, and re-educational measures available, as well as the physician's conception of the character of the disorder. Imhotep, the reputed surgeon-author of the papyrus, clearly lacked the knowledge and facilities for treating a major cause of speechlessness—that is to say, a head wound—and for staving off early death; restoration of higher cortical functions would scarcely have been even an academic matter.

From the point of view of aphasia therapy the Hippocratic Corpus is disappointing to read. It is often unclear from the original text whether the speech disturbances described are of language, articulation, or voice, or a combination of these, and treatment is largely confined to primary symptoms. Head wounds are to be "plugged with a plaster of dough from fine barley meal, kneaded with vinegar and boiled, to make it as glutinous as possible (Hippocrates, *On Wounds in the Head*, XIV, Withington translation, 1968, p. 33)." This treatment may have had some real beneficial effect; bread dough poultices can encourage the growth of penicillium moulds that could have inhibited bacterial infection. The author here, like the author of the Edwin Smith papyrus, noticed the association of these disturbances with paralysis of the other side of the body. Most of the cases in the Hippocratic Corpus where loss of speech is mentioned are poorly described and it is impossible to be sure whether a true language disorder was present; the case most likely to be an aphasia in modern terms is Case XIII in *Epidemics 1*. A pregnant woman developed a fever, and on the third day:

> Pain in the neck and in the head and in the region of the right collar-bone. Quickly she lost her power of speech, the right arm was paralysed, with a convulsion after the manner of a **stroke**; completely delirious . . . Fourth day. Her speech was recovered but was indistinct; convulsions; . . . (Hippocrates, Epidemics I; Jones translation, 1923, p. 13)

By and large, lack of precision in specifying which aspect of speech was disturbed limits the scientific interest of the cases in the Hippocratic

FIG. 1. The first written description of aphasia: Case 19 in the Edwin Smith Surgical Papyrus, reputed to have been written by the surgeon Imhotep in about 2800 BC. The top half of the figure shows a copy, made in about 1800 BC, of the original papyrus; this is in hieratic script—a fast, cursive form of hieroglyphics. The bottom half is the hieratic text transcribed into the corresponding hieroglyphics. The fainter parts of the text were written in red in the original papyrus.

Corpus and many subsequent accounts up to the early nineteenth century. There is indeed still lack of agreement on the nature of certain types of aphasia: for instance, whether they are primarily motor or primarily linguistic (a point of utmost important for therapy), and it could be that our successors with a finer diagnosis will criticise us in turn for ambiguity in reporting.

Some further discussion of prevalent conceptions of aphasia in the long period 30 to 1800 AD is a necessary background for the accounts of different types of therapy that will follow. Over succeeding centuries two primary notions of the nature of aphasia recur: first, as a disorder of memory for words; and, second, as paralysis of the tongue. This dispute still continues, in a somewhat different form. Many observers have stressed the **mnestic** aspect of acquired speechlessness. Pliny the Elder allocates his best-known descriptions of anomia, alexia, and agraphia to the section in his writings on memory in general, although he does maintain that disease or injury may affect a "single field of memory" in some cases (e.g., *Natural History*, Book VII, XXIV, 88). Johann Schenck von Grafenberg of Strasbourg (1530–1598), author of *Observationes medicae de capite humano* (1585) and other medical works, was, according to Trousseau, one of the early physicians who appreciated the essential nature of aphasia: in other words, he agreed with Trousseau. Schenck von Grafenberg observed that the patient's tongue was frequently not paralysed and he attributed speech disturbance to abolition of the faculty of memory:

> I observed frequent cases after an **apoplectic** attack . . . there being certainly no paralysis of the tongue, but an inability to speak; the faculty of memory was abolished and no proffered words came to help. (Schenckius, 1644, p. 180; our translation)

Many other physicians had long realised that speech could be lost without paralysis of the tongue. Nevertheless, throughout the Middle Ages and at times afterwards, speech loss following cerebral lesions was often ascribed to this cause, even when, as is clear from the context, the tongue was perfectly mobile and it was the linguistic code that was defective. The treatment was commonly **cauteries** and **blisters** applied to the neck in the hope of thereby stimulating the tongue. (And see Castiglioni, 1947; Critchley, 1970; Soury, 1899).

Soury (1899) draws our attention to some relatively encouraging reports by two sixteenth century doctors, both of which mention a successful treatment, although surgical rather than **logopaedic**. Nicola Massa, a Paduan physician and specialist in syphilology, described the case of Marcus Goro, a young man who lost his speech after a severe halberd injury, resulting in a fracture of the skull and damage to the **meninges** and the brain substance as far as the base of the skull. When Massa was called in some eight days later, after other doctors had attempted some surgical treatment, he found the young man still speechless. Although the other surgeons had seen no bone fragment in the brain substance, Massa was convinced that part of the bone must still be lodged in the brain. He was able to extract the fragment of bone from the open wound with a delightfully happy outcome. The patient immediately began to speak, saying *"Ad Dei laudem, sum sanus!"* ("God be praised, I am cured!"), or possibly the equivalent in the vernacular (Massa, 1558, pp. 90 and 91). This drew great applause and admiration from the doctors, senators, and others in attendance.

The second of these physicians, Francisco Arceo, described the head injury of a workman who was struck on the head by a stone, resulting in a depressed fracture, which left the patient motionless and speechless for several days (Arcaeus, 1658). Arceo then replaced most of the bone fragments, noting that the meninges were inflamed. Three days later the patient began to speak and in due course recovered completely.

Ambroise Paré (ca. 1509–1590), perhaps the greatest surgeon of the Renaissance, made important contributions to the treatment of wounds, including wounds of the head, sustained on the battlefield (Paré, 1628, pp. 321, 337 ff). The invention of firearms had produced new types of battle wounds and posed the gravest problems to surgeons at the end of the Middle Ages and in the Renaissance period. Paré discovered during a campaign that the conventional treatment of cauterising wounds by pouring on boiling oil and water was dangerous and ineffective in addition to being exceedingly painful and distressing. Desiring to do something positive as well as refraining from the barbarous application of boiling oil, Paré, ever a humane surgeon, substituted a digestive made of the yolk of an egg, oil of roses, and turpentine. At least two of his cases of battlefield head injuries, in those precarious times, had a relatively good outcome. One was a servant (*lacquay*) of Goulaines, who suffered a rapier wound to the left parietal lobe, and although seeming well immediately afterwards developed a fever later "and lost his speech . . . (p. 372)." The patient was bled and clysterised (given an enema) and the wound was opened to remove some diseased bone, whereupon he made a good recovery. Another case concerned a page of the Marshall of Montjean, who suffered "deafness" as a result of a temporo-parietal lesion from a blow from a stone. Paré again administered a successful surgical treatment and the page was restored to health, although the "deafness" persisted (p. 375). It is not clear whether this was a true deafness or a genuinely aphasic difficulty in language comprehension. Paré mentions that patients with head wounds progressed better in Avignon than in Paris. Eldridge (1968), in her history of speech therapy, gives a lively account of the ministrations of this barber-surgeon to war casualties, but confines it to his treatment of injuries to the peripheral speech organs and certain ingenious prostheses and offers us little on aphasia therapy for head injuries. It is probable that the great majority of such patients died within a short time—presumably, "an ailment not to be treated . . .," in the phrase of the author of the Edwin Smith papyrus.

More interesting in terms of aphasia therapy, with welcome precision of details, are accounts of Pierre Chanet (1649), Johannes Schmidt (1624–1690) and Peter Rommel (1643–1703). A reference of Critchley's (1970) leads the interested reader to the original account by the Sieur Chanet (1649). Here Chanet describes how a relation of his, wounded at the siege of Hulst in the Low Countries, "forgot" all kinds of words and the letters of the alphabet, although he could still copy letters. It is of particular significance for speech therapists that he was reported as:

> Now learning to read and speak . . . and making progress . . . for he could do neither the one nor the other, and it is hoped that, his brain being now strengthened, he will have a general recollection of what he knew before he was wounded. (Chanet, 1649, p. 208; our translation)

FIG. 2.   Head wounds: the causes of traumatic aphasia in mediaeval Europe. From Jacopo Berengario da Carpi's 1535 book on fractures of the skull.

DE L'ESPRIT. 207

au mefme eftat qu'il eftoit auparauant,
dés auffi-toft qu'il eut reparé quelques-
vnes de fes pertes, & qu'il fe fut confolé
des autres. La ioye rendit aux Efprits la
clarté que la trifteffe leur auoit oftée , &
reffufcita dans la Memoire , les Efpeces
qui y eftoient comme mortes & enfeue-
lies.
Il y a des maladies qui font plus puif-
famment le mefme effet, en diffipant les
Efprits du ceruean : cela eft fi ordinaire,
qu'il n'eft pas befoin d'en aller chercher
des Hiftoires dans Thucydide. I'ay vn
parent qui eftant au fiege de Hulft, y fut
bleffé à la tefte, & y perdit la Memoire. Il
n'oublia pas feulement fon nom, comme
Meffala Coruinus ; mais encore toutes
fortes de paroles, iufques à ne connoiftre
plus aucune lettre de l'Alphabet. Il n'oublia pourtant point à efcrire: c'eft à dire que
lors qu'on luy donnoit vne exemple , &
qu'on luy faifoit figne de là copier, il s'en
acquittoit fort bien : Mais quand on luy
euft dit faites vn A, ou vn B. il ne l'euft fceu
faire, fi en mefme temps on ne luy euft mis
deuant les yeux: car lors il faifoit bien voir
qu'il auoit autrefois appris à écrire. Cela

208 DES FONCTIONS

me confirme en l'opinion que i'ay prouuée
en mon Traitté de la Connoiffance des
Animaux, où i'ay monftré que nous auons
des habitudes inherentes aux organes ex-
terieurs, & differentes des Idées de la Memoire. C'eft ce qui eft bien clair en celuy-
cy, qui ne fe feruant plus des Images de fa
Memoire, auoit neantmoins, conferué cette facilité de la main , qui eft neceffaire
pour bien écrire. Il apprend maintenant à
lire & à parler, & y auance plus, que s'il
n'auoit iamais fceu ni l'vn ni l'autre : & on
efpere que fon ceruean eftant fortifié , il
s'y fera vne Reminifcence generale de ce
qu'il a fceu auant fa bleffeure.
Il eft donc bien éuident, que la diffipa-
tion & l'obfcurité des Efprits, empefchent
la Reminifcéce: d'où l'on peut inferer, que
leur clarté & leur abondance, contribuënt
beaucoup à cette action. Nous en auons
encore d'autres preuues tirées de la facilité
que nous acquérons à rencontrer les Idées
de noftre Memoire, lors que l'efperance
& la ioye réueillent nos Efprits, & les ren-
dent plus lumineux qu'ils ne font d'ordinaire. En ces occafions, les Imaginations
les plus pefantes, deuiennent ingenieufes:
c'eft

FIG. 3. The first description of re-education in aphasia; Pierre Chanet's account of his relative's aphasia after a head wound at the Siege of Hulst.

Johannes Schmidt's description (1676) of the patient Nicolaus Cambier, left with **motor aphasia** and **dyslexia** following an apoplectic attack, which is also of unusual interest in the history of aphasia, was cited by Bernard (1885). Therapy on a broad front was instituted, entailing abundant venesection (blood-letting); stinging enemas "to stimulate the faculties of sleep"; application of various oils and essences to the head, neck, and nose; and, finally, by dint of all these and "by the goodness of God," the patient improved vastly, albeit still troubled by **dyslexia without dysgraphia**. This is one of the earliest references to a patient who had severely impaired reading with writing unaffected. In this case some re-education of the disturbed language function was evidently attempted, but "no teaching or guidance was successful in inculcating an understanding of letters in him" (*"nullis enim praeceptis, nulla manuductione literarum cognitio inculcari iterum poterat"*). With another **cerebrovascular** patient, Wilhelm Richter, remediation was more successful and Schmidt was able to reteach the alphabet in a short time. The patient then "combined them [the letters] and reached a level of perfection in his reading" (*". . . combinavit sicque ad perfectam lectionem pervenit"*). (Cited by Bernard, 1885, pp. 75, 76)

Peter Rommel (cited by Gans, 1914) described a patient with evident aphasia that he called "aphonia" (De aphonia rara, 1683). Here again the terminology is confusing: "aphonia," or "alalia" was often used to describe speechlessness from any cause from the time of Hippocrates down to the nineteenth century; the distinction between disorders of the voice and the articulators, and disorders of language was not reflected in any consistent use of terminology. Rommel describes how the lady (*"uxor Dn. H. Senatoris . . . Matrona honestissima, 52. annorum"*) had a right-sided paralysis and had lost all propositional speech after a mild apoplectic attack, but had retained some automatic and serial utterances. She could, for instance, still recite a few prayers and certain passages from the Bible, but only in the order habitual to her. Dr Rommel apparently tried to help her by giving her a few phrases of this kind to repeat (removed from the context), but this proved too much for the poor lady, who after a number of attempts reacted **catastrophically** and burst into tears. Rommel stresses that her memory and comprehension were excellent. She was able to read but without perfect comprehension. Rommel adds certain details about the patient's satisfactory state of health and finishes his graphic and well-observed case history on the cheering note that, as far as possible, she managed to lead a contented life (*"forte contenta vivit"*). (Observation XVI, Petri Rommelii, 1734, cited by Gans, 1914)

The Swedish observer Dalin (1708–1763) reported a case with a more favourable outcome. A 33-year old Swede had a sudden attack of disease resulting in a right-sided paralysis and complete loss of speech. Two years later he was still only able to produce the one word *yes*, but could sing certain hymns that he had learnt before his affliction, seemingly with good articulation of the words, with a little help given in starting. He could also, again with some help, recite familiar hymns but he had to declaim these "with a certain rhythm and a high-pitched shouting tone." (Case cited by Benton & Joynt, 1960) A transition in treatment from speech sung along with the therapist, through speech with exaggerated intonation and rhythm, towards more normal speech is the foundation of the modern approach of **Melodic Intonation Therapy**—MIT (Sparks, Helm, & Albert, 1974).

Here and there in the past medical literature we can find really well-described cases of loss of spoken and written language, but on the whole the period up to about 1770 is unrewarding as a serious scientific introduction to the treatment of aphasia, partly because, as has been mentioned, the symptom-complexes of aphasia remained poorly defined.

Benton and Joynt (1960) provide a summary of the work of Johann Gesner (1769), as well as referring to a number of other early observers of aphasia (see also Benton 1964, 1965). In the history of aphasia, Gesner represents a significant advance. While attributing language deficits following illness such as stroke to a specific impairment of verbal memory, he took pains to point out that they were not part of a general loss of memory, nor due to paralysis of the tongue, but that the defect reflected a breakdown in the ability to associate *images* or abstract ideas with their verbal symbols. This view distinguishes aphasia from both a disorder of thought or concept, and a disorder of speech production, and locates the problem in the association between concepts and their symbols; it anticipates the basic position of the **associationist** neurologists of the nineteenth century (e.g., Broca, Wernicke, etc.). Gesner supplies many important details of his cases, noting how, for instance, written language might be impaired; how reading might be differentially affected in the various languages mastered by a patient; and whether patients were aware of their defects. Finally, there is a note on the treatment of a patient whose tongue became paralysed. After:

> **Spanish flies** and **venesection** he began to speak again but used the same words to name various objects, words that seemed to come from a foreign language. (Benton & Joynt, 1960, pp. 213–214)

There are a number of other vivid accounts of aphasia before the nineteenth century (for example, Oberkonsistorialrat Spalding's self-observations in 1772, cited by Eliasberg, 1950), but little evidence of any systematic and motivated attempts at language re-education. The story of Dr Johnson's transitory episode of aphasia is well-known, as is his attempt at assessing his own mental state ("the integrity of my faculties") (Boswell, 1791, p. 257 in 1901 reprint; see Critchley, 1970). Two days after suffering a sudden loss of speech, he wrote to his friend, Mrs Thrale, describing first how he had felt reasonably well on the day preceding the illness, and then continuing:

> Thus I went to bed and in a short time waked and sat up, as has long been my custom, when I felt a confusion and indistinctness in my head, which lasted, I suppose, about half a minute. I was alarmed and prayed God, that however he might afflict my body, he would spare my understanding. This prayer, that I might try the integrity of my faculties, I made Latin verse. The lines were not very good, but I knew them not to be very good: I made them easily, and concluded myself to be unimpaired in my faculties. (Boswell, 1901, vol. 3, p. 257)

Shortly afterwards he was able to write a couple of notes or letters:

> I then wrote a card to Mr Allen . . . In penning this note, I had some difficulty; my hand, I know not how or why, made wrong letters . . . I have so far recovered my vocal powers, as to repeat the Lord's Prayer with no very imperfect articulation. My memory I hope, yet remains as it was! (p. 257)

During the acute phase of his illness, Johnson made some suggestions about his own treatment:

> I think that by a speedy application of stimulants much may be done. I question if a vomit, vigorous and rough, would not rouse the organs of speech to action ... (p. 257)

According to Critchley (1970), Johnson's doctor, one Heberden, came and prescribed a mixture of aromatic carbonate and aloes and ordered blisters to be applied to his head and throat (p. 76); these were made from a "formidable diffusion of **cantharides** from which Dr Heberden assures me that experience promises great effects."

Critchley (1970) argues that Johnson's disability was not simply an articulatory disorder but also an aphasic one, as shown by defects in his written language, although a dysarthric component was also present. According to Critchley, Dr Johnson's ready fatiguability of speech was probably due to a difficulty in word-finding as well as the vocal effort. Critchley (1970) comments on "the muddled state of medical ideas on aphasia which existed up to the end of the eighteenth century (p. 89)." At that time, he maintains, no distinction was made between aphasia proper and impairment of speech due to dementia or delirium, hysterical aphonia and mutism, various types of **dysarthria**, or faulty articulation. With rare exceptions like Johann Gesner, inability to speak was attributed to paralysis of the tongue, and as a result, treatment seems to have consisted mainly of the application of blisters and other remedies aimed at the peripheral organs of speech.

At this period, as in our own, therapies for aphasia were limited by, and determined by, the conceptions of the nature of the disorder. Our account has not been a comprehensive history of early aphasia therapy but comprises selected illustrations of some of the views of the disorder and related attempts to help those who were, in the words of an anonymous ancient Egyptian commentator, "silent in sadness."

PHILOSOPHICAL AND PSYCHOLOGICAL DISPUTES IN THE NINETEENTH CENTURY AND THEIR INFLUENCE ON APHASIA THERAPY

Compared with earlier writings, the nineteenth century literature on aphasia contains much more that is of immediate relevance to modern aphasia therapists. Much of the debate among those investigating aphasia in the nineteenth century revolved around the neuroanatomical issue of **localisation** of higher cortical functions, especially language. This clearly has a bearing on one's orientation towards recovery and therapy. At one extreme there were the antilocalisationists like Gratiolet (1861), who declared:

In a general way I believe like Monsiur Flourens that intelligence is unitary, that the brain is one and that it operates above all as a whole organ. (p. 78; our translation)

If, as Flourens (1824), Gratiolet (1861), and more recently Lashley (1950), have argued, there is a large measure of equipotentiality of cortical substance, the prospects for spontaneous recovery, aided perhaps by systematic treatment, would appear to be brighter than if the extreme opposite is the case, and discrete verbal skills have their material substrate in narrowly circumscribed areas of the cortex.

The main course of this passionate controversy has been described over and over again (see especially Young, 1970). At the beginning of the century, Gall incurred the displeasure of the Catholic Church by asserting that the mind was a material consequence of the brain. He attempted to draw up a list of mental faculties and to correlate these with specific parts of the brain; he attempted to assess how well-developed different areas were by external examination of the skull—the discipline of *phrenology*. The idea that specific mental functions can be located in specific parts of cortical tissue was central to the work of Broca, Wernicke, and Lichtheim, and the other physicians whose views on aphasia have had an astonishing influence on our modern thinking on the subject. In 1861, Broca claimed that the faculty of articulated language lay in the third convolution of the left frontal lobe. The debate on localisation continued throughout the nineteenth century, through to Pierre Marie's attempted debunking of the whole localisationist position when he claimed that:

The left third frontal convulation has no particular role to play in the function of language. (Marie, 1906, p. 241; our translation)

The effects of the debate were far-reaching. Probably none of us is as free of prejudice and influence of the *Zeitgeist* ("spirit of the age") as we would wish to believe. Nineteenth-century physicians were no exception and the controversy between localisationists and their opponents was bound up with political, ideological, and theological attitudes; specifically, the mechanist or materialist school versus the vitalist. The mechanists wanted to describe all observable phenomena, whether inanimate or animate, whether non-human or human, within a physicochemical framework; the vitalists resisted all attempts to locate the soul in any square centimetre of crude body tissue whatsoever. Thought and language, for the vitalists, represented two sides of the same metaphysical coin, both belonging to the insubstantial, spiritual category of which the soul was the centre. In somewhat the same way, in more recent times, **dialectical materialism** has exerted a powerful, quite explicit influence on the scientific activities of its adherents, whether in physics, chemistry, or the biological sciences (e.g., J. D. Bernal, A. R. Luria, and others); adherents of other contemporary philosophies have also incorporated their ideologies into their "scientific" work—perhaps without being so clearly conscious of the way in which their values have shaped their science. The vehement and colourful language quoted by Bernard, commenting on the writings of G. Dax, is revealing of the extent of feeling generated by this controversy. Bernard writes:

> The author promises us a spiritualist phrenology aimed to confound materialism and atheism, "disgusting utopias." (Bernard, 1885, p. 29; our translation)

Marshall (1982a) reminds us that Gall, who promulgated the doctrine, at that time heretical, that the brain was the organ of the mind and was susceptible to analysis by observation, was prohibited from lecturing by a decree of the Emperor of Austria, Franz I, and finally expelled from Vienna in 1805. In 1817 he was excommunicated by Pope Pius VII and his books were placed on the Index.

The localisationists in the nineteenth century were anxious to confirm wherever possible by autopsy that the faculty of speech had a specific seat in the cortex. Thus Bouillaud (1825), an influential figure in French medicine, much impressed by Gall's approach (although remaining sceptical) insisted that the faculty of speech was to be found in the anterior lobes of the brain. He was able to produce evidence from post-mortem examination of his own cases and those of his colleagues that spoken language loss was associated with lesions of the frontal lobes. He had his critics —Flourens and Gratiolet in particular denied that functions could be localised in this way. Following a discussion at a meeting of the Société d'Anthropologie de Paris in April 1861, Paul Broca, who was both a surgeon and an anthropologist, had the opportunity to examine a speechless patient, who died shortly afterwards, allowing Broca to conduct a post-mortem. On the basis of this, and a second case later that year, Broca declared that the seat of articulate language lay in the third frontal convolution of the left hemisphere. Thus he was able to demonstrate for the first time that there could be an association between a higher mental function and an identifiable part of the cerebral cortex, on one side of the brain. Broca's discovery was a part of the advent of a new "scientific doctrine" that was to sweep over France, Germany, and even England as the ideas of the earlier French Revolution had almost a century before. In the wake of Broca's revelations, more systematic attempts at retraining in language began to be made. Broca himself was involved in attempts at retraining. Since the disability was a consequence of damage to a small area of tissue in the left hemisphere, he wondered whether, with proper teaching, the corresponding area in the right hemisphere would be able to take over the damaged functions (Broca, 1865). Proper teaching, as with a child learning to speak, would entail lessons every day, every hour. With aphasic patients, "treating them with the indefatigable constancy of a mother teaching her child to speak" (p. 119, in 1965 reprint) it would be possible to reacquire language, even without restoring that part of their intelligence that had perished with a part of their brain. During his time at the Bicêtre (a hospital in Paris), Broca had an aphasic patient under his care, and he tried to spend a few minutes every day helping him with his speech. He claimed to have enlarged the patient's vocabulary quite considerably. Broca also worked on the patient's reading problem; initially he taught him letter names, and then to point to short nonsense syllables when Broca named them. But at the next stage, combining nonsense syllables, the patient failed completely. In these procedures, Broca seems to have been following the usual methods used in France at that time for teaching children to read. In general he saw the process of therapy as closely allied to the process of child language acquisition, although he acknowledged that "it is probable that the adult and the child will follow different procedures to attain the same end." He saw the time he had available to spend in treatment as grossly inadequate, in comparison with the time a child needs to spend in learning to speak:

What is the point of such short lessons? Could one believe that a child would make progress, if one only made him speak for a few minutes each day? And do not believe that in this regard the education of a child will be more difficult than the education of an adult; on the contrary it is much harder for an adult. There are certain things which one does not learn easily after a certain age. (Broca, 1865, p. 119, in 1965 reprint; our translation)

Broca's complaint of insufficient time for the process of treatment will be familiar to almost all therapists working today!

Armand Trousseau (1801–1867) counted himself among the localisationists, but his interest in human lives was even deeper than his interest in dead brains, as his detailed and vivid case histories testify. As will be shown, he was deeply concerned with his patients' rehabilitation. Trousseau was one of the earliest systematic investigators of aphasia, which he held to be a disorder of memory for words. His picturesque observations of aphasic patients date from the 1850s or earlier, and 19 cases (not all his) are reported in his three-volume opus, *Clinique Médicale de l'Hôtel-Dieu de Paris* (first published 1861). Aphasia in these cases was usually secondary to some other disease: syphilis, heart conditions, gout, **Bright's disease**, and "intemperate habits" (presumably alcoholism); in some cases there was a history of milder cerebral attacks preceding a major one. He carefully notes the occurrence of paralysis and the side affected; he also records concomitant disorders of reading and writing, but regards impairment of these two skills as signs of defect of intelligence rather than as part of the aphasic syndrome as they are most frequently viewed today. That aphasia could involve impairment in the comprehension of speech was not realised until Bastian (1869) and Wernicke (1874), and although Trousseau was interested in the degree to which non-verbal intellectual abilities were affected in aphasia, his evidence was drawn only from vague observations of the patient's ability to play cards or dominoes, his retained reading skill, or simply the look on his face.

Treatment was largely directed at the primary cause, for example, mercury and potassium iodide for syphilis and bleeding for **cerebral congestion**. In many of these cases complete recovery of speech and other symptoms is reported within a short time; bleeding is certainly likely to have caused short-term improvement in some patients with cerebral congestion (raised intracranial pressure). Thus Trousseau cites the physician Rostan, who recorded his own aphasic episode, with complete inability to speak, comprehend written material, or write. Rostan responded immediately to bleeding, a treatment he prescribed for himself on judicious autodiagnosis; he indicated the treatment by gesture to others in the family circle. The bleeding had scarcely been terminated when "several words returned immediately" (p. 627; our translation). Twelve hours later every modality of speech had returned to normal.

With the 60-year-old Bright's disease patient (whose condition, Trousseau claims, was aggravated by excessive consumption of **Vichy water**), a sudden complete loss of speech occurred during a game of whist, followed by loss of reading ability. The leeches that were obtained by the family doctor on the patient's return home were not sufficiently keen (". . . they bit slowly and with difficulty") and the patient's gestures of impatience were misunderstood. However, when three of the leeches eventually bestirred themselves and tackled the task, the patient's words began to return and he was then able to make clear (in halting speech) his wish for some more efficient leeches. A new team of leeches was procured from the chemist, whose efforts were straightaway so therapeutic that the patient was soon even able to describe in precise words his earlier frustration at having his gestures misunderstood. His speech was completely restored. (Trousseau 1864, p. 672 in 1882 edn.)

In some of the cases described by Trousseau where the aphasia persisted, attempts at re-education were evidently undertaken, in addition to the use of leeches and other measures deemed appropriate to the underlying cause and a thorough investigation of what the patients could say, repeat, write, and copy. This applied, for instance, to the 30-year-old patient Marcou, with his *left*-sided paralysis and aphasia, who was unable even to give his name at the hospital registration office, his speech being restricted to stereotypes and oaths, with **echolalia** and **perseveration**. Medical examination disclosed an **indurated chancre** (a syphilitic ulcer), for which treatment was given, producing some general improvement, although speech remained severely impaired. Trousseau writes: "In spite of months of lessons and effort, poor Marcou never remembers the word 'hair' and of his nightcap (*bonnet de coton*) can only say the last part, *de coton*, which he produces with real satisfaction (p. 680)."

The outcome for Marcou was nonetheless more favourable than for 32-year-old Adèle Ancelin, a patient with **chronic endocarditis**, a right **hemiplegia** and **total aphasia** of two years' duration before admission to the *Hôtel-Dieu*. Trousseau and his colleagues were unable to teach her to name simple objects, either in confrontation or in repetition. She was a little better at recitation of serial numbers. She often pretended to be reading a certain religious book but was noticed to be in fact always stuck on the same passage. The doctors, students at the hospital, nuns, servants, and even her companions all exerted themselves in her re-education for the whole year of her stay, but when she left the *Hôtel-Dieu* for the *Salpêtrière*, now three years since the onset of her aphasia, her speech had hardly returned at all. There are a number of other instances in Trousseau of attempts to help patients to regain words by repetition after a clinician. These two cases suffice to show that 100 years ago speechless patients were not being written off as demented or hopeless, that the doctors themselves were spending a considerable amount of time at the bedside encouraging patients to talk, and that the nursing staff and others in the immediate environment were all being gathered in to stimulate speech or help in some way.

The English neurologist, H. C. Bastian (1837–1915) is now a rather neglected figure in the history of aphasia. As Wernicke acknowledged in 1906, Bastian, in 1869, was the first person to observe that aphasic disorders were not confined to language production, but there could also be difficulty in comprehension; this anticipated Wernicke's observation of a similar case in 1874. Bastian's real significance for this survey comes from much later in his career. By the end of the nineteenth century, a number of well-known physicians and psychiatrists such as Bristowe, Kussmaul, Déjerine, Féré, Danyou, Grashey, Mills, and André-Thomas, were attempting some sort of rehabilitation of spoken language, principally on **direct speech-training** lines. In 1898, Bastian described therapy in considerable detail. Working as he did in the heyday of localisationism, Bastian was obsessed with a scheme of cortical "centres" that he integrated with Charcot's doctrine of different individual types of mental imagery

—visual, auditory, motor. He based his interpretations of normal functioning and of breakdown of the four major verbal skills on a psychoanatomical model that revolved round four postulated centres: a centre for glosso-kinaesthetic impressions (articulation); one for cheiro-kinaesthetic impressions (writing); an auditory word centre; and a visual word centre. These centres, he explains, are not absolutely separated topographically but are "diffuse but functionally unified nervous networks"; they are repositories of impressions and images, and the mental processes that they subserve operate according to associationist principles. They are located, respectively, in Broca's area (the posterior part of the left third frontal convolution in right-handed people); in a more vaguely demarcated area somewhere around the second frontal convolution; in the posterior part of the first temporal convolution; and in the angular gyrus and part of the supra-marginal gyrus. The word centres are connected by "subcortical commissural" fibres. The auditory word centre he considers the most important for the revival of words, and, therefore, for high-level thought for the great majority of individuals. It should be noted that Bastian, unlike Broadbent, Kussmaul, and Lichtheim, has no conceptual centre *per se*. Centres in the psychological sense were a direct development of the **Reflex Arc Theory** of Johannes Muller; the Reflex Theory in respect of voluntary behaviour was eventually whittled away and with it the notion of psychological centres, with the realisation that higher mental functions were much more complex than simple reflexes.

Bastian considers it of "extreme importance" for understanding different kinds of speech defect that we should know in what region of the cortex words "are principally recalled to mind during ordinary thought processes (p. 20)." For him, words are the symbols with which our thoughts are inextricably interwoven.

Bastian's **aphasia classification** depends on the regions of the brain that are damaged; specifically, which of the four centres, or which of the connecting commissures, is affected. This view is still favoured by Geschwind and his disciples, and, like them, Bastian found the actual processing performed by the centres, of less interest than identification of the locus of breakdown.

Destruction of the auditory word-centre would impair comprehension of speech and affect verbal expression, the latter impairment depending for its severity on the individual's type of mental imagery. Bastian's hypothesis is that both hemispheres are educated concurrently by the advent of similar sensory impressions on each of them, although in articulated speech the muscles seem to receive their incitations mainly from one hemisphere (i.e., the left in right-handed individuals; the right in left-handers). The minor hemisphere has a latent centre of each of the four functions. In this way, with destruction of the principal (left hemisphere) centre for expressive

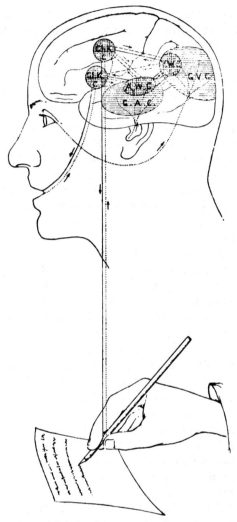

FIG. 4.   Bastian's language model: GAC = general auditory centre; AWC = auditory word centre;   GVC = general visual centre; VWC = visual word centre; ChKC = cheiro-kinaesthetic centre (for word writing); GlKC = glosso-kinaesthetic centre (for word articulation). This figure is identical with a diagram used by Charcot in 1888, apart from some trivial details. We assume that Bastian simply copied the diagram from Marié's (1888) report of Charcot's theory.

speech, recovery could take place through the intact left auditory word centre becoming more intimately connected with Broca's region on the right side or, less directly, by the left auditory word centre connecting with the right auditory word centre and thence with Broca's area on the right. In the case of agraphia, with the dominant (left) cheiro-kinaesthetic centre destroyed, the corresponding centre in the right hemisphere could be stimulated from the left visual word centre via the right visual centre. The act of writing with the left hand (necessitated by paralysis of the preferred hand) would in itself encourage the participation of the right visual centre and commissural fibres would gradually be formed between this centre and an embryonic cheiro-kinaesthetic centre in the minor hemisphere. This type of reconstruction of function, utilising the potentialities of the right hemisphere to take over higher functions, is the theoretical basis of Bastian's scheme of re-education.

Thus Bastian has a clearly defined theory underlying his scheme of language and speech rehabilitation. Unlike many of his predecessors, he also had a *detailed scheme of assessment* of speech disorders, linked to an examination of motor and sensory function of the limbs. Many of his suggested sub-tests are in use today, with slight modifications. He insists, for example, in his reading tests, that if a patient fails to read short words or letters one should examine whether he is helped by finger tracing.

Bastian is considerably more optimistic than the surgeons and physicians of antiquity about the outcome of an aphasia. He postulates two types of possible recovery: *functional restitution* (a type of "spontaneous recovery"), following amelioration of the primary cause; and *functional compensation*, brought about by the undamaged hemisphere gradually taking on new, or developing latent, functions. He considers that in spite of medical intervention, most improvements are due to functional compensation. A degree of ambidexterity is favourable for prognosis. Age is probably important, but Bastian refuses to dogmatise about this, reflecting:

> We have every reason for believing that plasticity of the nervous system is greatest in childhood, though it continues to a diminished extent well on into adult life, and is present still, for varying periods, even beyond middle age. This receptivity of the brain for new knowledge varies much, however, as we all know, in different individuals. The mental activity of some persons comparatively early moves in set grooves; while in others well on into a ripe old age a marked receptivity is shown, with interest in and power of acquiring new knowledge. (p. 342)

Bastian's re-education for aphasia makes use of methods originally evolved for teaching the deaf and dumb and also used widely with children suffering from severely delayed speech and language but having normal or near normal hearing. The most informative account of the system he favours is his summary of a case of Bristowe's (1880). The patient concerned may have been more dysarthric than aphasic, but Bastian categorically states that the method must be used for "all cases of **aphemia** and aphasia." (He may have intended to exclude the **amnesic** form.)

He [Bristowe] first got the patient to sound a laryngeal note, subsequently ... showing him how to modify the shape and size of the oral passage and aperture; and getting him to ... utter ... certain of the more simple and obvious vowel sounds ... At his next lesson he set to work to teach him the labials, and ... subsequently ... the lingual and guttural consonantal sounds; and thus in the course of four or five lessons, principally by making the patient watch the movements of his [Dr Bristowe's] lips, he regained the power of articulating all the simple vowel and consonantal sounds. He then began to teach him to combine letters, and eventually succeeded in making him talk well, ... the sister of the ward and nurses, and more especially three or four intelligent patients who were friendly with him and interested in his progress, giving him constant assistance. (p. 346)

It is not easy to see how the Bristowe method was expected to stimulate the centre for expressive speech in the right hemisphere. There seems no reason to assume that, when a patient repeats in this way, new centres in the right hemisphere will be involved.

There must have been an even greater exchange of ideas and methods in Europe than today, for all our plethora of conferences and symposia, and it is interesting to read that Dr Bristowe's "full oral method" had quickly spread to the *Salpêtrière* in Paris (once described as "the greatest neurological clinic of modern times"). Dr André-Thomas was treating a "typical case of aphasia", a woman of 34 who was trephined for a suspected brain abscess. This resulted in a right hemiplegia and complete aphasia. Five years later she entered the *Salpêtrière*, still only able to say *Yes* and *No*. She was unable to repeat words and could not read aloud, although she could understand a few common words in print. Dr Thomas applied the Bristowe method and taught her spelling and reading of the same syllables in the same way. The re-education period lasted six weeks. She was seen a few more times. A year later the patient could "reply without hesitation, and in words correctly pronounced to all questions put to her ..., she ... could make herself understood," although not yet framing sentences. She could repeat short sentences well, and could "read aloud correctly, pronouncing each syllable distinctly" and with improved understanding. Only in writing had she made no progress (p. 348).

This case is of especial interest in view of the length of time—five years—that had elapsed before the period of therapy, during which very little speech had been recovered by spontaneous restitution. A second dramatic case relates to a woman who had been aphasic for fifteen years before therapy was instituted, at which point she could still utter only three or four words. After a month of Bristowe treatment methodically carried out, she could repeat nearly all words without having to watch the teacher's mouth. She continued to improve without regular therapy and was later reported to pronounce many words spontaneously, although not a complete sentence. Understanding of written language had also improved. Not unreasonably, André-Thomas and Bastian both supposed that if similar treatment had been carried out within a few months of the onset of aphasia "the amelioration in the patient's condition might be very considerable (Bastian, 1898, p. 349)."

For the amnesic form of aphasia, Bastian prefers frequent stimulation of the "auditory word centre" by incitations to it from the visual word centre. Thus the elusive words might be written down for the patient to practice and the "superior performance in reading" used to compensate for difficulty in repetition as a means of improving word retrieval. **Word deafness** is treated by developing an auditory word centre in the right hemisphere. A modification of Bristowe's oral method is used, concentrating on vowels, then syllables, and finally words. Reading is incorporated where possible, to create a relationship between the left visual centre and the glosso-kinaesthetic area. Reading and writing disturbances are treated on the same principle of training appropriate centres in the right hemisphere. When developing a right visual centre for dyslexic patients by bringing it into functional relation with the intact left auditory word centre, the patient is treated "as though he were a young child learning to read for the first time (p. 353)."

Much of the treatment would not be considered applicable to aphasic patients today, although possibly to some types of dysarthria, and we would certainly quarrel with his insistence on treating an aphasic adult as a child, whether hearing or deaf. Certain of his techniques might, however, be adapted for specific purposes. The importance of Bastian to aphasia therapy lies in his having a clearly formulated theory (even if wrong) on which to base a system of re-education. A prototype of the localisationist school, and, psychologically, an associationist, he believed firmly in the possibility of transfer of function from one part of the dominant hemisphere to another and from the dominant hemisphere to the minor hemisphere.

The type of didactic training, or drilling, advocated by Bristowe and Bastian, working up from what were conceived as the simplest units of language, was shared by a number of physicians of the day—Goldscheider (1902), Wyllie (1894) and others. These men were also believers, like Bastian, in the possibility of re-educating new parts of the damaged hemisphere or of the minor hemisphere by stimulating verbal exercises. Many of these workers reported improvement in the patients they treated. With minor modifications in technique and a slightly different interpretation this was the approach widely favoured in several countries right up to the First World War and even beyond, both with vascular and traumatic patients.

For a time localisationism and associationism continued to flourish, in

France represented *par excellence* by Charcot, in Germany by Wernicke and Lichtheim (1885). Wernicke, partly under the influence of Finkelnburg, developed a more sophisticated analysis of language. Finkelnburg (1870), drawing on Kant, suggested that aphasia involved a general loss in the ability to use symbols—an "asymbolia"; this widened the concept of aphasia far beyond the field of language. Kussmaul (1876) found Finkelnburg's notion of asymbolia too wide and general and preferred the philologist Steinthal's (1871) term "asemia," which implied a disorder specifically of word concepts, thus confining the disorder to language alone. Kussmaul's classification included word deafness, **word blindness**, **paraphasia**, **agrammatism** or akataphasia (defects of morphology and syntax).

The effect on therapy of these rather broader views of the nature of aphasia—we have come quite a long way from Broca's aphemia (later renamed aphasia) that he defined as loss of the faculty of co-ordinating the movements necessary for articulate language—was disappointing in the short term. Aphasia therapy, for which there was growing enthusiasm, remained somewhat inflexible and lacking in insight. Those Germans who were most active in elaborating methods of aphasia therapy inherited a long tradition of philology and of systematic speech training evolved for other groups of subjects. Kussmaul's stimulating book *Die Stoerungen der Sprache* (1876) tackles a great range of problems of speech and language, as well as the psychology of normal speech and its acquisition and, finally, aphasia. Chapter 31 includes the topic of aphasia therapy. Kussmaul recommends first treating the primary causes, weakness, inanition, syphilis, saturnismus (lead poisoning), hysteria, cerebral congestion or inflammation. If medical measures to not alleviate the aphasia, he is confident that systematic speech training can be beneficial. The motor co-ordination of speech sounds or words must be "grasped in vision or verbal memory." This is consolidated by methodical practice of pronunciation of sounds, syllables, words, and sentences with attentive watching of the teacher's lips and face. The wording, such as *"methodischer Unterricht"* (methodical instruction), underlines that the whole approach is much more akin to speech training than most aphasia therapy practised today. For vocabulary work the most frequent words are singled out for training by repetition, and as words are "reacquired"—apparently almost wholly by dint of repetition and not in any context or as parts of sentences—so new ones are introduced. According to Kussmaul this was the method used by Broca, Trousseau, and Ramskill, and he asserts that this was effective in amelioration and even cure of the impairment. In the case of amnesic aphasia, the elusive words must be practised daily with a therapist, who first pronounces the whole word for repetition, or provides the initial syllable (clearly a form of phonological cueing) or letter. (When various writers refer to "letters" one is never sure whether letter-names or **phonemes** are intended—probably the latter—cf. Abercrombie, 1965.) This is combined with the use of dictionaries where patients can look up the meaning of words ("which they have forgotten"); it is assumed that they can read.

The nineteenth century saw the triumphant rise of an associationist neurology, which located psychological functions within different portions of the brain. With this came a specific approach to aphasia treatment where new centres and associations were to be developed in the other, undamaged hemisphere, by getting the patient to relearn language, in much the same way as a child did. Although at the end of the century the localisationist position was predominant, it was not without its critics. The English neurologist John Hughlings Jackson (1878, 1932) pointed out that observing that a particular deficit followed a lesion in a particular area did not necessarily mean that the (impaired) function was located in the (destroyed) tissue. He argued that the symptoms observed in a patient were not a consequence of the lesion, but a result of the concerted action of the unimpaired remainder of the brain. In consequence, Jackson saw higher mental functions, not as a function of discrete centres, but as a result of a set of interacting systems. By the end of the nineteenth century, he was one of few voices critical of the localisationist position, and his ideas had little impact. Only when his ideas were developed by his admirers including Pick (1913), Isserlin (1922), Goldstein (1948), and Head (1926) at the time of the First World War, did Jackson's critique begin to take effect.

TREATMENT OF APHASIA IN THE EARLY TWENTIETH CENTURY: THE RISE AND FALL OF SPEECH GYMNASTICS

By the end of the nineteenth century, the German-speaking world was playing a leading role in the development of speech therapy. Perello (1976) in his history of the International Association of Logopaedics and Phoniatrics reminds us that at the turn of the century the Austro-Hungarian Empire, and especially its capital city Vienna, was the medical capital of the world, Germany had close medical and scientific links with Austria, not only on account of the common language. Eldridge (1968) comments, furthermore, that "Germany and Austria were especially prolific in literature concerning the many varieties of speech and voice disorder before the First World War (p. 5)." This dominant role was to be lost under the Hitler regime, when most leading aphasiologists, for instance, Goldstein, Froeschels, Quadfasel, and Weigl, were forced to emigrate. After Hitler's death, and Germany's defeat in 1945, German neuropsychology slowly re-estabilished itself, until, as we shall see in our discussion of contemporary schools, in the 1970s the output of some centres marked them as some of the most active contemporary practitioners of aphasia research and therapy.

Clinics for correction of speech defects existed well before the beginning of our century in Germany and Austria. They were presided over by "phoniatrists," that is to say, medically qualified specialists with a basic ENT (Ear, Nose, and Throat) orientation, who treated the entire range of disorders of "human communication." This wide experience had advantages but also resulted in a tendency to apply methods, which had been found useful with children or the deaf, rather indiscriminately to aphasic adults.

The phoniatrist Hermann Gutzmann senior (1865–1922) directed a clinic for speech and voice disorders in Berlin towards the end of the nineteenth century, which attained worldwide fame. He had been working with aphasic patients (mainly vascular cases) since 1894 or earlier; he had also written a thesis on stuttering. By some he has been regarded as "the father of modern speech therapy," by others as the epitome of a particular orientation towards language re-education that found favour for a long period but is now as unfashionable as the Homburg hat. This is not to suggest that neither will be resuscitated at some future date. Hermann Gutzmann had no doubt inherited an interest in speech disorders from his father Albert Gutzmann, who was principal of the Berlin School for the Deaf before turning his attention to speech disorders in the hearing population.

The First World War prompted a more urgent look at what might be attempted in re-education for the increasing number of soldiers who survived head injuries from bullets or shrapnel in Germany and, of course, in other combatant countries. During the war Gutzmann maintained a centre in Berlin for battle casualties with speech and voice disorders and treated a whole range of organic and functional conditions. He took on teachers of the deaf and dumb as speech therapists in this clinic and pronounced them suitable; he did, however, give them extra training in treating aphasics.

The methods Gutzmann used in the war were based on a system he had elaborated nearly 20 years earlier with a different patient population consisting mostly of people who had become aphasic as a result of cerebrovascular accidents. His earlier paper (Gutzmann, 1896) contains details of five patients with motor aphasia and two with sensory aphasia, his treatment and its outcome. All the cases were fairly longstanding (6 months to 10 years post-onset) and neurologically stable. One example of these is a 40-year-old officer who had had a series of cerebrovascular accidents (possibily as a consequence of syphilis) and had been aphasic for 10 years; his speech was very indistinct and incorrect (*undeutlich, verschwommen und fehlerhaft*) and he so confused his words that he was unable to tell the horse-tram conductor that he wanted a 10-*pfennig* fare and simply had to hand over the money in silence (p. 355). After three months of Gutzmann's therapy in 1890, the officer was able to express himself so lucidly that even strangers could understand him immediately, and he "could perfectly well explain to the Droshky driver or horse-tram conductor where he wanted to go." Here one only has to substitute "answer the telephone" for "state one's journey to a horse-tram conductor" and one has the elements of an up-to-date **Functional Communication Profile** (FCP) (Taylor, 1965; see the pragmatic school in Section 2). Gutzmann admits that his patient's speech was not yet absolutely fluent. Two years later, during which time the officer had continued Gutzmann's exercises regularly, but without any personal contact, they met and the officer declared that his speech was so much improved that a stranger could hardly detect any residual language peculiarity. Gutzmann's own verdict was that he "was surprised that, after about two years, he had made quite extraordinary progress in his speech (p. 355)."

The other four motor aphasic patients, who received relatively short courses of therapy (between one and three months), all showed improvement, even if in limited aspects of language. The two sensory aphasics, with short-term memory problems in addition to receptive loss for single words and connected speech, also improved with two to three months' intensive therapy.

Gutzmann sees the importance of recording the time lapse between aphasia onset and initiation of therapy and it is interesting to find also in his later accounts (particularly during his war work) that a gap of several months or a year might ensue after the head injury or stroke. There is, for instance, the case of Offizier von U., wounded in September 1914, and left with a total aphasia that in the initial phase resolved only minimally, leaving dysarthria and dysphasia. The condition then remained static for eight months, when von U. was referred to Gutzmann, who gave him a short course of therapy and declared that "he improved greatly." That improvement was genuinely a result of Gutzmann's treatment and not due to **spontaneous recovery** gains in credence, because the treatment began some time after onset, and improvement followed a relatively short course of therapy (Gutzmann, 1916).

Since Gutzmann's re-educational system long remaind the pattern to be emulated both in German-speaking countries and the United States, it will be described in some detail.

Following Kussmaul's injunction, Gutzmann recommends for motor aphasics that speech movements should be visually apprehended and "fully remembered". Repetition of speech-sounds and whole words by the patient and close watching of the therapist's mouth movements figure prominently in the treatment. But for longstanding cases special systematic "drill" in the "elements of speech" has to be undertaken. Gutzmann maintains that we do not know which sounds are the easiest or most difficult for patients and suggests that we must be guided by the order of acquisition of speech sounds by children. He, like Bristowe 25 years before, begins with vowels and proceeds to plosive consonants and then fricatives, teaching those that are most clearly visible first. Later on simple consonant-vowel units are introduced. Some of this progression is fairly logical by our reasoning today, but his comment that the sound "M" is especially difficult is surprising. In 1941, the linguist Jakobson also suggested that aphasics should learn phonemes in a developmental order, but his order, in which / m / is one of the easiest phonemes, is derived from much more accurate observations of child development. Gutzmann advocates the use of a mirror for comparison of the patient's lip movements with the teacher's. Patients with right hemiplegia are taught early to write with the left hand, and writing reinforces articulation practice. Moreover, like Bastian and others, he believes that left-hand writing activities may stimulate right brain centres for speech-sound movements. For word-finding tasks he trains association of the visual perception of objects (or object pictures) with word movements, realising that a patient may be able to repeat a word but not retrieve the same word when asked to name an object. Much of the material he recommends is that originally designed for deaf and dumb children. We can hardly criticise this when the majority of therapists today are using much material not specifically designed for aphasic adults.

For receptive problems he again leant heavily on methods for teaching the deaf and dumb, demonstrating to the patients visible articulations of the speech sounds, especially consonants (Gutzmann, 1896), as well as of the most frequent words in the language. He observed that patients with auditory receptive loss might, after some re-education, sometimes be able to repeat a word correctly (by the lipreading technique) without grasping its meaning. To overcome this problem he resorted to the use of his so-called "phonetic script" developed earlier, an ingenious system of representing each phoneme by iconic diagrams of the position of the articulators. His total therapeutic plan also includes exercises in "memory training": he attributes a number of defects in articulation and comprehension to memory impairment. Finally he describes exercises for restoration of syntax, this time with methods used in schools for normal children.

One could quarrel with much in his approach—not a difficult feat nearly a century later—but he was at least systematic. One can, further, be struck by his many acute observations of patients. He noted, for example, how certain patients had difficulty in finding the generic name of objects (furniture, clothes, and so on); in this connection he quotes one of Neumann's patients who, when asked to write the German word for light (*Licht*)—a relatively "generic" word—wrote the more specific and con-

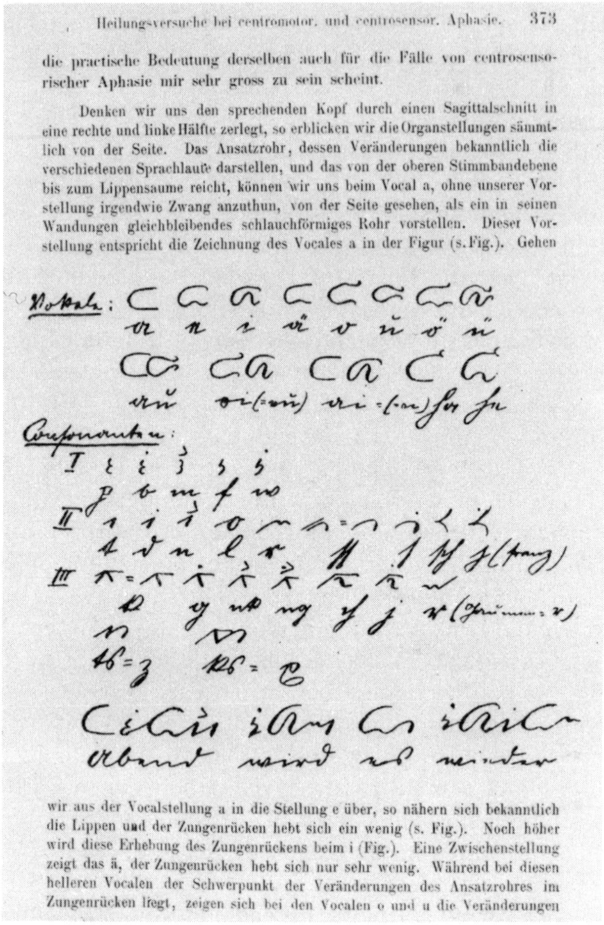
Heilungsversuche bei centromotor. und centrosensor. Aphasie. 373

die practische Bedeutung derselben auch für die Fälle von centrosensorischer Aphasie mir sehr gross zu sein scheint.

Denken wir uns den sprechenden Kopf durch einen Sagittalschnitt in eine rechte und linke Hälfte zerlegt, so erblicken wir die Organstellungen sämmtlich von der Seite. Das Ansatzrohr, dessen Veränderungen bekanntlich die verschiedenen Sprachlaute darstellen, und das von der oberen Stimmbandebene bis zum Lippensaume reicht, können wir uns beim Vocal a, ohne unserer Vorstellung irgendwie Zwang anzuthun, von der Seite gesehen, als ein in seinen Wandungen gleichbleibendes schlauchförmiges Rohr vorstellen. Dieser Vorstellung entspricht die Zeichnung des Vocales a in der Figur (s. Fig.). Gehen

wir aus der Vocalstellung a in die Stellung e über, so nähern sich bekanntlich die Lippen und der Zungenrücken hebt sich ein wenig (s. Fig.). Noch höher wird diese Erhebung des Zungenrückens beim i (Fig.). Eine Zwischenstellung zeigt das ä, der Zungenrücken hebt sich nur sehr wenig. Während bei diesen helleren Vocalen der Schwerpunkt der Veränderungen des Ansatzrohres im Zungenrücken liegt, zeigen sich bei den Vocalen o und u die Veränderungen

FIG 5. The phonetic script invented by Hermann Gutzmann.

crete word lamp (*Lampe*). Here he foreshadows Goldstein's observations that some patients find particular difficulty with category names that are relatively abstract (see Goldstein, 1948). It is easy to browse through the works of our scientific forebears with amused condescension, nonetheless many of their methods must have been helpful—if only for a limited group of patients. Some of these early papers contain detailed observations of the behaviour of individual aphasic patients, which can still be of importance today.

One of many followers of Gutzmann's methods was the Viennese physician Emil Froeschels (1884–1973). Early in his career, Froeschels was professionally involved in psychotherapy and the treatment of a vast range of disorders of communication and in Vienna, like Gutzmann in Berlin, conducted an outpatient clinic for voice and speech disturbances, especially for children. In 1914 he was active in treating war casualties, including aphasia and voice disorders, many of the latter functional, and in 1917 was appointed senior physician to the Department of Head Injuries in the Central Hospital, Vienna. In 1921—we are anticipating a little—he founded a logopaedic training school in Vienna. In retrospect it is interesting to note to what extent study and remediation of speech disorders generally were the preoccupation of medical men in Germany, Austria, and a few other European countries, who were also actively and personally involved in the minutiae of therapy. In Great Britain, with a few exceptions (Wyllie, Bristowe, Bastian, and later Worster-Drought), the initiative often came from elocution teachers and those who had originally been concerned with the aesthetic aspects of voice production. For this reason therapy for stuttering, for the dysphonias and certain types of articulation defect was relatively thoroughly undertaken early on in a number of "speech clinics" whereas more central disorders were only very superficially treated. This was not altogether true of the West End School, London, where there was considerable emphasis on neurology and psychotherapy in the training back in the 1930s, and there were other exceptions among training schools.

Froeschels must be remembered for his detailed accounts of therapy for aphasia (Froeschels, 1914, 1916), which with Gutzmann's served as a model for a long time to come, but not only for that: for speech therapists all over the world he is to be remembered as the founder of the International Association of Logopaedics and Phoniatrics, in 1924. Froeschels read a report on aphasia at this first meeting, at which the disciplines of neurology, psychology, laryngology and **paedogogics** were represented.

Like Gutzmann, Froeschels recommended separate approaches to motor aphasia and **sensory aphasia** and was *au fond* a localisationist at a time when this doctrine in its purest form had lost much ground. Like Gutzmann, he based his therapy for motor aphasia on the conviction that the essential problem was an articulatory one and that techniques evolved for teaching speech to the deaf were appropriate for acquired aphasia. But he went even further than Gutzmann in his use of highly synthetic measures for retraining articulation and included the component of moulding the shape of the articulators with both hands to achieve the units of the phonemic repertoire one by one, the so-called "optic-tactile method". This approach was subsequently criticised by Froment and Monod (1914), who pointed out that very few motor aphasics are completely speechless, the majority managing to produce words containing many of the desired phonemes in certain circumstances (as, of course, Hughlings Jackson had stressed years before) and that the underlying problem is not an articulatory one (see also Froment, 1921). They also rejected Froeschels' contention (shared by Gutzmann and many others at the time) and this is how children acquire lanaguge in the first place, and is therefore the "natural" way. Froment and Monod approached language re-education in a manner reminiscent of the approach that Schuell was to develop in the United States 40 years later (Schuell, Jenkins, & Jimenez-Pabon, 1964; and see the stimulation school in Section 2). Like Schuell, Froment and Monod believed in using intensive auditory stimulation by presenting the target word innumerable times in the auditory modality. They further objected that the "optic-tactile method" did not sufficiently exploit the factor of association between word and concept. Replying to Froment and Monod's (1914) article, Froeschels (1916) accepted many of their views, but claimed that in his experience many patients suffered from defective **kinaesthetic** sensation, rendering them unable to imitate speech in a more natural manner; consequently the therapist was obliged to resort to the complete optic-tactile method. Furthermore, he claimed considerable success with his approach.

Froeschels' system for treating sensory aphasia was not dissimilar from Gutzmann's, but he distinguished between two sorts of sensory aphasia: (1) where the *Wortklangbild* (acoustic word image) is not comprehended, due to a difficulty in word-sound perception, and the patient cannot repeat; (2) where the word's *Lautklangbild* (phonemic image) is correctly identified, but is disconnected from the conceptual speech centre and the patient can repeat. The idea of more or less concrete images continued to dominate thinking at this time. These two patterns correspond to word-sound deafness and word-meaning deafness respectively (cf. von Monakow, 1914; Kohn & Friedman, 1986). In the first case the patient is taught to recognise motor speech images once more as relating to specific phonemic images, and if this fails, lipreading is taught. This is an early example of "reconstitution of function" (cf. Luria, 1947). For the word retrieval problems, the teacher must try to improve the patient's memory by practising words with their corresponding pictures. Continual practice in naming and pointing to pictures named may serve to bring back meanings of words where repetition is preserved without comprehension.

The above account highlights Gutzmann's and Froeschels' fundamental approach to rehabilitation of spoken language, but omits their treatment of other aspects of aphasia, which on the whole followed schoolbook methods.

The practice of presenting words to the patient for repetition and of **phonemic cueing**, seen here in an extreme form, in fact remained a staple of treatment in many countries until very recently. Its possible value was based on faith rather than demonstration of its efficacy; recent experimental work has shown that repetition and phonemic cueing have, at best, short-lasting effects (Patterson, Purell, & Morton, 1983). Techniques that involve word-meaning are of much more substantial benefit (Cohen, Engel, Kelter, & List, 1979; Howard et al., 1985a). Furthermore, from the standpoint of articulatory facilitation, words may often be elicited in their correct phonemic form in familiar phrases and stereotypes more easily and painlessly than by practice of phonemes in isolation. Obviously, one must take the nature of the "word-formation" difficulty into consideration.

W. Poppelreuter (1917) was active in the First World War in Cologne, in one of the several centres for treatment and rehabilitation of the head-injured. Many of his practical, effective, and ingenious exercises concern problems of reading, visual agnosia, and constructional apraxia, rather than aphasia, and interest in him as a rehabilitation therapist lies in these rather than his treatments of aphasia. Other rehabilitation centres were run by Isserlin in Munich, and Goldstein in Frankfurt; considerable numbers of patients were treated in these units, and many improved even where the treatment began long after onset when spontaneous recovery could be assumed to be complete (cf. Feuchtwanger, 1935).

The American neurologist C. K. Mills can be classed, in our opinion, among the German practitioners of speech gymnastics of which Gutzmann was a protagonist. The remedial system he describes in detail (Mills, 1904) is fundamentally the same as Gutzmann's and Froeschels'. It is based on gradual introduction of speech-sounds, syllables, and words, which the patient has to repeat. Mills, like the German therapists, was also a localisationist.

Mills had been treating patients since 1880, probably even before Gutzmann. He used Wyllie's (1894) "physiological alphabet," a forerunner of Daniel Jones' International Phonetic Alphabet, in reconstructing an executive phonemic system for his patients, in conjunction with a "phonetic" reader, where patients practised newly-acquired phonemes in words linked together in rather artificial sounding sentences. (For example, for posterior linguopalatal consonants: "Can Gilbert bring Loch Hourn youths?"; for linguo-dentals: "Thinkest thou so, zealot?", and so on.) The highly segmental application of the physiological alphabet was designed to give patients conscious control of their articulators, as we might today in cases of dysarthria or **articulatory apraxia**. Patients had to understand fully how all individual phonemes were made, as a student of phonetics might. With one of his patients, a predominantly motor aphasic with well-depicted agrammatism (cf. Howard, 1985; Kean, 1985), and possibly a **deep dyslexia** and **deep dysgraphia** (cf. Coltheart, Patterson, & Marshall, 1980), the treatment instituted by Mills, with the help of his assistant Weisenburg, 18 months, post-onset, comprised repetition by the patient of "letters, words, and the names of objects." One is directly reminded of Kussmaul's exhortation to consolidate motor co-ordination of speech-sounds or words by systematic practice of sounds, syllables, words, and sentences (". . . all patients will improve through methodical practice in saying, sounds, syllables, words, sentences." Kussmaul, 1876, p. 218; our translation.) The same progression has been seen in the systems of Gutzmann and Froeschels. Mills does, one is relieved to see, bring in the dimension of grammar and syntax. He observed agrammatic features in at least one of his patients and included a language primer, a grammar, and a dictionary (also recommended by Kussmaul and Froeschels) along with the physiological alphabet in his retraining battery. Mills, like Gutzmann, believed that the patient should be instructed "much as a child would be in the nature and use of the parts of speech." Mills is inconsistent: in the same article he twice advocates an approach "as one would teach a child," but contradicts this in the discussion that follows his printed talk, where he states that aphasic patients do not relearn language as a child learns it.

In fairness to Mills, it should be recorded that he did not altogether neglect the **propositional** aspect of language. This is, however, discussed in far less detail than the articulatory, or phonemic, aspect. Reading aloud was also important in the re-education of spoken language. Object-names were retaught through encouraging the patient to handle the objects as well as look at them. Mills reports improvement in a number of cases he treated.

These were the types of remedial approaches to aphasia fashionable during the early years of the twentieth century, up to and including much of the First World War, with disparate patient populations. They were strongly biased towards didactic training, or drilling, utilising highly synthetic methods. This orientation was shared by a number of physicians of the day who were also re-educators. They were mostly believers, like Bastian, in the possibility of re-educating new parts of the damaged hemisphere or the minor hemisphere. There were, of course, critics of this position, including Hughlings Jackson (1878), Freud (1891) and, at the turn of the century, Marie (1906). Their turn was to come in the twentieth century, where the history of aphasiology was to move off on a different tack.

The tremendous flowering of the French school of aphasiologists and "neurophysicians" in the mid-nineteenth century—taking in Bouillaud, Flourens, Auburtin, Gratiolet, Trousseau, Charcot, Broca, and others—has been related by some historians (for instance, Castiglioni, 1947) to the military, political, and social achievements at Napoleonic France. In the second half of that century we see German physicians and psychiatrists coming to the fore (Wernicke, Finkelnburg, Kussmaul). It would be tempting to seek a link with the pronounced military, scientific, and industrial successes in Germany during that period. Indeed, according to Hécaen and Angelergues (1965), the Germans took the lead with Wernicke's publication of 1874. And up to the time of Marie at the beginning of the twentieth century:

... the German school, whose power was demonstrated in Lichtheim's synthesis, influenced all studies of aphasia. Trailing in its wake was the French school, which had lost its inspiration after the military disaster of 1870 [The French defeat in the Franco-Prussian War]. Meanwhile the English school of Jackson remained a local and ignored event, whose impact was not to be felt across the Channel until very much later. (Hécaen & Angelergues, 1965, p. 37; our translation)

NEW DEPARTURES IN THERAPY AND ASSESSMENT AFTER THE FIRST WORLD WAR

The obsession with cerebral localisation that dominated the latter part of the nineteenth century and the first years of the twentieth gradually yielded to an interest in more dynamic functions of the cortex. There were a number of reasons for the decline and fall of classical localisationism: one was the withering away of psychological centres with the realisation that voluntary action was essentially different from reflex physiological activity; another was that localisation frequently failed to predict the clinical symptoms of aphasia and other neuropsychological disorders, and that the prototypes of, for example, **Broca's aphasia** or **Wernicke's aphasia** seldom occurred. Moreover, beyond the vague idea that you needed to "stimulate" the right hemisphere, which generated no particular methods beyond the peculiar advocacy of writing with the left hand, localisationism had no systematic relationship to the practice of therapy. According to Weisenburg and McBride (1935), by the 1930s "the majority of recent investigators have joined the dynamic school" (represented by Jackson, Pick, Goldstein, and Head, among others). Jackson's emphasis on aphasia as a psychological problem and his insistence that aphasia could involve loss of power to "propositionise" had an important influence on therapy, but not until several decades later. Pierre Marie's tests, described by Moutier (1908), were a substantial advance on those used previously. The greater interest in cognitive and behavioural factors was to lead to more profound insight into the nature of aphasia, and this was a pre-requisite for more enlightened re-education.

Right up to the First World War, with a few exceptions, such as the work of Froment and Monod, methods used in aphasia rehabilitation were largely those elaborated for teaching children with retarded or defective speech or the deaf and dumb. These approaches seem to have been adopted because techniques of language teaching had been developed for disabled children, and aphasia therapy was viewed primarily as a process of *re-learning* lost language. Weisenburg and McBride (1935) see Mills as an improvement on most of his German contemporaries, but on close scrutiny his methods are seen to be equally artificial and narrowly didactic, with much emphasis on articulation and wide reliance on simple repetition of stimuli and little realisation that a special approach is needed for aphasic adults differing in essence from that suitable for other groups. Among the latter are, for instance, schoolchildren with normal brains but without that long apprenticeship in use of language that has been experienced by most aphasic adults.

In the nineteenth century, Jackson's ideas had very limited impact. In 1868, at the British Association meeting in Norwich, he had debated with Broca, an arch localisationist, about the nature of aphasia. He pointed out that demonstration that a particular lesion caused a particular deficit did not mean that this "function" was located there. For him aphasia was, essentially, a defect in the ability to encapsulate thought in verbal propositions, and he observed that while the more automatic aspects of language (serial speech, cliché completion, singing the words of familiar hymns, and so on) were often retained, voluntary and purposeful use of language was lost, at least to some extent. Even in England, localisationism, represented by Broadbent and Bastian, was the dominant position. The critique of the localisationist position gained force at the end of the nineteenth century; in the German-speaking world, Freud (1891) and Pick (1898, 1913) developed Jackson's position. In France, Marie (1906) expressed the disillusionment with simple localisationism in denying Broca's original localising claim. In England, Henry Head reprinted all Jackson's work on aphasia in a special 1915 issue of the journal *Brain*, and in his 1926 book, in a chapter entitled "Chaos", delivered a devastating critique of the worst theoretical excesses of localisationists of the nineteenth and early twentieth century. Aphasia was no longer seen as a loss of memory images, and Head's view that it was fundamentally a disorder of symbolic formulation and expression gained considerable ground (as we have seen, a view already anticipated by Finkelnburg). In Germany, Goldstein, who had originally been a student of Wernicke's, was meanwhile applying a modification of **Gestalt theory** (which he called "organismic psychology") to language and language disturbances (cf. Goldstein, 1948), and in the 1930s Vygotsky and Luria in the Soviet Union began to develop a very different view of the nature of aphasia (cf. Luria, 1979).

The importance of assessing more objectively the effects of language therapy began to gain attention. As has been described, Gutzmann frequently began his courses of re-education a considerable time after his patients had suffered brain damage; he recorded that during this time they had regained very little useful speech and then gave them a relatively short course of re-education, the details of which he related with characteristic thoroughness. He then reported improvement, very often in general terms such as "quite exceptional progress." Other clinicians were less explicit about what they did and in what way the patients' speech had improved. S. I. Franz of California was dissatisfied with these ways of reporting progress.

Franz's main contribution to aphasia therapy in the 1920s—note that he had written a paper on the re-education of "an aphasic" in 1906—was his precise tracking of the course of improvement with minute and yet copious details of the therapeutic algorithm and goal (Franz, 1924). Some of his therapeutic activities had the sole noble aim of helping the patient to regain some useful speech, but some were undertaken unapologetically "for the demonstration of the course of relearning" and thus had a scientific as well as therapeutic character. The three patients selected for the experiment were all fairly young soldiers, suffering from syphilis. At that time, syphilis was a common cause of aphasia, whereas today cerebrovascular accident associated with hypertension, faulty diet, and so-called "stress" is the commonest aetiology of cases of language loss referred to speech therapy clinics, while head wounds from road traffic accidents are far commoner than those inflicted by rapiers or halberds. Franz's experiment was carried out many years post-onset of aphasia, but the patients had received some unspecified and apparently fairly unsystematic and unintensive help with their speech from time to time—indeed, because family, friends, and professionals always try to help, that is inevitable.

Comprehensive assessment was carried out before the experiment. This included tests of repetition, word-finding, copying of writing, selection of written words, and non-verbal tasks, for example, for **apraxia**. In connection with the latter it is interesting to read Franz's observation of Infantryman G: "When told by the physician to put some oil in the oil reservoir, a job which he had seen done and had also done . . . a number of times, he put oil in the gasoline tank (Franz, 1924)." (We are moving into a motorised era, nearer our own.) Franz took this to be a sign of diminished intelligence.

The experiment concentrated on the learning, or re-learning, of object names. The procedure was as follows: 60 objects were selected for the subject to learn their names by the technique of hearing and repeating the names. Of these 60, Franz initially selected 20 that he placed one by one before the subject and named, requesting the patient to repeat the name. The objects were then presented in a different order for the subject to name. If he gave an incorrect name, the correct one was given and he had to repeat it. This was carried out several times for all the objects. "Learning" of any one object name was judged complete when on each of six days scores of seven or more out of ten trials were attained; thereupon that object was removed and a new one substituted. When an object name had been "learnt' by this criterion, seven days elapsed and then the subject was re-tested on that object. If the re-test score failed to reach a predetermined criterion, practice along the same lines was continued until the criterion was achieved. There was then a further rest period (of two weeks), followed by a further re-test and extra practice if necessary. At the end of trial experiment there was a further week of "rest" and then a re-test of all

60 items. In this way, naming performance on each one of the 60 items was plotted throughout the entire period of the experiment. Franz was able to observe that it took the patient much longer to master the names of some objects than others, using exactly the same method (repetition) for each, but he could offer no satisfactory explanation why this happened.

After the end-of-series post-test, a further period of 120 days ensued before a final "memory test" was administered. A similar procedure was carried out with names of colours and, finally, with certain reading tasks (both reading letters of the alphabet and matching printed names with object-pictures). The learning procedure was also extended to simple writing tasks and learning the names of shapes.

There was nothing particularly novel or enlightened about the teaching procedure which Franz used, that is to say, having the patient repeat a word after him and then requiring the patient to produce the name himself after a short interval, and then giving the patient the name again if he failed, and so on; the principle of repetition was part of the whole associationist philosophy. What was significant was Franz's meticulous attention to a methodology for measuring changes in performance, plotting accurate "recovery curves" for each target item; indeed this achievement is unique in the annals of aphasia therapy, with a few exceptions, the most notable being the "recovery curves" of a patient's reading ability, carried out by Newcombe, Hiorns, Marshall, and Adams (1975). (See also Elvin & Oldfield, 1951; Lapointe, 1977.) Apart from observation that the names of some items were considerably more difficult to learn than others, Franz made two further observations of particular relevance: first, that the re-learning process was slow to begin with but became easier as the experiment progressed, with newly introduced items being acquired more rapidly; second, that the three subjects responded differently to identical tasks and learning conditions. He realised that any treatment plan would have to take individual differences in learning behaviour into account. It is easy to sneer at this boring and theoretically trivial type of therapy. However, the reader at least knows exactly what was attempted and by what method, and this contrasts quite favourably with many references to aphasia today (in particular in studies comparing groups of patients having "conventional speech therapy" with patients having no "professional" speech therapy, or "no therapy at all"), where the reader has little or no idea of the actual content of the treatment sessions.

By the 1930s, many workers in aphasia were breaking out from the localisationist mould. Weisenburg and McBride (1935) represent an uncompromising departure from the localisationist tradition of Broca, Wernicke, Trousseau, and the Gutzmann-Froeschels-Mills group. Avowed followers of Jackson's doctrine, they criticised the method of investigation of the **diagram makers**, who, they alleged, were more interested in the problems of cerebral localisation than in clinical manifestations. Their attitude was considerably more favourable to re-education. Weisenburg (the neurologist of the pair) had, incidentally, been Mills' assistant at an earlier period. The latter was, as has been seen, a "firm believer in localisation" (Weisenburg & McBride, 1935, p. 24), with faith in *centres* for speech and related functions, and all the usual images. Weisenburg cast most of this aside and regarded the study of psychological changes by means of *better designed tests* as more important than locating the seat of the disorder, although that was to be included in the investigation.

Weisenburg and McBride were impressed by the new views of Head (1926), of Goldstein (1916, 1919, 1924, 1925), and, to a certain extent, of Marie (1906). Their theory of recovery from aphasia includes the belief that this recovery partly results from lessening of physiological pathology; like Goldstein, they believed that improvement also takes place through readjustment of the individual to the abnormal condition and an adaptation of the behaviour that is still within the patient's power. The brain-damaged patient seeks a situation that he instinctively feels he can cope with and shuns those where he anticipates failure; if forced into the latter he may exhibit extreme signs of physical and psychological distress. They accepted, almost as an afterthought, the possibility of extension of cortical activity to areas that have long been closely related to the function disturbed, whether elsewhere in the same hemisphere or in corresponding areas in the opposite hemisphere, but they still declared themselves a trifle sceptical of that possibility. They considered that major factors in this recovery also embraced the condition of the brain and the individual as a whole, his age, his intelligence, and his interests. Weisenburg and McBride rejected any simple localisation of higher cortical functions, preferring instead a degree of **holism**:

> It is widely believed now that mental functions, even the simpler speech processes, cannot be related to any strictly defined cortical areas but involve unified activity of many areas, if not of the whole brain. (p. 92)

Weisenburg and McBride made an outstanding contribution to the design of tests for aphasia. A number of test batteries had been drawn up especially for aphasics from the time of Bastian (1898) onwards, including Rieger's (1888), Marie's (1906) and Head's famous tests (1926). However Weisenburg and McBride felt that most of these were narrow and superficial. Psychometric testing had advanced during the First World War, particularly in some of the German institutes that were established to care for and rehabilitate patients with head injuries. Weisenburg commented:

> The construction of tests . . . has now run parallel to the recognition of aphasia as a psychological problem and, furthermore, as a disorder extending *far beyond simple speech processes*. (p. 91)

AT-D

For the first time, they collected information on normal levels of performance on their clinical tests. Based on such thinking, their test battery adds to many "verbal" tests of the types we are by now familiar with—tests of spontaneous speech, of naming of objects, of serial speech, of repetition of speech, of comprehension of spoken language (including Head's **hand, ear and eye** test), and so on—an interesting group called "language intelligence tests"—finding opposites, analogies, spotting absurdities, sentence completions, reproduction of digits and nonsense syllables, and so-called "non-language" tests. Furthermore, they felt that tests "in vivo" —for example, domino playing (Trousseau), travel by public horse-tram (Gutzmann), filling up one's automobile with gasoline in the right place (Franz)—were as important as formal, clinical tests, but opined that "one must have balance." Thus they stressed the importance of *practical* as well as *clinical* testing (cf. Taylor, 1965).

Finally, their new, more flexible classification into four loose forms of aphasia—predominantly **expressive**, predominantly **receptive**, expressive-receptive, and amnesic—allowed clinical psychologists to plumb many more of the complexities of language disturbances than the more constraining, cut-and-dried classification that saw the subtleties of language as being mapped on to motor and sensory activities in the same way as the cruder activities of locomotion or grasping.

They reported in minute detail their patients' responses to a wide range of tests, and the course of parallel improvement on different tasks over a fairly long period, with two or more administrations of identical tests. All this time "training" was being carried out.

Weisenburg and McBride have plenty to offer in ideas for re-education. As a generalisation, they insist on a degree of individuality for each treatment plan. They also, in contrast to the Gutzmann–Froeschels–Mills trio, insist that the exercises should be meaningful and of personal interest to each patient. Practice of verbal skills should be related to the performances that the patient has to regain and, presumably, should be *seen* by him to be related.

They still see expressive aphasia—correlating only approximately with Broca's aphasia in classical terminology—as primarily a problem of articulation, or at least containing a major articulatory component, and therefore recommend that training for this type of disturbance should always include exercises for articulation as such. Nonetheless, the form of exercise they recommend is in general carried out in a way that takes more note of *linguistic* principle than those so far described (with the possible exception of Froment and Monod, 1914). For example, where confusion or substitution of similar phonemes occurs, these are taught as "oppositional pairs" (e.g., /f/ and /v/ are presented in a sentence containing both). Mastery of the articulated form of words and sentences is emphasised rather than drill in isolated sound formations. Most of the time Weisenburg and McBride had in mind patients who had already regained a modicum of articulatory skill and presumably some word-finding ability, and they allowed that in more severe cases it may be necessary to "drill" the correct production of single sounds, but they prefer to embody the target sounds in meaningful utterances whenever possible.

Writing is retaught by getting the patient to copy individual letters while "saying them aloud" (presumably the letter names) or tracing them with a finger before writing. For spoken word-formation they recommend breaking the word up into its component "letters" (sic) or syllables (this for expressive and occasionally for receptive patients as well), and they add that exaggerated emphasis on rhythm may be of assistance. Many little touches suggest, perhaps for the first time in the history of aphasia therapy, this awareness of certain essential parameters of spoken language. They like the patient to practise writing and saying the target words simultaneously, sometimes dividing the word into syllables and pronouncing each syllable separately while putting hyphens between them in writing. Occasionally it is necessary to go further and break the words down into their "letters" (presumably here they mean phonemes, not letter-names).

For vocabulary as such, they favour more or less traditional methods, by which the patient is shown an object (or its picture) and has to pronounce and write its name. This is part of the "multisensory" approach, which is not new. But they also wish to incorporate Goldstein's newer approach, according to which object-naming is different in different situations. They refer occasionally to "drills" for word-formation and vocabulary, showing the persistent influence of the Gutzmann–Froeschels school—that is, without any suggestion that a subject has in some way to "process" the information or motor acts that he must acquire. They recommend beginning with the most frequently used words (using perhaps for the first time a standardised word frequency count; Thorndike, 1927); this is done so that newly-acquired items would be of greatest immediate use for the patient, as Franz had also stressed. Their patients seem to be considerably better than many of ours, and Weisenburg and McBride suggest that one should start with the "500 or 1000" most frequent words. In addition, the words are practised in tasks involving their meaning, the patients having to define them and construct sentences around them. They encouraged patients to take an active part and show initiative, which was quite a new departure, and note down any particular words they had difficulty in pronouncing or evoking. Patients were encouraged to look up the more abstract words in dictionaries. This aspect of rehabilitation—that is to say, in crude terms, passing the responsibility to the patient—has been relatively neglected in the past 50 years, although it has been revived today by some contemporary schools. For sentence structure the same training is used both for the expressive and the predominantly receptive, consisting of construction by the patient of oral and written sentences using a small number of given words. One cannot quite see the logic of this, but it is still often advocated.

Weisenburg and McBride have a number of delightfully practical suggestions. Patients are encouraged to do their own shopping or marketing by consulting magazines or newspaper advertisements and making up their shopping lists themselves (see also Singer & Low, 1933).

Another new dimension of Weisenburg and McBride's therapy is attention to "changes in language and thought processes which cannot be isolated for separate study or training." Among the "more complicated training methods" were summarising stories and short newspaper articles, orally or in writing; this they look on as "a half-way stage between propositional speaking . . . which is so difficult for the patient, and oral reading, which is easier, and satisfactory as practice for articulation but not for the more complex processes of expression (Weisenburg & McBride, 1935, p. 389)." Their treatment plans also attend to understanding of spoken language and printed material. Longer and longer utterances or texts were read to the patients, who had to extract the essential points. Although Weisenburg and McBride mainly saw "complexity" or "difficulty" in terms of the length of the passage—that is to say, it was largely a question of auditory memory—they found that this type of exercise gave them the opportunity to observe "particular difficulties in understanding certain turns of speech or grammatical constructions (p. 390)."

As we mentioned, they sat on the fence as regards the possibility of re-educating the right hemisphere by language exercises such as left-hand writing. Accepting this hypothesis momentarily, they pushed writing with the left hand to its logical conclusion and trained two patients who did not need to use the left (because there was no paralysis of the right) to write with their left hands. They did not report the outcome of this "experiment"; indeed, if the patients' oral speech had improved *pari passu*, they could hardly have logically attributed this to the direct effect of left-hand writing practice, since there would have been so many other (more plausible) explanations.

Finally, they consider it an important goal of aphasia re-education to make a contribution to the patient's "sense of well-being and to increase his morale. The training must be adapted to arouse his interest and to make him feel reasonably encouraged (p. 391)."

Much of Weisenburg and McBride's approach to therapy can be seen as a substantial advance on the earlier, more didactic, approach, and shows considerable psychological and linguistic insight. No doubt this was largely the direct outcome of the swing away from the excesses of localisationism—regarded in the mid-nineteenth century as the height of progressive thought—and of associationism.

If Weisenburg and McBride brought a veritable gale of fresh air into aphasia therapy, we cannot be sure how much credit they deserve for the new outlook in general. One tends to think of Kurt Goldstein as a man of the 1940s, but in fact, chronologically, he almost belongs to the turn of the century; he had published two papers on aphasia in 1906—the year of Pierre Marie's bombshell into the localisationist camp. By 1914 Goldstein (a former student of Wernicke) had published some nine papers on the subject and by 1935 (the year of Weisenburg and McBride's major work) when Gestalt psychology was at its zenith, nearly thirty. By that time Goldstein, who was a Jew, had emigrated to the United States to escape political and racial persecution under the Nazi regime, along with Froeschels and a number of other significant neurologists, psychiatrists, and psychologists from Germany and Austria. They were more fortunate than Branco van Dantzig of the Netherlands, a leading pre-war logopaedist, who died a few years later in a concentration camp gas chamber.

The views of Kurt Goldstein, the epitome of holistic and organismic aphasiology, are still well-known even to the younger generations of aphasia therapists. With the decline of Gestalt psychology, and the return of a form of localisationism that happened in the late 1950s, Goldstein and his views have undergone an eclipse, but it would fit the pattern of scientific history if the 1980s saw some form of comeback. It is necessary only to summarise his attitude to aphasia before attempting to assess his contribution to therapy. He believed that alterations of performance following brain damage could only be understood in relation to the *total organism*. He did not consider it fruitful to look for specific impairments of individual performances, but rather to comprehend these as part of a general dedifferentiation of function; this could also be seen as a blurring of the boundaries between **figure** and **ground**—a Gestalt concept. This did not mean that aphasia was a unitary phenomenon, as he posited "performance fields" in the brain and claimed that according to which part of the brain is injured, the reduction or dedifferentiation affects one performance field more than the others. In the most *central* types of aphasia (which correlate in a very general way with those parts of the cortex "which are relatively independent of the projection systems and the peripheral cortex"), he attributed many of the manifestations to an underlying impairment of **abstract attitude**.

In his new approach, many symptoms of brain damage are seen as expressions of the change that *the patient's personality as a whole* undergoes as a result of a disease, and also as expression of the struggle of the *changed personality to cope with the defect* and with the demands it can no longer meet (Goldstein, 1942). When the patient is confronted with a task he cannot perform, he has a **catastrophic reaction**, a temporary emotional collapse often accompanied by physical signs, such as pallor, sweating, and tears. Much of the behaviour of sick people can only be understood as an unconscious defence against catastrophic situations; they therefore seek out un-taxing environments and are excessively orderly, rigid, and unadventurous. So, where pathology cannot be removed, it is the physician's responsibility to secure the best possible milieu for the patient.

Goldstein had a word of caution on psychological testing: the important aspect is not whether a patient can do task A and/or task B, in terms of plusses and minuses, but *how*—in what way is the patient's performance modified, and what means, or strategies, does he/she employ in doing the task. As a result his case descriptions show remarkable attention to detail in the patients' performance in a wide range of tasks.

Among the principles underlying his therapy is his denial that performances related to a particular cortical substrate can, after its destruction, return by taking over a tissue that was not previously related to this function before. Thus, for Goldstein, re-education cannot develop new capacities in the minor hemisphere. Put in the most general terms, Goldstein's attitude towards therapeutic intervention is that even if some spontaneous restitution can be expected "exercises are of help." In particular, they may prevent a patient from developing undesirable reactions or unproductive compensations. Furthermore, special rehabilitation methods may have to be applied that the patient cannot find for himself, "because these methods must be based on psychologic and biologic knowledge concerning the nature of the defect." *A fortiori*, when very little spontaneous restitution occurs the clinician is needed to help the patient to elaborate useful compensations. Goldstein outlines several types of compensatory performances for each type of impairment. These differ according to whether the patient is satisfied with a reduction in a particular skill and wary of any further effort which might result in anxiety or disappointment, or whether he or she wishes to aim higher and risk a catastrophic reaction. Thus there is no one goal or one retraining technique for a specific defect, but a different goal for each unique case. This is the "treat the whole person" philosophy *par excellence*. Goldstein indeed had the necessary training and understanding to put it into practice.

Like Gutzmann and Froeschels, Goldstein had run a rehabilitation unit at the end of the First World War; his methods of treatment are developed from a basis of their traditional **direct method**. For dysarthrics and motor aphasics, whom he tends to bring together, Goldstein includes certain Froeschels-type articulation exercises, consisting in practice of isolated phonemes, and adds some devices of his own, such as eliciting a P sound by pretending to blow out a candle or puff out smoke, as when smoking a pipe, or achieving the vowel U from the "moo" of a cow. Such devices are, however, only to be used when all else fails and he warns that:

> We should never forget that the sounds acquired by this method are not
> equal to the sounds we use in speech, and, further, that the sounds which one
> produces separately are not the same as those used in words. (Goldstein,
> 1948, p. 329)

Having some linguistic insight, he adds: "In real language, we do not speak
by combining sounds into words." As far as possible, therapist and patient
should proceed along "physiological," that is to say, more natural, paths;
wherever possible the therapist should elicit words using Froment and
Monod's (1914) stimulation method. Only when this "physiological"
approach fails, should one introduce more formal exercises in the articulation of single sounds. In some of the more severe cases, where the patient
can repeat sounds more naturally, words are soon introduced for repetition. (One notes no attempts at getting patients to repeat phrases—seemingly Goldstein has patients in mind for whom this would be impossible.) If
the patient is able to speak words "so clearly that he is able to make himself
understood, and only his pronunciation is incorrect, we should not torture
him in this period of training with phonetic exercises (Goldstein, 1948,
p. 329)." Goldstein anticipates Schuell by reflecting: "It is much more
important for him [the patient] to be able to use his speech for comprehensible communication than to speak correctly (p. 329)." Goldstein
has great faith in conversation and communication with one's fellows as a
form of therapy and incentive for "motor speech." He goes on:

> Because the goal is to gain a language which is suited to express definite
> thoughts, training with words which have meaning for the patient, or mean-
> ingful sentences, as soon as possible is preferable. This does not mean that
> the patient should learn to build correct sentences. But he should learn to use
> words as sentences . . . (p. 331)

He is totally opposed to learning of nonsense syllables, and says, "words
derived from senseless syllables do not exist either in our consciousness or
in our motor action (p. 331)."

As far as the actual re-acquisition of phonemes goes, Goldstein points to
the hierarchical organisation of speech sounds and accepts Jakobson's
(1941) formulation by which acquisition of certain phonemes presup-
poses acquisition of certain others. Thus Goldstein was a pioneer in trying
to apply linguistic principles to the treatment of aphasia at a relatively early
date in the history of aphasia therapy. He also realised—like Froment and
Monod (1914), and earlier Gesner (1769), and Jackson (1878)—that
articulation in **serial speech** (numbers, days of the week, etc.) or in singing
may sometimes be superior to articulation in more conscious, deliberate,

utterances, and urged that use should be made of this fact in the early stages of helping a patient towards control of his/her articulation.

He interprets agrammatism in the patient's connected speech as due partly to loss of certain automatisms that are necessary for fluent speaking, and he emphasises the effortful character of this type of motor aphasia. His treatment of this disorder, which is not particularly profound, involves some rote learning and learning of grammatical rules, but he urges that as soon as possible the patient should use what he has learnt in meaningful sentences.

Goldstein has a number of roundabout ways of reteaching the reading of letters and words, including tracing movements which, as we have seen, was not new. In mentioning some techniques that are also used in teaching children, he says, characteristically:

> ... a simple carrying over of the methods used in child training would be wrong and disappointing. This refers not only to retraining in reading, but is valid generally. I stress this point because it is often overlooked, and the disappointment which naturally follows may cause all attempts to retrain patients to be discredited. (1948, p. 336)

For word-finding defects, the first step is to ascertain the cause in the individual case, whether it be memory impairment, impairment of abstract attitude, or something else. Where little spontaneous restitution occurs, a "pseudo-improvement," i.e., building of "associations" between objects and words, can sometimes be achieved, but seldom directly by rote learning. Rather, the patient may relearn names in a roundabout way; for instance, learning a number of names of objects having a "natural, concrete, relationship;" the patient recites the whole series until he comes to the one he seeks. An even better way is for the patient to find the word in a concrete situation to which it belongs. He adds such techniques as sentence-completion, but he maintains that all these ways "are not real word-finding" and immediately afterwards the patient is unable to retrieve the word unaided. He sees it as the therapist's task to find the best methods that the individual patient can apply. But as long as the patient does not recover his abstract attitude he never regains real knowledge of word meaning, although, in spite of this, he may perform better by improving his associations and learning external associations (p. 344).

An account of the first major contribution of a British team to aphasia therapy in the twentieth century requires a brief introductory note on the state of speech therapy in Great Britain in the 1930s and 1940s. As a profession speech therapy had crystallised out of the efforts of a comparatively small number of individual practitioners who had come from "among those working in some field of voice production, or speech training, from an artistic rather than a scientific angle ... (MacLeod, 1945)." Thus

Courtland MacMahon, who was appointed to the first hospital speech clinic in England (at St Bartholomew's Hospital, London) in 1911, was a "teacher of voice production and public speaking (Eldridge, 1968)." These "therapists" with a background of elocution teaching co-operated with medical officers in the treatment of a wide spectrum of disorders of speech and voice. From the literature of the period immediately before the Second World War it would appear that neurological disorders had a minority role in the caseload. An article in the official journal of the British Society of Speech Therapists in 1937 by the neurologist William Johnson presents, rather disappointingly, the old model of strictly anatomically localised centres, more or less as if Bastian had had the last word after all. His recommendations on therapy are either negative or purely speculative. For severe disorders of "the sensory speech centre," he considers that "treatment can effect little" as mental capabilities would be impaired; for more favourable cases, "it is interesting to speculate what result might be obtained by a method of re-education, which literally would mean re-teaching the patient his own language by ordinary school methods (Johnson 1937, p. 12)." All the work on aphasia therapy in the twentieth century—including Weisenburg and McBride in the United States, Goldstein and Isserlin in Germany, and Froment and Monod in France—would seem to have passed him by.

However, a more constructive attitude towards aphasia therapy began to gain ground and the disasters of the Second World War increased the urgency to offer treatment for traumatic aphasia. By the end of the war various training schools for speech therapists had been established in England and Scotland and the courses had become more structured and academic. The more experienced speech therapists who lectured on aphasia were aided by such neurologists as Worster Drought and Colin Edwards. Among the speech therapists was Butfield, whose rehabilitation work with Zangwill will be discussed in detail in the next section. In 1940 British approaches to treatment had not advanced since Bastian's work 40 years before. The next 40 years were to see extraordinary changes in the training of speech therapists and in attitudes towards the re-education of aphasic patients.

Under the direction of Professor D. K. Henderson and Mr (later Professor) Norman Dott, the psychologist Oliver Zangwill was concerned with the assessment and re-education of head-injured patients in Edinburgh during the Second World War. The hospital was organised under the Emergency Medical Service. The rehabilitation work was undertaken with the collaboration of two young speech therapists, H. Micheltree, and subsequently, E. Butfield. Their caseload included a number of servicemen and civilians. In 1946 they reported briefly on their methods of retraining 70 cases of dysphasia and in greater detail on the outcome

(Butfield & Zangwill, 1946). This paper was to become a classic because, with a few exceptions (e.g., Franz, 1924) re-educators had up to then been satisfied with quite general and unsubstantiated claims of success. Their techniques of therapy were largely based on Goldstein (1919, 1942), and carefully tailored, as Goldstein himself would have recommended, to each patient, with his or her individual language disturbances and unique personal problems and interests. The Weisenburg and McBride classification was used. For patients with predominantly expressive speech disorders rather more attention was focused on the articulatory aspect, for which direct exercises in speech sound production were used, than would normally be the case today. This had also been seen even in Goldstein's own battery of therapeutic procedures, in spite of his insistence on following the "natural," "physiological" way. Butfield continued for a long time in this field and was later to elaborate a number of new techniques and to modify her approach considerably to so-called expressive or executive disorders of language (Butfield, 1958, 1960).

At Edinburgh the speech therapists were as a rule able to give the patients two half-hour sessions daily, and this therapy was supplemented by work carried out by the patients on their own or in the occupational therapy department. Therapy was thus reasonably intensive.

An attempt was made to assess more accurately than usual the effect of the re-education. The cases were divided into two groups, according to whether the re-education was begun less than, or more than, six months post-onset. The criterion of six months was chosen since Dott believed that spontaneous improvement is "in general liable to be both limited and slow after six months." Patients were exhaustively assessed before and after their course of treatment. The courses varied in length, being mostly between about three and eight weeks or somewhat longer, and were terminated when "little or no practical disability" remained or the patient's condition remained stationary for a considerable period. The functions of speech, reading, writing, and calculation were rated on a three-point scale as "much improved," "improved" or "unchanged." Taking both groups together, the authors found that 40% of the severe cases, 56% of the moderate cases, and 58% of the mild cases underwent a marked improvement *during* the course of their therapy. Patients with predominantly expressive dysphasia tended to do better than other types and the traumatic patients made better progress than the vascular and **neoplastic** groups. The authors found that patients as a whole made more improvement in speech than in reading, writing or calculation. The group with re-education delayed for six months post-onset was unfortunately too small to allow a statistical comparison of results of therapy between the two groups. It was, however, an important part of the methodology of assessing efficacy of therapy, although it sets up a conflict that is difficult to resolve. Goldstein insisted on early initiation of therapy, in the belief that it would accelerate "spontaneous" recovery and also prevent undesirable attitudes and compensatory techniques from developing. This latter recommendation has been followed—more on the basis of intuition than any scientific "proof"—by probably the majority of therapists in the years 1950–1980. Apart from Feuchtwanger's brief report in 1935, the Butfield and Zangwill paper of 1946 was the first published attempt to evaluate the efficacy of therapy properly, and to assess also the significance of specific factors, such as the form of aphasia and its aetiology. The neurosurgeon Dott and his team were, furthermore, strongly interested in their patients' eventual resettlement in employment. Zangwill long retained this interest, and carried out a further study much later in collaboration with one of us (Hatfield & Zangwill, 1975).

Another interesting figure in aphasia therapy during this period was the American L. Granich (1947). Granich was an educational psychologist who became a captain in the United States Medical Corps during the 1940s and was occupied in the retraining of Second World War casualties, mainly the victims of gunshot wounds. Like Poppelreuter in the First World War and Butfield and Zangwill in the Second, he had the aim, for many of his patients, "to restore them to normal functioning and to economic independence." This was no mean goal. A subordinate aim was to help the surgeon to localise the lesion, by means of a precise analysis of the neuropsychological symptoms. This was indeed regarded by neuropsychologists as perhaps one of their main functions for quite a long time to come, right up to the arrival of the computerised tomographic scanner.

Granich's brief was to look after 300 brain-injured soldiers in Atlantic City Hospital, New Jersey, of whom one-third were aphasic or had related disorders. He was able to carry out intensive re-educational work with 38 men, many of whom he saw daily over a period of months. He was familiar with Goldstein's work and incorporated a number of Goldstein's therapeutic techniques into his retraining. But he was also to a certain extent influenced by Nielsen, one of the few at that juncture to remain faithful to the localisationist doctrine (see Nielsen, 1946).

Granich abandons the notion of broad aphasic syndromes and favours a factor analysis. He postulates some 14 factors, including low-level impairments such as hemiplegia and visual field defect. The others include the factor DTR (dysarthria and verbal dyspraxia); OWF (difficulty in oral word formulation, characterised by **phonemic paraphasia**); AGR (agrammatism); AND (anomia); ARA (auditory receptive aphasia); and a number of factors germane to reading and writing impairments. He recognises that each language function may involve two or more basic abilities. Granich is opposed to standardised tests and regards the individual investigation as therapeutic in itself (p. 32).

Granich, like Goldstein, is particularly interested in observing the strategies and compensatory methods that the patients hit on by themselves; these he considers provide the models for therapy: "Most new techniques for retraining are invented for us by the desperate and more intelligent patients (p. 35)." His approach to retraining is basically didactic and he harps throughout on "taxing drills," which are in themselves considered to improve concentration, a prerequisite of improvement.

Granich pushed his mania for hard work on the part of others to the utmost limit. He urged: "In the brain-injured patient it is well to develop compulsive-obsessive habits of work at an early stage (p. 39)." It is all-important for patients to develop attitudes to tolerate taxing drills and good concentration. In spite of his faith in drills and working the patient hard, he declares that we will make only slow headway unless the patient develops strategies or undergoes substantial "spontaneous recovery." Granich made an earnest effort to tease out a number of basic factors underlying various aphasic manifestations. Moreover he recognised the importance of programming an action like speech production and of feedback and self-monitoring.

As specific therapies he advocates the automatisation of limited responses, for instance, the learning by heart of the names of parts of the body, or writing one's signature, or memorising the spelling of the 500 or 1000 most frequent words in the language. His treatments are on the whole fragmented and ad hoc, with a poorly conceived rationale and reiterated emphasis on "taxing drills." For articulatory disorders he uses Froeschels-type techniques, but without suggesting any useful hierarchy of phoneme acquisition.

For OWF (oral word formation), where he surmises the defect to be in auditory word imaging, he relies on kinaesthetic motor control, although he asserts that this only really applies to short words, longer words needing the auditory pattern. Persistent taxing drill with polysyllabic words is essential. Rhythm and emphasis on the words are used in addition. (He also mentions roundabout ways of producing sounds and words.) If the pronunciation of words is combined with their writing: "There will be a better reaction from the patient." This sort of assertion, without any scientific evidence, is an attitude of faith that we do not find especially helpful today. We are similarly told that "the patient will be helped . . ." by reading the word. Nonsense syllable repetition is a staple for treating this factor—"taxing drills in repeating nonsense syllables bring improvement here (p. 51)," even though he admits that patients are able to imitate familiar words more easily (but perhaps that would not be sufficiently "taxing" to be beneficial). For agrammatism he recommends "memorisation by repeated drill" of sentences and paragraphs—an approach that must have been sadly out of date even in the 1940s. Thus the patient is required to memorise the sentence: "The apple tree makes a cool, pleasant shade on the ground where the children are playing." If he omits the prepositional phrase, this serves as a "lesson" in use of prepositions, the teacher beginning by asking: "Makes a shade where?" The teacher may then succeed in getting the patient to express "ground" and even, on further questioning and priming, "on ground," while still omitting the article. The function of the article is then explained. Such a superficial and unsystematic way of restoring grammar and syntax is surprising at this date and compares poorly with the understanding shown by his contemporary Luria in Moscow (Luria, 1947). For the word-amnesic factor, which is subtly different from the anomic factor and implies a difficulty in "word ideas," he encourages the patient to find an effective preliminary association for the object name and then memorise these associations. He utilises context and cliché at times to facilitate word-formation and word-retrieval.

For dyslexia he had three factors, four if one includes VFR (reduction of the visual field). For homonymous hemianopia he suggests that the patients should turn the page sideways and read from top to bottom (cf. Romanian **lecture verticale**, Gheorgita, 1981; Doms & Bourlard, 1982). Finger tracing and various Goldsteinian methods are proposed for treating defect of the visual recognition factor. Another factor is PLS (loss of phonetic associations), which in a very tentative way foreshadows the condition now called deep dyslexia (Coltheart, Patterson, & Marshall, 1980). Granich attributes the disturbance to a "loss of associations between visual-recognition areas and areas for the recall of sounds" (as contemporary workers might express it, loss of the grapheme-to-phoneme route). He questions whether this is technically an "aphasic" loss, "since it seems to be a loss or a reduction in associations between two major sensory areas." Recognition of whole words is still possible, as he puts it, "by visual-to-visual association of whole-word form . . . with revisualisation of the object." Patients with severe PLS may make semantic errors in reading (Granich does not use this term), and read, for example, the word *sea* as "ocean," or *car* as "auto." Granich explains that the patient "recognises a word form, evokes a picture or perhaps a 'meaning,' then names the picture or idea." In a further sub-type Granich says the patient may omit or find difficulty in reading prepositions and "other connecting parts of speech." Retraining generally involves roundabout methods and Granich admits that attempts to teach letter sounding by repeated drill of letter-to-sound associations are often absolutely fruitless.

Granich gives us some detailed accounts of the retraining of some of his soldiers. Case No. 2, for instance, was wounded in action by shell fragments in the left parieto-temporal region. Although motor speech "had never been impaired" the ability to speak seemed to be almost totally lacking. The patient had severe word-finding problems and was also agrammatic. Details of reading and writing disturbance are of particular interest. The patient could read about 20 words, all nouns, and when he had learnt to copy writing with his left hand, could write about a dozen words from dictation, again nouns only. He learnt to read more nouns by visual-to-visual associations (studying pictures with the words beside them), but made frequent "bizarre" errors, such as reading *road* as "street." Phonetic associations of all types needed for reading and writing were lacking—in modern terms, this patient was a deep dyslexic (Coltheart et al. 1980). Reacquisition of vocabulary and syntax were trained along the lines described above, namely by memorising word lists, learning single words with mnemonic associations and memorising of paragraphs for sentence formation. Case No. 7, with a parieto-occipital lesion, was left wih a number of impairments including a severe dysgraphia. He could later write purely by phonetic association, but without any notion of "what the word might look like." He wrote "shoe", *shu*, for example (a typical **surface dysgraphic** spelling). The treatment for this was study of the 1000 commonest words and learning of "verbal-motor habits," as repeating aloud "tear," T.E.A.R.; "bone," B.O.N.E. and so on.

In Granich's work the direct, didactic treatment of the German school of the nineteenth century was continued. As with all approaches, it was enriched by ideas from other schools; Granich was aware of Goldstein's contribution, and tried to incorporate his insights into treatment. In essence though, Granich belongs to the past, even though the essential elements of his, and Gutzmann's, approach formed the basis of the contemporary didactic school which we describe in Section 2. At the same time as Granich continued (and regenerated) the old traditions, Wepman in the United States, and Luria in the Soviet Union were laying the foundations of radically different, and much more dynamic, approaches to aphasia therapy.

THE END OF THE PAST: THE BEGINNING OF CONTEMPORARY APPROACHES

This section summarises the diversity of approaches to the treatment of aphasia through the centuries, from remote antiquity down to 1947, the year of publication of Luria's *Traumatic Aphasia*. It includes general medical and surgical treatments, on the one hand, and specific re-educational measures on the other. The general remedies, or palliatives, range from application of gazelle, crocodile, or hippopotamus grease to sojourns in Avignon and use of Spanish flies and well-motivated leeches, and have little relevance to aphasic patients today. We have often mentioned the use of cauteries and blisters applied to the tongue and mouth, from the Middle Ages right down to Samuel Johnson's aphasic episode at the end of the eighteenth century. This was, of course, motivated by belief in paralysis of the tongue as the cause of loss of spoken language. Various forms of blood-letting were also frequently resorted to. Alongside these it becomes easier and easier to find references to attempts at re-education, both of spoken and written language. All these measures must be seen in the light of available knowledge at the different periods and of prevalent beliefs and attitudes. We have, in addition, referred to the variety of primary causes of loss of language—head injury (e.g., from the halberd in the sixteenth century; from bullet wounds or shell fragments in later wars), apoplexy, Bright's disease, Saturnismus, syphilis, and so on. This, of course, affects the type of lesion as well as the condition of the rest of the brain, with implications for therapy.

With little still agreed on today about the nature of this baffling symptom-complex, it is not surprising that early attempts at re-education of aphasia drew heavily on methods used with the deaf and dumb. More disturbing are reiterated exhortations to treat aphasic adults as one would non-brain-damaged children. Among remedial measures, we have described in some detail the techniques that we have called "speech gymnastics." Here Gutzmann the elder (to distinguish him from his son Hermann, who was long active as a phoniatrist in Berlin after the First World War) was one of the principal proponents, but the general approach was not limited to German therapists. Gutzmann's re-training system was probably much more thoroughly worked out than those of most of his immediate predecessors (although many of these fail to supply enough detail to be properly judged) but it roughly follows in the tradition of Bristowe and Bastian. These methods were founded on the neuropsychology of the physicians whom Henry Head aptly described as the "diagram makers"—including Broca in France, Wernicke in Germany, Lichtheim in Switzerland, and Bastian in England—which was based on localisationism and associationism.

As we have explained, these doctrines were already on the wane by the first years of the twentieth century; their decline, however, was neither uniform, nor absolute. Some followers of this approach continued to exercise a certain influence right up to the Second World War, and, as we shall demonstrate in Section 2, the **Wernicke–Lichtheim model** was to be revived by the neo-classical school in the 1960s.

Localisationism in itself was relatively sterile as an inspiration for therapy. If important verbal functions are subserved by narrowly circumscribed cortical areas and these areas are obliterated by damage to the brain, there would seem to be little to hope for from speech exercises. The sole reason for attempting specific re-training would be the assumption, which Bastian made, that there are duplicate, but subsidiary, cortical areas in the right hemisphere subserving the identical functions. As is well-known, the whole notion of narrow neuroanatomical regions subserving specific cognitive functions was rejected by Hughlings Jackson and a growing number of others. Not only was the doctrine itself challenged, but scientific interest and curiosity became channelled into entirely different pathways. To people such as Head the principal task was to describe and try to understand different ways in which language and other symbolic systems could break down after brain damage. This necessitated far more sensitive tests than had been used in the past and Head criticised many of his predecessors for superficiality in defining the symptoms or symptom-complexes that they then set about attempting to correlate with a discrete neuroanatomical substrate. A number of theorists today adopt an explicitly **dualist** position and have gone so far as to deny the relevance of anatomical localisation to understanding cognitive impairments as long as these latter remain inadequately analysed in psycholinguistic terms (e.g., Mehler, Morton, & Jusczyk, 1984).

Many of the techniques used in therapy ignored not only essential characteristics of aphasia and the implications of a partially damaged brain but also the nature of the learning process in general. Associationism, as still adhered to by Thorndike in a modified form, was partly responsible for faith in simple repetition as a method of learning. Later psychologists realised that some sort of "processing," whether expressed as "insight" on the part of the learner, or as the discernment of patterns or Gestalts, was a prerequisite of true learning. Here Goldstein appears to have had substantially more understanding of the brain-damaged individual and of the learning process than most of his predecessors in aphasiology.

Attention has been paid in the last part of this chapter to figures, beginning with Bastian, who represent specific trends, innovation or contributions relevant to aphasia therapy. Bastian himself was selected as an extreme localisationist and one who at a relatively early period spelt out a re-educational system in detail, even if the connection between the types of exercise he advocates and his theoretical model is at times difficult to follow. Gutzmann, Froeschels, and Mills elaborated their re-training schemes still further, but on the whole without any explicit theory; this may have been because localisationism and associationism were losing much of their popularity, and the trio had, at the time that we have reported, not yet been introduced to one of the newer doctrines, or philosophies, such as Gestalt theory, or holism. As early as 1914, Froment and Monod were developing a quite new approach that took account of patients' ability to produce well-articulated words in some conditions, without any specific articulatory training. However aphasiological doctrine and re-educational systems were going to develop, it would be necessary to assess the results more precisely than had been done before the First World War, and Franz of California was a pioneer in that field.

Goldstein and Weisenburg and McBride represent in their different ways a new departure, with improved methods of testing (especially Weisenburg and McBride) and emphasis on the individual's own reactions to the impairment and the importance, in re-education, of ensuring that the items to be practised are meaningful to the patient. Goldstein drew attention to particular difficulties that certain aphasic patients experience with tasks that require them to assume an "abstract attitude."

The amount of space devoted to individual aphasiologists does not necessarily represent even our own personal evaluation of their respective importance; in certain cases extra space has been accorded to figures whose published work is, for various reasons, less readily accessible; while the work of others, where a fair measure of familiarity is assumed, has been more briefly summarised.

Granich represented in some ways a step backwards and a return to some of the Gutzmann approaches. Although his "taxing drills" are of little theoretical significance, many of his observations and asides are of interest, and the idea of breaking down language skills into essential components was a productive one. His descriptions of dyslexia and dysgraphia were unusually detailed for that time.

Granich had some influence abroad and possibly at home, but Weisenburg and McBride and Goldstein had considerably more. After Weisenburg and McBride and Goldstein the stage was set for a more mature type of therapy, such as that carried out by Butfield and Zangwill during the Second World War, who subjected their results to a more or less quantitative analysis. By this time the rather rigid motor–sensory or Broca–Wernicke classification had yielded to the more flexible system of Weisenburg and McBride. The pre-eminence of a localisationist approach was at an end. In the period after the Second World War, the modern schools of aphasia therapy began to develop. A number of very different approaches, which gained their inspiration from a variety of outside fields—including linguistics, behavioural and cognitive psychology—were to take their place. Issues of the relationship between brain and language became less central, and in 1947, Luria published his *Traumatic Aphasia*. This book, which offered a new view of the relationship between brain, thought, and language, bore the seeds of a major doctrinal upheaval, but being written in Russian (and not translated into English until 1970), the book took some years to scatter its seeds. The flowering of those seeds belongs, however, to the next section.

Section 2
Competing Approaches to Treatment: Aphasia Therapy in Modern Times

INTRODUCTION

The development of methods, schemes or schools of aphasia therapy since the Second World War has not proceeded in a smooth, regular way. As with earlier approaches, some of the methods have been pure hit and miss; others have rested on a definite theoretical position. It is possible, however, to distinguish certain patterns and to group most of the systems under a small number of headings, each unified by a more or less common view of the nature of aphasia and process of therapy. This is a more productive way of reviewing trends than treating the different methods as a chronological succession, or else looking at national trends.

In the nineteenth century aphasiologists were usually therapists as well; since then the two trades have gradually separated. In some areas of science, neuropsychology is now seen as a hard-nosed respectable discipline; some branches of cognitive psychology, for instance, take the patterns of impairment in aphasic patients as one empirical test for theoretical models (cf. Coltheart, 1985). Therapy, by contrast, is often seen as intuitive and imprecise; as neurologists have increasingly abandoned aphasia therapy for the diagnosis and investigation of lower-level brain functions, aphasia therapy has increasingly become a specialist, but rather less respectable occupation in the eyes of the scientific world. Treatment has become much less closely tied to neurology and medicine; instead many therapists frame their ideas in terms of theories from the different psychological and linguistic sciences. Since the Second World War, therapists have attempted to incorporate and use a large number of neuropsychological and neurolinguistic findings—but the relationship is entirely one way. Outside the Soviet Union and Eastern Europe, neuropsychology has, as far as we know, scarcely ever used any therapeutic findings as evidence, nor shown signs of any interest in developing theories that could predict or explain the process of therapy itself. This, we believe, need not and should not be so (cf. Beauvois & Derouesné, 1982). Therapy that is clearly and specifically related to a neuropsychological analysis of deficits will be both precise and testable; a theory that can predict how a deficit can be alleviated and the pattern of changes that will result will be very much more powerful than one that does not.

We want to distinguish eight main schools of aphasia therapy:

1. *The didactic school*. This is the direct descendant of most language therapy of the nineteenth and early twentieth centuries. Language is essentially re-taught using a number of practical methods, most of which seem to work, which have evolved partly on the basis of common sense and clinical intuition and partly on *traditional* patterns of teaching reading, writing, and grammer to schoolchildren and non-brain-damaged foreigners.

2. *The behaviour modification school*. Like the didactic school this views therapy as a process of re-learning language. It is distinguished by a particular prescription of how things should be learned, which is drawn directly from behaviourist psychology. Many of the proponents of this approach doubt the value of theoretical accounts of the nature of aphasia, and concentrate in particular on the *methods* that should, they believe, be used in therapy.

3. *The stimulation school*. This was largely developed by two famous American therapists of the 1940s and 1950s—Joseph Wepman and Hildred Schuell. Therapy is seen as a process of providing the appropriate stimulation to enable the aphasic to regain access to language abilities that remain largely intact but unusable.

4. *The re-organisation of function school*. Dominant in much of Eastern Europe and the Soviet Union since the Second World War, this school views language ability as a number of quasi-independent physiological sub-systems. Therapy is tied closely to this theory developed by Alexander Luria and his colleagues, and depends on learning to use intact sub-systems in different ways to bypass those that are impaired.

5. *The pragmatic school*. These therapists view the problem in aphasia more as one of communication than of language. Most proponents take the view that therapy should concentrate on developing optimum use of unimpaired abilities to compensate for the language problem.

6. *The neo-classical school*. The renaissance in the 1960s of the **Wernicke-Lichtheim model** was mainly led by a group of neuropsychologists based in Boston, Massachusetts. This has contributed much to neuropsychological theory, and a few specific methods of treatment have been developed by therapists in this group. These mainly use relatively intact abilities of the aphasic patient to *support* the uncovering of inaccessible language abilities.

7. *The neurolinguistic school*. A number of therapists working principally in West Germany and France have, in recent years, attempted in incorporate relatively sophisticated linguistic theories into the process of therapy.

8. *The cognitive neuropsychology school*. Complex theories of language processing have been developed by applying models generated on the basis of laboratory studies of normal subjects to the performance of aphasic patients. The earliest applications of this approach to treatment were to acquired disorders of reading, but these have more recently extended to other areas.

It will be seen that elements of all the eight schools were present in the treatment systems of the early re-educators, although sometimes for quite different theoretical reasons from those of their modern advocates. In the following sections we critically evaluate the approaches to therapy of these eight schools.

THE DIDACTIC SCHOOL

We have used the term "didactic" in a rather loose way to cover a fairly wide range of approaches evolved partly out of experience and intuition and partly out of traditional teaching, where the therapist aims at some form of specific language re-training, in contrast to the methods of the stimulation school (see p. 69). All of these approaches assume that the task in treatment is to relearn missing information. Although most of these remedial methods derive ultimately from the traditions of Gutzmann and Froeschels (see p. 28) they have come to be applied much less rigidly, and multiple repetition no longer takes so central a role in treatment. Indeed, there is considerable emphasis on tailoring the therapy to the individual, his/her wishes and interests. Therapy is down to earth, and not related to any theoretical formulation; rather it is taken as obvious that for any particular problem a certain course of therapy is required. In some cases a certain rank order of difficulty of items to be re-taught is also assumed without adequate justification. Much of this has a strong empirical as well as didactic flavour. Many adherents of this school, in Britain and elsewhere, have not in general even felt the need to describe their methods in print. However, without testing individual methods they often report generalised improvement on standardised language assessment batteries.

We mention accounts of therapy by Braun of Bonn (1973) and by Lhermitte and Ducarne of Paris (1965) as some of the best examples of this school. Both are exceptional in the amount of detail they provide. Braun's short monograph (1973) contains various practical suggestions. Different exercises are prescribed for seven different forms of aphasia—or, rather, *described*, since she warns that it is impossible to follow a preconceived plan. In her introduction she says that each individual treatment should proceed from easy exercises to more difficult ones. This procedure one can hardly quarrel with, but the matter of deciding which skills or sub-skills for each aphasic group or individual aphasic patient are "easier" than others has been shown in the past ten years—and was indeed shown by Goldstein—to be a complex problem.

Braun's suggestions for each of the seven forms of aphasia are accompanied by details of treatment of actual cases, with a variety of aetiologies. Although there is little statement of underlying principles, she gives a number of references to Leischner (Leischner, 1959, 1960, 1972, etc.) and presumably expects the more scientifically curious reader to turn to these. For motor aphasia she emphasises the feature of greatly reduced lexicon; disturbances of grammar are also dealt with. In total aphasia there is a comprehension deficit as well as a severe expressive disorder. Expressive speech is regained in the most severe cases by conventional kinds of facilitation—completion of word-pairs, sayings, etc.—as well as simple repetition. She makes considerable use of singing: patient and therapist sing folk songs and suchlike together, the patient being urged to "read" the consonants (or words) from the therapist's lips. The phrases gradually merge into speech, both in tone and by actual variation of the words (as one might in English proceed from "Down by the old Bull and Bush" to "Down by the old Bull and Field," "Down by the old stream and field," and so on, first keeping to the original melody and later making the intonation more speech-like). This is reminiscent of Vargha and Gereb (1959), but even they were far from being the first to exploit their patients' residual singing talents. In vocabulary building, picture-naming with repetition, lipreading, and the accompaniment of written words is used. The progression is from nouns (especially concrete ones) to verbs (infinitives before conjugated forms), adjectives, prepositions, adverbs, and so on, and this progression is assumed throughout except for amnesic aphasics. The agrammatic patient (in motor aphasia) will proceed from simple subject-verb-object sentences to re-master some of the intricacies of German grammar—conjugation of the verb, use of prepositions, declension of the articles, and, at a more advanced stage, inversion of word order ("then answered Peter . . ."). Object-verb-subject structures, where the object is marked for the accusative case and the subject for the nominative, use of "separable" verbs (where the affix of a verb such as *auf*stehen or *ein*giessen is separated and relegated to the end of a simple sentence), and other refinements follow. The patient exemplifying this type of aphasia later progressed to picture description, retelling of short narratives, and dialogue, thus adding the level of text to the linguistic progression. For correct word-retrieval in sensory aphasia, Braun advocates assiduous imitation of the therapist's visible articulations of the word, coupled with rhythm to prevent the addition of unwanted syllables, so characteristic of this group. She stresses the lack of self-monitoring of speech in sensory aphasia and uses constrained picture-naming tasks to inhibit overproduction of utterances; this is coupled with playing back to patients tape recordings of their own speech to develop self-criticism.

Use of phonological cueing and of the usual facilitations is attempted by Braun for various groups, this for the articulatory rather than the word-retrieval aspect. For amensic aphasia, however, she cautions that the goal is word-finding (*Wortfindung*), without perpetual dependence on a therapist to provide the cue, and aims at developing associations that the patient will later on be able to initiate for him/herself.

We are using this monograph mainly as an example of an approach that has enjoyed very widespread popularity, although often carried out in a less systematic way than Braun's approach in the early 1970s.

That the re-education of aphasics in France was rigorous and exacting in the late 1960s and possibly still is today will surprise no one who knows anything about the French educational system. Patients came to the rehabilitation centres already well programmed into the work ethic and prepared to expend much effort, time, and money on their re-education just as, in the past, their parents had on their education. Given such motivation and preparedness for large doses of rote learning and occasional doses of boredom, they already had a head start. To this was, and probably still is, added the important factor of support from the extended family, practical, financial, moral, and remedial. Lhermitte and Ducarne (1965), emphasising the family's role, say:

> It is desirable that one of the family members takes on the role of *repetiteur* (assistant teacher) and assists at all (therapy) sessions . . . in addition, the family members, must, at all times, stimulate, listen to and correct the patient's language. (Lhermitte & Ducarne, p. 2345; our translation)

Lhermitte and Ducarne preface their language re-education courses by a period of "non-linguistic" excercises, with the aim of improving concentration, attention, and co-ordination. These comprise classification of objects; copying writing patterns; geometric shapes of increasing complexity; reproduction of various gestures, both symbolic and arbitrary; and a number of other "pre-linguistic" tasks. The treatment of motor aphasia subsumes the articulatory, lexical, and syntactic aspects. Exercises for buccofacial apraxia are thorough and intensive with auditory input supported by a stylised visual representation of the movements. The patient's attention is commanded by "varied and even excessive stimulation." Reacquisition of a "phonetic" system follows a functional hierarchy from "the simple to the complex." Each stage of phonetic elaboration has to be mastered "without escape (p. 2347)." The postulated hierarchy assumes vowels to be more elementary than consonants, followed by "simple" syllables, then consonant clusters, and so on, up to "words." All the same, higher linguistic units, as in short social formulae and semi-automatised utterances, are introduced fairly early; these serve as a framework for articulation practice. Lhermitte and Ducarne emphasise that good articulation in itself is not the aim but rather the recovery of propositional speech. Nevertheless they pay great attention to articulation, and specific exercises are proposed for paralysis of the speech organs, **dysprosody** and "dystonic anarthria;" for the latter a number of useful exercises in speech relaxation are prescribed.

Re-education of language has at least two goals—restoring a lexical stock and improving situation-related language. The former is approached in a fairly didactic way. The latter refers to dialogue and narrative speech, and retraining was carried out for a considerable time using an audiovisual series designed for teaching French as a foreign language; this in spite of reiteration that language re-education for aphasics is quite different from teaching a normal subject a foreign language. A comparatively advanced exercise is summarising a heard or read text. Here the patients were to have recourse to manuals "destined for foreigners." At this stage, clear and creative thinking is required, and the authors declare that "explicit formulation of thought and thought itself are indissociable (p. 2350);" the re-education therefore goes beyond what is normally understood by "speech therapy."

Jargon aphasia is overcome by constraint and discipline. Lhermitte and Ducarne see the linguistic part of it as a breakdown between the **signifié** and the **signifiant**—between concepts and words. One ingenious technique to regain conscious control of the phonological form of a word involves the therapist suggesting a series of acoustically similar words for each target word. Repetition of syllables, words, and short sentences is also used. Then, for this form of aphasia (as well as for the Broca form), the tape recorder is switched on so that the patient may hear his own errors and correct them. Lhermitte and Ducarne quote certain patients who report: "I have practised them a hundred times since the last session." No further evidence of their patients' conscientiousness and persistence is required.

In re-education of written language, Lhermitte and Ducarne consider that written automatisms differ from oral automatisms. After training in certain written formulae such as signature and address they suggest copying of regular verb paradigms followed by reciting them without the model, sentence completions, naming of pictures with prior verbalisation to establish correspondence between *signifiant* and *signifié*, and dictation of words. Acquisition of grammar and syntax is one of the most difficult steps; here contextual and semantic cues are provided. For the category **aphasic alexia** they based re-education on the *signifié* in order to reach the *signifiant*, so that the more analytical side of reading is left to the end. Analysis of the *signifiant* follows acquisition of the semantic value of the words. Some patients never get beyond a semi-global method of reading, a "spectacular dissociation which confirms the essentially different nature of the processes of acquisition and re-acquisition (p. 2355)."

The strongest critic of this school of therapy was the neurologist Bay of Dusseldorf (1973), who objected that aphasia therapy lacked a theoretical basis, that it lacked a system—there were as many methods as therapists—and, finally, that therapy could achieve nothing since aphasia is incurable. Braun and Lhermitte and Ducarne could hardly be accused of working in an unsystematic way, although it is sometimes unclear why they choose the methods they do.

The views of Lhermitte and Ducarne (1965) are developed further in an informative chapter on re-education by Lecours, Coderre, Lafond, Bergeron, and Bryans in a comprehensive textbook on aphasia edited by Lecours and Lhermitte (1979). They make a number of generalisations about the hierarchical order of various linguistic and psycholinguistic elements, some of which still await confirmation, and suggest certain ways of facilitating word-retrieval that later work has shown to have only short-term effect. Their plans for therapy show very much more linguistic sophistication than the Lhermitte and Ducarne article and include a progression of syntactic structures for agrammatic patients to follow. **Paragrammatism** is partly treated by the reading, repetition, and reproduction from memory of a correct version, orally and graphically. Lexical semantics are reconstituted in a systematic way.

Their attitude shows considerable development of the didactic line described earlier and embraces many elements of neurolinguistics (see p. 94) and a certain partiality for programmed instruction. They lay less stress on the complete mastery of isolated linguistic segments than on the re-acquisition of meaning-differentiating features.

In spite of certain similarities in the fundamental approach to re-education, there are many differences in technique and this "school" is evidently not a completely homogeneous group.

THE BEHAVIOUR MODIFICATION SCHOOL

In a general sense all forms of aphasia therapy constitute attempts at behaviour modification, because their aim is at most improvement in verbal behaviour, and at the least a change in the patient's attitude towards greater relaxation and acceptance of far-reaching limitations.

But in its most rigorous sense behaviour modification derives from Skinner's theory of **operant conditioning**, which stresses only the importance of **reinforcement** in **shaping** and producing verbal behaviour. (See Skinner, 1957, for an operant account of language and Chomsky, 1959, for a thorough critique of its inadequacies.) This extreme approach has generally led to a sterile view of aphasic language, defined for example in terms of stimulus-response channels and eschewing **mentalist** (and useful) terms such as meaning (see e.g., Sidman, Stoddard, Mohr, & Leicester, 1971; Sidman, 1971); as a result apparently simple statements can become engulfed in a fog of **behavourist** jargon. For example Bollinger and Stout (1976) take the premise that "the brain injury has resulted in a lessening of the ability cognitively to organise covert and overt responses" and suggest that:

> When the goal of communication management is considered to be the facilitation of more efficient covert and overt symbol manipulation by the patient, then the role of the speech clinician must be to teach the patient retrieval strategies designed to achieve that end. (p. 43)

This presumably means "a therapist can improve a patient's language by teaching strategies."

Therapists who have used behaviour modification do not necessarily believe in a Skinnerian account of language, or use pseudo-scientific jargon to describe their methods. In general this approach has been used as a teaching *method*, not as a theoretical account of aphasia (Goldfarb, 1981; Packman & Ingham, 1977). Programmed instruction requires the specification of a target behaviour (i.e., what is to be learnt) and accurate assessment of the patient's existing abilities and disabilities. The patient moves from one to the other by a series of small steps; correct responses are immediately and clearly reinforced; stimulus support is gradually faded out; opportunities may be provided for the patient to miss out stages if they are unnecessary ("feed-forward") and to revise earlier stages if he/she is having difficulty ("feed-back") (Costello, 1977; Holland, 1967, 1970).

As Holland (1967) points out, this requires careful and systematic analysis of a patient's abilities and it is "not accidental that similar ability and patience are important characteristics of the competent clinician (p. 12)." It also has the potential advantage that by precise specification of the aims and methods of therapy and the aphasic's reaction to it, we can learn more about how to do therapy (Seron, 1979). To the aphasic it offers the advantage of immediate knowledge of results, and if the appropriate therapy is being used the patient gets the reinforcement of knowing that he/she has improved; particularly if, as Lapointe (1977) suggests, 10 items are worked on in one task and their day-to-day improvement plotted on a graph.

One of the crucial questions for the behaviour modifier is how to choose the appropriate reinforcer. In general authors have maintained that it is an empirical question—suggesting (circularly) that whatever it is that changes aphasic behaviour is the reinforcer of choice. Holland (1970) claims that, in general, giving knowledge of results (saying "yes" when patient is correct) or "forward progression through a programme" is adequate, and suggests that using money or cigarettes is inappropriate and insulting. Goodkin (1969) found his patient's spontaneous speech changed most in response to self-punishment, **modelling**, and delayed feedback. "Punishment" of "mal-adaptive" behaviour has generally been thought non-ethical (and counter the principles of Skinner); according to Holland (1967), simple extinction (ignoring an undesirable behaviour until the patient stops doing it) does not work. This is perhaps not surprising where a patient has available only one way of responding to a task; Holland suggests that the best solution is to reinforce the correct response until it takes over.

Perhaps because behaviour modification emphasises the importance of breaking a task down into its "simplest elements" early efforts of programmed instruction were aimed at non-linguistic tasks like visual discrimination (Edwards, 1965; Filby & Edwards, 1963; Rosenberg, 1965; Rosenberg & Edwards, 1964, 1965). An initial enthusiasm for teaching machines (Holland, 1969; Holland & Harris, 1968; Keith & Darley, 1967; Sarno & Sands, 1970), has generally declined, partly because of the lack of flexibility inherent in the machines and because many patients prefer interaction with a human therapists.

Machine programmes were used with global aphasics by Sarno, Silverman, and Sands (1970) without conspicuous success; Holland (1969, 1970) described a variety of programmes for use with less severely affected patients; Culton and Ferguson (1979) describe automated programmes for comprehension deficits; Goodkin, Diller, and Shah (1973) trained aphasics' spouses to use operant methods to modify the patients' speech production; Smith (1974) gave aphasics coins for selecting the correct written prepositions; Ayres, Potter, and MacDearmon (1975) describe the use of reinforcement schedules to aid articulation, sentence completion, and pointing to auditory command; and Pizzamiglio and Roberts (1967), Schwartz, Nemeroff, and Reiss (1974), Hatfield and Weddell (1976), Seron, Deloche, Moulard and Rousselle (1980) have developed programmes for teaching spelling. DiCarlo (1980), following in the spirit of Gutzmann and Froeschels, has even described using language programme filmstrips for the deaf with aphasics, but without success.

Aphasia therapy is treated by behaviour modification as a *learning* process; as a result a considerable volume of work has been devoted to describing the conditions under which aphasics will learn non-verbal tasks (Brookshire, 1969; Carson, Carson, & Tikovsky, 1968; Tikovsky & Reynolds, 1962, 1963). It is not at all clear why learning a new non-verbal task has any relevance to aphasia therapy where the patient is reacquiring or even regaining access to language abilities he/she once had; it is a very open question whether this can profitably be viewed as a learning task.

One lasting contribution of the behaviour modification school to aphasia therapy has been in the development of experimental designs for examining the effects of specific treatments with single subjects (McReynolds & Kearns, 1982). A variety of studies of treatment that adopt a broadly behaviourist methodology have emerged from the United States over recent years (e.g., Burger & Wertz, 1984; Kearns & Salmon, 1984; Moyer, 1979; Thompson, McReynolds, & Vance, 1982). Increasingly, these studies have explored the use of microcomputer-based programmes for the treatment of specific problems: for example written word recognition (Katz & Nagy, 1982, 1983) or auditory word comprehension (Mills, 1982); or an intriguing approach where a microcomputer was used as an aid to word retrieval where the patient could only retrieve partial information about sought-for words (Colby, Christinaz, Parkinson, Graham, & Karpf, 1981). In general, though, this neo-behaviourist work, while concerned to establish the empirical utility of its treatments, adopts methods with no theoretical justification; the only assumption made is that practice on a task where performance is impaired will lead to improvement.

The potential for microcomputers in aphasia therapy may not yet have emerged; machines currently available at reasonable cost are very limited in their input, output, and processing capacities. Fifth generation computers with good word production and comprehension, and the ability to run programmes that can respond flexibly and intelligently to a patient's progress in treatment, may make it possible to make much more intensive "expert" treatment available to many more aphasic patients.

Programmed learning has not proved to be the "solution" for aphasia therapy that its early proponents appeared to hope. The vision of the future where all the therapist had to do was select the appropriate programme(s) and slot them and the aphasic into a machine and then sit back and wait for them to get better has manifestly not arrived and shows no signs of doing so. The reason is probably that the principles of behaviour therapy—that correct responses should be rewarded (reinforcement); that you should go in small carefully-graded steps from what a patient can do to what he/she would like to be able to do (shaping)—are probably what careful therapists were doing anyway. And behaviour modification provides no principled answer to what the hierarchy of progression in therapy should be, beyond the repeated injunction that they should be small, carefully worked-out steps. In practice these often turn out to be different from what supposedly "logical analysis" may have deduced (Sarno, Silverman, & Sands, 1970; Sidman, 1971). Reading accounts of the application of behaviour modification methods to aphasia therapy is often daunting. An obsessional concentration on the minutiae of "contingency management," with baselines and small steps—in general with the *hows* of the approach—contrasts with a blithe disregard for the question of *why* treatment was being done this way. The whole subject of "reinforcement" is much overplayed; one does not need to have spent long with aphasics to realise that *successful communication* is a highly rewarding thing for both patient and therapist. Aphasic patients' motivations are complex, and we do them a disservice if we treat them in a simplistic or manipulative fashion.

Behaviour modification is a method of therapy, but not a theory; it tells us how to do something but not what to do. It is to the other schools that we must turn to find therapy motivated by theory.

THE STIMULATION SCHOOL

In 1914 Froment and Monod attacked what they described as the classical "pedagogic" method of aphasia therapy, in which articulation was laboriously retrained, as if, they say, the patient was a child. They point out that nearly all aphasics can produce correct phonemes in some task (e.g., counting, **automatic speech**) and argue that to treat aphasics as if they have articulatory problems misses the point. Instead they propose the "psychophysiological method" that "provokes directly or indirectly the reawakening of auditory verbal images." To do this they advocate what were to become the two cardinal principles of stimulation therapy for aphasics: auditory stimulation and the progression in language from involuntary responses elicited by the therapist to voluntary and appropriate speech. This they base on the fundamental premise that language procedures are not lost, only inaccessible to the patient (Froment, 1921).

What happened to this approach we do not know (although they had some influence on German contemporaries of theirs), but it was to be recreated in the renaissance of aphasia therapy in the USA that followed the Second World War.

After the First World War there were isolated attempts in the United States at rehabilitation of aphasic soldiers with head injuries (e.g., Frazier & Ingham, 1920). Between the wars speech therapy in the USA developed principally in university clinics where the patients were mainly children and adults with functional speech disorders, and the myth arose that organic cases of aphasia were rare (Peacher & Peacher, 1948). Interest in aphasia therapy seems to have been kept alive by neurologists such as Weisenburg (Weisenburg & McBride, 1935), Low (Singer & Low, 1933), and the psychologist Franz (1924). In the Second World War many more soldiers with head injuries survived and with a large population of young, healthy aphasics in need of rehabilitation, aphasia therapy had to be forcibly reborn (Backus, 1945; Blackman & Tureen, 1948; Huber, 1942; Sheehan, 1946).

American therapists of this period saw themselves as pioneers; in part this was due to an extraordinary degree of ignorance. Wepman (1953) states that "the history of aphasia therapy for any large number of patients does not extend beyond the early 1940s (p. 4)."

Presumably he was unaware of the large numbers of aphasics treated after the First World War by Isserlin, Gutzmann, Froeschels, Goldstein, and Poppelreuter (see p. 35). In another sense these American therapists were pioneers; they were the first therapists to popularise the view that treatment was not teaching but stimulation. The two outstanding therapists of this period were Joseph Wepman and Hildred Schuell, whose methods and theories evolved in this period were to dominate aphasia therapy, in the United States at least, for a quarter of a century.

Wepman's methods were developed in a rehabilitation programme in an army general hospital, where aphasic soldiers were treated intensively (30 hours per week) over periods of 18 months (Wepman, 1951). Perhaps the most significant aspect of this was that improvement was monitored using standard Progressive Achievement Tests of reading, writing, spelling, and arithmetic; the measurement of language gains, though, remained impressionistic. Wepman's therapy was based on the three concepts of *stimulation*, *facilitation*, and *motivation* (Wepman, 1953). *Stimulation* is the therapy that results in changes; these depend not on what you do but how you do it:

> The content of therapy served only to stimulate the patient to produce the integrations necessary for language, but did not convey specific new learning of new vocabulary to the patient. (Wepman, 1953, p. 8)

In order for stimulation to work the aphasic must be in a state of *facilitation*, an internal condition of "physiological" readiness to use the information from the stimulation; the state of facilitation can itself be a result of appropriate stimulation. And for the stimulation–facilitation diad to work the aphasic must be motivated, which is in part a result of previous success in therapy, and of the patient's perception of his problems—"we must be prepared to accept as our goal what the patient feels to be his greatest need (p. 11)."

For Wepman, then, therapy is an active process on the part of the patient to forge new integrations on the basis of the stimulation provided by the therapist; language is recovered—or rather uncovered—in therapy rather than relearned. In the early stages the patient is bombarded with oral language, based heavily on object names; no response is demanded, but any attempts at speech are at least acknowledged. Written words and objects are used as well; verbs, adjectives, and adverbs are introduced, and reading and writing begin early on to supplement the other channels of stimulation (Wepman, 1951). Therapy has moved away from the concept of specific techniques aimed at specific linguistic difficulties of the patient, to an emphasis on the whole patient, with his/her needs and wishes. Treatment is less task oriented and more person oriented; as Wepman (1958a) put it, therapy has to take the "whole person concept" as primary. Indeed for Wepman (1958b) it is not the specific deficits of an aphasic that determine the prognosis, instead it is the way in which the patient reacts to his/her problems; whether he/she recognises and attempts to correct errors indicates how the language disorder will progress.

Later Wepman (1972) moved away from this initial formulation of aphasia as a language deficit, which needs general language stimulation related to the patients' psychosocial situation, to considering aphasics as having an impairment in thought that results in a language problem. Emphasising that "word finding is not the only source of difficulty in aphasic speakers (p. 207)," he suggests that therapy could be best directed at "stimulating the individual to think, letting whatever verbal behaviour follow that the patient is capable of producing (p. 208)." This proposal at first sight is so vague that it seems to be a recipe for almost total non-therapy; you could do almost anything and maintain that this was thought stimulation. Yet Schwartz, Saffran, and Marin (1980) and Saffran, Schwartz, and Marin (1980) have produced evidence that for agrammatic patients there is a problem in relating meaning to word order—precisely at the level of the relationship between thought and language that Wepman suggests that therapy should be pitched. The change to "thought-centred therapy" made communication rather than language the focus of treatment (Martin, 1981a), a view that has recently been developed by the pragmatic school.

The language stimulation approach of the young Wepman was developed by Hildred Schuell. Solidly, in her view, an empiricist, she rejected all previous formulations of aphasia, believing that our concepts should come only from "objective" test results. She imported the methods developed in IQ testing to aphasiology and tested large numbers of patients on her standardised test. Factor analysing the scores, she came up with one main factor that she claimed represented the overall severity of aphasia, and a series of subsidiary factors reflecting difficulties in particular peripheral processes—visual, visuospatial or sensorimotor (Schuell, 1965; Schuell & Jenkins, 1961; Schuell, Jenkins, & Caroll, 1962; Schuell, Jenkins, & Jimenez-Pabon, 1964). Aphasia is, then, a general and unitary problem varying only in severity; this is a point of view we find baffling—there seems little in common between a Broca's and Wernicke's aphasia—and the one never evolves into the other, which it must if they were simply different points on a continuum of severity (Leischner, 1976). If aphasia is a single problem, therapy needs to be basically the same for all patients, with some additional tasks for any of the other processes that are impaired. Schuell was impressed by her finding that all aphasics have difficulty in auditory comprehension at some level which she attributes to a deficit in auditory–verbal short-term memory (Schuell, 1953) and therefore suggested that therapy should be based or "intensive auditory stimulation," with visual stimulation as well if the patient found it useful. The therapist must ensure that the stimulation is "adequate"—sufficient to elicit a response—by varying rate, loudness, and length and using high frequency material interesting to the patient. Every stimulus should elicit, but not force, a response, and errors should not be corrected, but more responses should be elicited instead. The aphasic should produce the maximum possible number of "verbal attempts" in each session, and auditory stimuli should be repeated by the therapist as much as possible—she suggests 20 times is much better than 10 or less (which she says is really rather useless!) The influence of behaviourism, which dominated American academic psychology at the time, is shown by Schuell's insistence that it is the production of as many correct responses as possible that is critical. Treatment should focus on using patients' remaining strengths, and not draw attention to their weaknesses (cf. Holland, Swindell, & Fromm, 1983).

Schuell's theory is based on an idiosyncratic "functional schema for the communication process," which specifies a variety of different modes, or levels of processing. The source of the schema is obscure, although it resembles in some ways the associationist speculations of the nineteenth century diagram makers. No attempt is made to relate this level of speculation to empirical results or to the selection of tasks to be used in therapy. The primary weapon in the therapist's arsenal, should, she maintains, be intensive auditory stimulation. Like Bastian (1898) she sees auditory comprehension as the centre point of the language system; not only is language acquired by auditory input but the auditory system provides feedback control of performance in other modalities. Her finding that all aphasics are impaired in sentence comprehension was taken to confirm this.

Schuell's justification for this approach is no longer particularly convincing. Language acquisition requires auditory input, but there is a great deal more to it than auditory stimulation (Brown, 1973). Aphasics may fail in sentence repetition tasks for a number of different reasons (Shallice & Warrington, 1977), and in any case normal spontaneous speech is possible when repetition is severely disturbed (Shallice & Butterworth, 1977). The nature of the role of auditory feedback processes in monitoring other language systems remains to some extent unclear (Levelt, 1983). But there is no evidence that disturbance of external auditory monitoring ever causes aphasic symptoms in normals. The primary position that Schuell gave to auditory comprehension cannot be sustained—it certainly cannot in any simple way mediate other language systems; if it did we could not, for example, tell from the written words that BEAR and BARE had different meanings (Henderson, 1982), nor would there be aphasics with severely impaired auditory comprehension but (relatively) intact reading and writing (e.g., Michel, 1979).

It is easy to criticise Schuell for the theoretical content of her approach, but it is important to remember that she was a product of American psychology in the 1950s, when it was dominated by behaviourism and theory was frowned upon. Her impact and appeal do not depend on this. Her treatment approach was sensitive and practical; she produced a rich catalogue of therapeutic techniques and materials. All aphasics, apart from the **global aphasics** who suffered from an "irreversible aphasic syndrome," could and should be treated, and even they were sympathetically advised and consoled/counselled.

Schuell's doctrines still have many devoted disciples (see e.g., Darley, 1982); this is because her test provides a diagnosis and prognosis and she suggests a wide variety of treatment methods—although because of her lack of theory there is no principled way to choose which are appropriate.

Much of the research on the general effectiveness of aphasia therapy with groups of patients has used a general stimulation approach to therapy (e.g., Smith, 1972), and Schuell herself related test results to progress achieved in therapy (Schuell, Jenkins, & Jimenez-Pabon, 1964). Wiegel-Crump and Koenigsknecht (1973) used the whole gamut of therapeutic techniques recommended by Schuell for anomia in the treatment of picture-naming for four anomic aphasics; they showed substantial improvement in naming the pictures that were the focus of treatment, which generalised to other pictures that were not involved in the process of therapy (cf. Seron, Deloche, Bastard, Chassin, & Hermand, 1979). But because of the emphasis of the school on the use of "abundant and varied materials" in each session (Schuell, Caroll, & Street, 1955, p. 45); and because, as long as responses are elicited it doesn't really matter how, there has been little research on which particular techniques are useful.

Schuell's prescription for massive and repetitive auditory stimulation (Schuell, Jenkins, & Jimenez-Pabon, 1964) was tested by Helmick and Wipplinger (1975) in the treatment of picture-naming with a single patient. They compared progress on items where each name was repeated by the examiner a total of 24 times in a session, with those where the aphasic heard the name only 6 times, and found no suggestion that massive amounts of auditory stimulation resulted in greater improvement, in therapy which extended over four weeks. Two other techniques for naming therapy were studied in Patterson, Purell, and Morton (1983): repetition and phonemic cueing. Both were very effective in enabling the patient to produce the picture-name immediately, but 30 minutes later they were no more likely to name the picture than if nothing had ever happened. This suggests that simply eliciting responses in any way possible is not necessarily therapeutic, although it may have an effect on morale as Schuell, Caroll, & Street, (1955) suggest: "The fact that he has spoken a hundred or more times during the clinical hour gives the patient confidence in his ability to talk (p. 45)." (Although patients may soon become dissatisified with elicited and involuntary speech.)

The importance of motivation was demonstrated by Stoicheff (1960), who found that when aphasics were told that they would find the task hard and perform poorly, they performed much worse on both word reading and picture-naming than when they were given encouraging instructions emphasising how well they were doing and would do. And the aphasics rated their performance much worse under the discouraging conditions.

The influence of the stimulation approach remains widespread, particularly in the United Kingdom and the United States. Many therapists still consider that the crucial process in treatment is to elicit responses by whatever means possible; although many have used a relatively eclectic approach, especially, in recent years, influenced by the neo-classical school that emphasises the differences rather than the similarities between groups of aphasics.

Possibly the best example of an eclectic approach is the work of Jon Eisenson (1973, 1977). Stimulation is related to an analysis of the patients' problems, and should use whatever input modality is least impaired; in the early stages repetition is often of particular use. He suggests that programmed learning and group therapy have their parts to play, but only as an adjunct to specific individual therapy; and Beyn's "preventive method" (see p. 79), should be used. His distinctive contribution lay in his attention to the importance of the aphasic patient's needs, aspirations, and emotional state.

The Milan school see therapy as "a stimulus–response situation in which the therapist endeavours to elicit and consolidate language responses by giving stimuli and reinforcements (Basso, Capitani, & Vignolo, 1979, p. 192)." They use stimulation to shift aphasic responses from relatively automatic actions elicited by the therapist towards increasingly voluntary and purposeful use by the patients themselves. Like Eisenson they warn against the dangers of excessive amounts of "auditory stimulation," and base their methods explicitly on the hypothesis that intentional production of a response makes it more likely that it can be produced later. As they put it, "this assumption awaits empirical verification" (see the discussion of evidence on this issue on p. 128ff).

A neuropsychologist from a very different tradition, Egon Weigl, working in Romania and East Berlin, provided some interesting evidence in support of this fundamental assumption of stimulation therapy. Viewing the linguistic abilities of aphasics as fundamentally intact (Weigl & Bier-wisch, 1970), he argued that particular deficits resulted from impairments in individual input and output modalities. He discovered a facilitation process which he called **deblocking** (Weigl, 1961). Use of a word, or syntactic structure, in an unimpaired task could temporarily make it available for an aphasic to produce in an impaired modality. This tempor-ary availability only lasted for a few minutes (Weigl & Kreindler, 1960), but once it had been produced in the impaired modality the response could remain available for a considerable length of time (up to two years). Not all performances were equally good at deblocking other tasks and the patterns of deblocking varied from patient to patient, and needed to be empirically discovered for each one.

Until 1980, Weigl's works were not widely available in English (see Weigl, 1980), and as a result several important differences between deblocking and classical stimulation methods have not always been appreciated. While stimulation therapists argue that the most effective facilitation is by auditory input, Weigl claims that any relatively intact ability may be used to deblock any impaired one. So, for example, if a patient is good at naming but poor at auditory comprehension, naming a picture may improve comprehension of that name a few minutes later. Crucial to Weigl's approach is that the deblocking stimulus should *precede* the performance to be deblocked, and that the aphasic should be *unaware* that deblocking is happening. In contrast stimulation therapists claim that facilitation is greatest when stimuli are presented in several modalities simultaneously (e.g., Ulatowska & Richardson, 1974); presumably then the aphasic is also aware of what is going on.

While deblocking appears to provide a systematic rationale for one form of stimulation therapy, Weigl's empirical results have not always been replicated. What appears to be crucial is *how* a performance is deblocked; this evidence is discussed in more detail later. In general it appears that picture-naming is only facilitated in the long-term when the aphasic is deblocked by a task that requires *semantic* processing of the picture name, for example spoken word-to-picture matching, written word-to-picture matching, or even yes/no semantic judgements; neither hearing the word, nor speaking the word, nor seeing the picture is necessary to get substantial and long-lasting facilitation effects (Howard et al., 1985a). In contrast, exercises such as repetition, rhyming or phonemic cueing that emphasise the *phonological* structure of the name have only very short-term effects (Patterson, Purell, & Morton, 1983).

Weigl (1970, 1979) claims that deblocking can apply to a whole seman-tic field; so for example reading *dog* might then deblock *dog, puppy, kennel, bone,* and *cat.* However, Howard et al. (1985a) found no evidence of facilitation spreading to closely associated members of a semantic category, and Podraza and Darley (1977) found that when patients heard the words "sting, honey, hive" just before they named a picture of a *bee*, they performed worse than when they had heard nothing at all. So, just as with normal subjects in a "tip-of-the-tongue" state, semantically-related items can block the retrieval of a target word (Reason & Lucas, 1984).

The stimulation school no longer holds the predominant position in aphasia therapy that it did 10 years ago. Its great contribution was to capitalise on the observation that much more language may be intact in aphasics than appears on the surface; practical and straightforward therapy methods were devised and used, with, as far as one can judge, sensitivity and compassion. Fundamental to the approach was the feeling that relatively small amounts of stimulation, if of just the right kind and applied at just the right time, could make a critical difference to the outcome; if the therapist could only find the correct fulcrum, the patient's language system could be levered back towards normality. The stimulation school has, to some extent, been hampered by general mistrust of theory, a failure to put its methods to detailed empirical test, and adherence, in the face of a growing body of contradictory evidence, to its two principle tenets—that aphasia is a unitary, undifferentiated disorder, and that auditory stimulation is *the* method for treatment.

RE-ORGANISATION OF FUNCTION: APHASIA THERAPY IN EASTERN EUROPE

The adherents of the other schools somehow skate over the implications of a physiologically damaged brain. The school which could loosely be called the Lurian school after its progenitor meets this awkward fact head on. Followers of this school draw attention to the unavoidable fact of irreparable damage to areas of the brain crucial to language and other higher functions after stroke, gunshot wound, or other causes. Recent evidence of some limited form of neuronal regeneration (e.g., Devor, 1982) does not affect the position fundamentally.

The heart of Luria's conception of **reconstitution** of higher **functions** is I. P. Pavlov's view of the nature of organic function itself (Pavlov, 1949) and Anokhin's more recent elaboration of this view (Anokhin, 1935, 1974). Pavlov looked at an organic function as an organism's activity directed towards the performance of a particular biological task; as a further development, the physiologist Anokhin formulated the concept of *functional systems*, consisting of groups of interconnected acts incorporating a network of neurological structures whose dynamic functions are united in a common task. The implication of a system viewed thus is that it enjoys a measure of plasticity: the initial and final links of the system (the initial conditions and the result) remain fixed, while the intermediate links may be modified within wide limits. As a result a functional system can be re-created or re-organised in a different form where one component has been impaired or destroyed. The notion of *centres* is thus replaced by the view of *neural networks* comprising a number of components that together subserve a complex "function."

This view of functional systems operating within brain substance that has some degree of neuroanatomical specificity allowed Luria to resolve the conflicting doctrines of localisationism and anti-localisationism in a dialectical **synthesis** (Luria, 1966). His resolution, moreover, both accounts for the selective impairment of intellectual activity by brain damage and includes the possibility of restoration of function under certain conditions. The new functional system will differ from the original but will accomplish the same task, if less efficiently. A degree of plasticity exists even for the more biological functions such as respiration, and for the higher cortical functions an even greater degree of plasticity obtains. (Readers are reminded how damage to the diaphragm may be compensated for by greater involvement of the intercostal muscles, in respiration, or, in the last resort, the mechanism of air-swallowing may be brought in. Luria, 1947, 1948, 1962, 1975.)

The higher cortical functions, according to Sechenov (1891, 1962) and Pavlov, are responsible for reflecting the outside world; they also have a mediating, creative-productive aspect, which enables the performance of previous tasks by new methods. Examples of this are the use of tools to extend motor potential, of a variety of devices within and without the organisms as mnemonics and, *a fortiori*, of speech, in the mediation of mental processes.

Pavlov's model of cortical analysers (or concentrations of receptors in the primary sensory projection areas)—auditory, visual, motor, cutaneous-kinaesthetic—is fundamental to Luria's interpretation of specific impairments of skills and their reconstruction. In this way, Luria examines the primary cause of different forms of language breakdown, mainly in terms of which of the cortical analysers is implicated, and then devises remedial measures that endeavour to utilise intact analysers to reconstitute the impaired function. Even extraneous components, that is, outside the system and in the world beyond the organisms, may be drawn in and with practice the new system becomes integrated as a specific functional organisation.

Luria, and Vygotsky before his early death from tuberculosis, had become interested in the problems of aphasia in the 1930s (see Luria, 1979). During the Second World War, Luria was responsible for running one rehabilitation hospital for soldiers with head injuries. In 1947, he published *Traumatic aphasia* and in 1948 *The restoration of function after brain injury*, which were the results of his experiences in working on rehabilitation of these brain-damaged soldiers. With his sophisticated synthesis of anatomical and psychological analysis of patient's impairment, and the application of specific treatment techniques founded in a theory of therapy, his views were much in advance of the understanding of aphasia in the West. Clinicians in the West were not, however, aware of this; it was only 20 years later that Luria's works started to appear in English translation.

A well-known example of a Lurian reconstitution is his treatment of certain types of breakdown of syntax occurring in the aphasic forms called, in his classification system, **efferent motor aphasia** and **dynamic aphasia**. In addition to relatively "low level" or peripheral impairments, such as inability to switch rapidly and smoothly from one link in coherent speech to the next, there is the deeper problem of a disturbance of "propositionising" (in Jackson's phrase), with loss of the predicative component. This manifests itself in the surface phenomenon of "telegraphic speech," consisting mainly of nouns in the nominative case (in an **inflecting language** such as Russian). Vygotsky, one of Luria's early colleagues and his mentor, claimed that "inner speech", which evolves out of the social speech of early childhood via "egocentric speech", is predicative in character (Vygotsky, 1962) and Luria considered that, with these patients, the underlying defect lay at the level of inner speech. Luria used various auxiliary, visual schemes to restore inner speech and achieve target sentence structures. One such scheme brings in the "auxiliary external aid" of three blank pieces of paper that serve as a frame for moulding the proposition, corresponding to a certain "thematic picture." These three papers stand for the three fundamental components of the sentence (as in *deti sobirajut gryby*—the-children are-gathering mushrooms—in Russian it can, conveniently, be done with three actual words).

Luria (1947, 1948) describes a variety of treatment approaches for other types of aphasia. With *afferent motor aphasia*, where the primary defect is identified by Luria as residing in the kinaesthetic basis of speech articulation, he uses the intact visual analyser as a new, extra support for production of articulemes; for *sensory aphasia*, where the acoustic analyser is at fault, the sounds of speech must be analysed consciously, with the help of kinaesthetic and visual images. This form of reconstruction is not a *compensation* in Goldstein's sense, but is a reorganisation that at a later stage can become internalised and automatised. Luria was one of very few psychologists to attempt to create psychological theory from clincial practice and practice from theory, and for a long time he was unique in evolving a thoroughly worked-out system of speech therapy with a rational basis.

That A. R. Luria achieved a unity of theory and practice is not to be doubted. Furthermore, although he accorded great attention to the minutiae of language re-education, he succeeded in integrating all his ingenious remedial devices in a coherent system. Nonetheless it cannot be claimed that his approach was "scientific" in the western sense of the term, if by that one understands proceeding beyond hypothesis and inferences to verification by experimentation and measurement. Luria has been criticised by some as over-emphasising relatively low-level biological operations in his model of cognitive functioning and of over-simplifying the linguistic complexities of speech production and comprehension, particularly at the syntactic level (Hatfield, 1981). In addition, it must be noted that other researchers have been unable to replicate some of Luria's findings of specific impairments, with specific groups of patients. For example Brown (1972) and others were unable to confirm the existence of two distinct forms of motor aphasia (efferent and afferent), while Blumstein, Baker, and Goodglass (1977) failed to find any increased difficulty in specific deficit in phonemic discrimination among "sensory" aphasics—in fact, in their study Wernicke patients (Luria's sensory aphasics) were found to be superior in this skill to other groups.

Luria's doctrines, interpretations, and classification spread very widely throughout East Europe. After some delay partly due, ironically, to the communication barrier, in a profession whose very business was the study and remediation of disorders of communication, Luria's philosophy eventually also penetrated to the West.

A second significant figure in Soviet aphasiology, and especially in aphasia therapy—the two go hand-in-hand in the USSR—is E. S. Beyn, once a student of Luria. Her early work was concerned with problems of sensory aphasia and their remediation (Beyn, 1947). A little later she turned her attention to breakdown of syntax and morphology (Beyn, 1957). Using the same classification and theoretical orientation as Luria, she went on to elaborate various methods of re-education of her own. Her method of treating efferent motor aphasia and precluding the development of agrammatism that inappropriate therapeutic measures might provoke (the so-called "preventive method," Beyn & Shokhor-Trotskaya, 1966) is by now well-known. Beyn and Shokhor-Trotskaya recommend remedial measures that concentrate on the predicative aspect of speech from the outset. They begin with verbs in the imperative and adverbial particles such as here, there, down, no, maintaining that with appropriate intonation such words are equivalent to sentences. Gradually verbs in the conjugated form are introduced. The introduction of nouns is delayed—this is diametrically opposed to standard practice elsewhere (e.g., Taylor & Marks, 1955; Wepman, 1951)—and when finally introduced they are presented in oblique cases, thereby representing "dynamically mobile parts of the sentence." Their aim is to prevent the appearance of "telegraphic speech" by ensuring that the patients from the earliest stages produce sentence-like utterances. Beyn says: "We have tried to advance from the sentence to the word." This is a case where the theory leaves the facts trailing somewhat behind. Many researchers have confirmed the common observation that for many severe Broca's aphasics verbs are more difficult to retrieve than nouns (Miceli, Silveri, Villa, & Caramazza, 1984; Myerson & Goodglass, 1972; Wales & Kinsella, 1981). One could question the logic, for a stage when any kind of verbal utterance is a hurdle, in adding to the difficulty. An alternative would be to retrain a small number of nouns and try to introduce verbs, adjectives, and adverbs as early as possible but not be too purist about it; then, as soon as a modicum of nouns and verbs or nouns and adjectives has been reacquired, to introduce the idea of basic syntax and word-combinations (cf. Hatfield, 1979). Beyn goes on to point out that "word denotations by themselves do not constitute speech" and accords primary status to the grammatical aspect of language. Like Luria, she was far ahead of most of her contemporaries in her application of ideas from structural linguistics to the problem of aphasia. Like Luria, she is adamant that therapy must be specifically geared to each identifiable form of aphasia. Her 1962 *Manual of aphasia therapy*, which she co-authored with Gertzenshtein, Rudenko, and Shiaptanova, contains a set of exercises in phonemic discrimination that aim at underpinning restoration of impressive speech in "sensory" aphasia (cf. Gielewski, 1983), as well as a range of remedial language exercises for other forms of aphasia, at various stages. Her later work focused attention on morphology and phrase analysis (ability to operate the formal grammatical rules of the language). She and her colleagues found by experiment that patients able to assess the correctness of auditorily-presented word-combinations, such as prepositional phrases, can on the whole perform tasks based on orientation in their acoustic-rhythmic form (and vice versa). The tasks comprised division of words into syllables, making rhymes, and producing word-forms by analogy. These findings then formed the basis for further therapy for efferent motor aphasics, who were given "pre-grammatical" training on word-stress and the above mentioned tasks (Beyn & Vizel, 1979; Beyn, Vizel, & Hatfield, 1979). Both in the case of the earlier **preventive method** and the more recent work, Beyn tried to demonstrate the efficacy of these procedures, using small groups of matched patients (Beyn, 1964; Beyn & Shokhor-Trotskaya, 1966; Beyn & Vizel, 1979).

Tsvetkova and Glozman (1975), reared in the Luria tradition, carried out further investigations of grammatical problems in different forms of aphasia and made use of their findings in improving the design of plans for therapy. One such task involved assigning words to different surface grammatical categories where the deep semantic correlates violated the formal designation (as the "verb" *to blush*, or *redden*, contains the "adjectival" concept of *red*—this is particularly marked in Russian). More recently they have explored the use of group treatment where language can be used in a motivating social context (Glozman, 1981; Tsvetkova, 1980). A number of other Soviet Russians were involved during this time in the practice of aphasia therapy, whose names are perhaps less well-known outside Eastern Europe: Akhutina (1978): Kogan (1947, 1969); Tonkonogii (1968, 1973); Vinarskaya (1971); and many others. The Soviet psychologist/therapists have not been coy in describing exactly what they do in therapy for their aphasic patients, nor why.

In Poland, Klimkovski (1966), Maruszewski (1975) and Mierzejewska (1978) received their basic training in the Luria tradition but went on to develop an individual style.

In Romania, Kreindler (Kriendler & Fradis, 1968) applied Pavlovian concepts of conditioned reflexes to his interpretation of aphasia. Among his pupils, Voinescu and Gheorgita have elaborated methods of therapy. Voinescu has a number of techniques for reconstruction of the sentence in agrammatism (Voinescu, 1971; Voinescu, Dobrata, & Gheorgita, 1971) and Gheorgita has recently evolved a system of "vertical" reading for certain types of dyslexia in addition to new types of remediation of dysgraphia (Gheorgita, 1981; Gheorgita & Fradis, 1979).

THE PRAGMATIC SCHOOL

In recent years a number of therapists have argued that the focus of therapy should be on communication rather than language *per se*. Treatment should not concentrate on production and comprehension of normal and correct language structures, but on enabling aphasic patients to make optimal use of all their available resources in communication. The development of this approach indirectly reflects increasing interest in **pragmatics** in academic linguistics since the mid 1970s, just as increasing interest in syntactic aspects of linguistics during the 1960s and 1970s was reflected in the development of the neo-classical and neurolinguistic schools.

The approach is essentially atheoretical, and is based around one particular observation: that aphasic patients in real-life situations are often able to communicate very much better than they can speak/understand (Prinz, 1980; Wilcox, Davis, & Leonard, 1978). Formal language tests of the traditional kind (e.g., the **BDAE, WAB** or **MTDDA**) may fail to capture important aspects of communication. As Davis and Wilcox (1985) argue, there are a variety of aspects of communication that are not present in the literal text. These include implications from the message that involve inference from the context (cf. Grice, 1975) both linguistic and non-linguistic, use of prosodic information (intonation, stress), gestures, facial expressions, and situational context. Information of all of these kinds can be used in communication: for example, on first meeting someone it is almost inevitable that their first utterance will be some kind of greeting. Given all the contextual information, one can with some accuracy predict the subjects of conversation. Aphasic patients do indeed use a variety of contextual, situational, and pragmatic cues when dealing with language; for example when patients cannot use the syntactic structure of a sentence they will use the overall plausibility of a situation to come to an interpretation (Caramazza & Zurif, 1976; Heeschen, 1980; Schwartz, Saffran, & Marin, 1980). And, in expression, aphasic patients will use a variety of channels of communication to supplement and correct their speech in communicating particular messages. When patients' performance is observed they are found to use a wide variety of communicative resources to convey a full range of messages—commands, requests, questions, performatives, as well as propositions (Guilford & O'Connor, 1982; Holland, 1982; Meuse & Marquardt, 1985; Prinz, 1980).

One consequence of this change in emphasis is the development of a variety of formal aphasia assessments that measure patients' ability to communicate rather than technical language proficiency. Rather than trying to assess separately the patient's ability to use each individual aspect of non-linguistic and paralinguistic communication (e.g., facial expression, gesture, etc.) the assessments all try to form a global impression of the effectiveness of communication. The assessments include the Functional Communication Profile (**FCP**; Sarno, 1969) that is based on observation of patients in communication; Communicative Abilities in Daily Living (**CADL**; Holland, 1980) that widens the range of contexts sampled by including some role play situations; and the Edinburgh Functional Communication Profile (**EFCP**; Skinner et al., 1984) that is intended to give a picture of the communicative resources of elderly patients. These tests suffer from some problems: while it is easy to grasp the overall concept of "communication" it is not easy to quantify, especially when you consider that people potentially need to convey or understand an unlimited number of different messages conveyed in a variety of different ways in an unlimited range of contexts. There is no obvious principled way in which a sensible sample can be made. And, more important, communication is part of interaction, and how effective it is depends on who the other communicator is. A number of studies have found that spouses of aphasic patients generally see the communication problems as less severe than therapists (Helmick, Watamori, & Palmer, 1976; Linebaugh & Young-Charles, 1978, 1981). The usual interpretation is that spouses can be unrealistic in their appreciation of the patient's problem; another viewpoint is that patients will communicate more effectively with members of their families because of the range of shared knowledge and assumptions that they can bring to bear.

For some years therapists have argued that treatment should focus on providing patients with strategies that they can use themselves to circum-vent their problems. Aphasics use very different methods of self-cueing in word-retrieval, compared with those provided by therapists. Clinicians find that phonemic cueing and clichés are particularly effective (Pease & Goodglass, 1978), but these presuppose information that aphasics them-selves generally have not got (Bruce & Howard, 1987); when trying to find words the simple strategies of delay or description are most likely to lead aphasics to successful retrieval (Farmer, 1977; Marshall, 1976; Marshall & Tompkins, 1981, 1982). So therapists have encouraged aphasics to develop whichever of their own strategies seem to be most effective; this, of course, results in word-retrieval methods that the patients themselves can use rather than being dependent on the therapist. Berman and Peelle (1967) found each of their patients benefitted from different self-cueing techniques: one, for example, was often able to write the first letter of a word he could not find and use this to cue himself phonemically; while another was able to use description to create a contextual cue.

The pragmatic approach broadens the whole context of therapy. The focus of attention is how successfully the aphasic uses his/her resources to *perform a communicative act*, which will depend on the whole range of verbal and non-verbal strategies that are brought to bear, and on the ability of the other person to use and interpret the information. Prinz (1980) investigated the ability of aphasics to communicate requests and found that all were able by verbal and non-verbal means to make the pragmatic force of their intention clear, irrespective of the severity of their aphasia. And Martin (1981b), discussing therapy of jargon aphasia, points out that despite the flow of **neologisms** and paraphasia it is often possible to extract the general thread of meaning; the focus of therapy can be both on improving the aphasic as communicator and on training others to be good interpreters.

Treatments have been developed to improve patients' communicative abilities. Aten, Cagliuri and Holland (1982) treated a group of seven aphasic patients who were at least nine months post-onset. In two weekly one-hour sessions, the patients and a therapist discussed the strategies that they could use in communicating in a variety of contexts (e.g., going shopping, greeting someone, supplying personal information), and practised them in role play. At the end of the period all seven patients had improved in the CADL (which samples role play behaviour in just this range of contexts) by an average of 12.3 points, while their scores on the **PICA** remained unchanged.

Davis and Wilcox (1981, 1985), Davis (1980), and Green (1982, 1984) have taken this approach a step further. Not only do they argue that therapy should aim to provide the patients with the most efficient com-municative strategies available, but also that this should be done by therapy in which all tasks involve the patient in conveying new information. Davis and Wilcox describe the paradigm of this approach (which they have named **PACE**—promoting aphasics' communicative efficiency [sic]): the therapist and patient each have a pile of object pictures, and take turns to communicate to each other what is the object on their card which the other cannot see. The patient is encouraged to convey the message by whatever means are available; in turn the therapist models techniques that the patient may find useful. According to Davis and Wilcox (1985), four principles are fundamental to their approach:

1. The clinician and [aphasic] client participate equally as sender and receiver of messages.
2. The treatment interaction consists of an exchange of new information between clinician and client.
3. The client is allowed free choice with respect to selection of communicative channels.
4. Feedback from the clinician is based on the client's success in communicating a message and is characteristic of receiver feedback occurring in natural settings. (pp. 89–90)

These therapists argue that formal exercises designed to teach and elicit particular linguistic structures or items focus on the patients' disabilities, prevent the use of non-verbal communication, and fail to carry over into everyday life. They claim that if therapy consists of sending and receiving communicative messages then these problems are avoided. Currently there is no evidence to support this set of claims, or the implication that therapy should be "naturalistic" (Green, 1984). It is not immediately obvious that treatment aimed at communication need always involve communication; in other areas people may use exercises for particular aspects of a skill in isolation and build from these elements towards their aim. Thus, for example, physiotherapists working with hemiplegic patients will work on balance in sitting, and muscular control in standing before practising walking; they do not develop patients ability to walk by only practising walking. (In fact most physiotherapists would claim that premature practice of walking can be an obstacle to progress.) The PACE method, apparently, involves no direct instruction; patients have to infer from the behaviour modelled by the therapist what is intended that they should do. Many patients may find this difficult; again it is not clear why Davis and Wilcox feel that direct instruction is not appropriate.

Davis and Wilcox (1985) report a preliminary study of whether PACE therapy is effective. The subjects were eight aphasic patients at least one year post-onset. Four subjects were treated for two sessions a week over four weeks by "directed stimulation of impaired communicative modalities" (p. 116; which is defined no further), followed by four weeks of

PACE; the other four patients just had a period of PACE. Improvement was assessed on a "role playing battery." There was no improvement in overall PICA scores after treatment of either type, but PACE treatment resulted in improved scores in the "role playing battery" that was not observed with "direct stimulation."

It is, probably, inevitable that treatment approaches to aphasia will reflect the ideological preconceptions of the society in which they are developed. PACE therapy is extraordinary as a treatment, because it takes a situation (client and therapist in a room with a stack of picture cards) that is as far from true communication as one can imagine. Communication is seen as an individual performance with one other person; group treatment is only mentioned in a very short section right at the end of Davis and Wilcox's (1985) book. At the same time as Green, Wilcox, Holland, and their colleagues were discovering pragmatic approaches to treatment in Australia and the USA, Tsvetkova (1980) and Glozman (1981) were exploring the uses of group treatment in the Soviet Union. For Tsvetkova (1980) language is essentially a social tool; groups can work together in mutual co-operation to deal with the communicative challenges that aphasia brings. They claim that group treatment incorporating drama, role play, and discussion can result in both more self-confidence, a positive self-image, and improved desire to communicate, as well as technical improvement in language.

Pragmatically-based approaches to treatment are a valuable counter to treatments that concentrate exclusively on linguistic skills, while forgetting that the ultimate aim must be to improve patients' ability to communicate. But, some pragmatic therapists confuse questions of the *aims* of treatment with the *means* used to achieve those ends. Pragmatic therapy develops patients' overall ability to communicate by using whatever verbal and non-verbal means are available to *compensate* for their disabilities. Whether this is best done in exercises to teach particular strategies, or by ensuring that all therapy consists of communication of new information, awaits empirical test.

The pragmatic school reflects the growth in interest in pragmatics among linguists in the last decade. As an approach it is, unlike the others we have discussed, in a very early stage of development; it involves a radical change of emphasis in therapy, with the aphasic as a much more active utiliser and developer of strategies aimed at communication. Its view of aphasic patients' potential is essentially limited; the patients' language disabilities are taken as given and treatment aims to ensure that the patients can use other sorts of information as effectively as possible to supplement their failed linguistic skills. The results of treatment studies confirm this view; patients' linguistic disabilities remain unchanged while their communicative abilities in role play improve. Other schools aim to provide specific treatments aimed at the aphasic difficulty itself.

THE NEO-CLASSICAL SCHOOL

The diagram makers of the nineteenth century (Wernicke, Lichtheim, Bastian, etc.) with their wide range of pure aphasic syndromes, each associated with particular cortical or sub-cortical lesion sites, were temporarily eclipsed by the vociferous attack of Henry Head (1926), and to a lesser extent Pierre Marie (1906). Then, as we have seen, the notion of differentiable aphasic syndromes was completely rejected by Schuell and other American aphasiologists of the 1950s. Meanwhile, of course, in the USSR and elsewhere in Europe, aphasic syndromes lived on, being described, re-described, differentiated, and re-analysed.

The classical localisationist doctrines were rediscovered by a group of workers based in Boston (USA) from the early 1960s onwards. Prominent among them were Harold Goodglass and Norman Geschwind. They rediscovered Broca's and Wernicke's and anomic aphasics, pointed out that **conduction aphasics** were by no means as rare as had been previously thought, and observed examples of other rarer syndromes, such as the transcortical aphasias and pure alexia, agraphias, and word deafness.

But this did not simply constitute a revival of the elegant schemata of Wernicke, Lichtheim, Charcot, Bastian, and others. The Boston School took as fundamental the division of aphasics into **fluent** (associated with post-Rolandic lesions) and **non-fluent** (pre-Rolandic lesions) *on the basis of the characteristics of their spontaneous speech*. A new sophistication from post-Chomskyan linguistics was put to use, and aphasic deficits were re-described, and syndromes defined both in terms of *localisation* and impairment of *linguistic levels*. Thus, very crudely, Broca's aphasia was identified with impairment on a syntactic level with problems present in both input and output, and a lesion in the inferior part of the frontal lobe; Wernicke's aphasics showed fundamentally intact grammar and deficits on a lexical–semantic level with temporal lobe lesions; conduction aphasics show a predominant deficit in repetition, and literal paraphasia in spontaneous speech, which can be characterised by an output phonological deficit, and is associated with lesions deep to the supramarginal gyrus. **Anomic aphasia** is milder and not associated with a particular locus of lesion, and represents a breakdown at the level of lexical retrieval. In addition a number of less common but specific aphasias have been described—or rather re-described, as both the names and the symptoms are much the same as those proposed by the Wernicke-Lichtheim model (see Albert, Goodglass, Helm, Rubens, & Alexander, 1981; Goodglass & Kaplan, 1972; Lichtheim, 1885).

Of course all aphasics do not fit neatly into these categories. Albert et al. (1981) suggest that only 30% of patients are ideal types of particular syndromes; the remainder represent mixtures of pure deficits (cf. Benson,

1979b). The value of the syndrome system is, they argue, that it provides a framework against which other symptom patterns can be described. The fundamental assumption is that some aphasics at least can, on the basis of the characteristics of their spontaneous speech output, be classified into different *diagnostic groups* that are *homogeneous*; that is, the aphasics in one group may show differences in degree of deficit, but all will show the same qualitative pattern in different tasks. So, unlike their nineteenth-century predecessors, the Boston school usually argue from performance of groups rather than individuals.

The attempt to characterise a school in general will always do violence to differences between different members of it. For example, within the neo-classical school, there is a wide range of opinions on the precise status of neurological lesion localisation. While Geschwind (1965) would consider localisation fundamental to the explanation of aphasic deficits, Gardner (1977) maintains that the presence of similar lesions will define a group of patients with common neuropsychological deficits, whose problems should be explained on a psychological, rather than neurological, level.

The neo-classical school has rapidly grown to become a major influence on neurolinguistic theory, with a prolific output of studies of performance of aphasic groups in a wide variety of tasks (see Albert et al., 1981 for a review). Much of this has had little direct application in aphasia therapy, but there have been some valuable contributions, particularly in devising treatment programmes that use relatively intact non- or meta-linguistic systems to *support* the production (and comprehension) of language.

In general their approach owes much to the stimulation school. Sparks (1978) states that:

> A realistic and somewhat delimited concept of language therapy for aphasics places the language therapist in the role of a catalyst helping the aphasic realise the maximum improvement that an ongoing process of spontaneous recovery will permit. (p. 135)

He argues that therapy must be based on the diagnostic group to which a patient belongs, but that standardised assessment must be supplemented by detailed observation of the patient's behaviour and reactions to therapy. The importance of this is to observe the factors which influence the patient's behaviour—for example, self-correction, responsiveness to different varieties of cues, perseveration, and the effects of changing task. Having found these out, therapy seems to be largely a matter of intuitively directing intervention at the functions that are impaired. The importance of the supplementary tasks is that all factors that improve a patient's performance should be used; for example, Broca's aphasics should be helped to produce syntax in output by "liberal phonetic cueing (p. 141)."

The fundamental assumption is the same as for stimulation therapy; correct responses should be elicited by whatever means possible.

The observation that aphasics often have relatively well-preserved abilities to produce serial speech, nursery rhymes, poems and prayers, songs and rhythm, dates back at least as far as Dalin (1745) and Gesner (1769). Many clinicians have used these skills as a basis for therapy (e.g., Baldi, 1936; Keith & Aronson, 1975; Ustvedt, 1937; Vargha & Gereb 1959). The earliest description of singing used in treatment that we have found is Sharpey (1879), publishing a manuscript that he wrote in 1824. In it he describes a patient who suddenly became mute. As her speech improved:

> The reacquisition of her reading was eventually facilitated by singing the words of familiar songs from the printed page, while she played on the piano. (p. 8)

Goldstein used rhythm and singing in treatment:

> Sometimes they can only say a word within a song. While in singing they may make no mistakes in pronunciation, they may have the greatest difficulty in pronouncing one of these words individually. Later the word has to be freed from its relation to the rhythmic context. (Goldstein, 1948, p. 332)

> A patient unable to find the words hunter, hare, shoot, learned in a **deposited rhythm** "The hunter shoots the hare". Later he could find all these words with the help of this sentence. (Goldstein, 1948, p. 343)

Backus (1945) suggested that instead of teaching grammar to aphasics it was easier to train them in the rhythm of speech. Starting off with singing, the patients then progressed to speaking in unison and beating out the rhythm. And Gerstman (1964) described how one mute aphasic in a psychiatric hospital was befriended by another non-aphasic patient. As she pushed the aphasic around she would sing songs and sentences to her; the aphasic started to sing along and gradually transferred this into ordinary speech.

The concept of using intact rhythmical and intonational ability to develop oral expression in aphasics is not new. The contribution of Sparks and his colleagues in the development of Melodic Intonation Therapy (Albert, Sparks, & Helm, 1973; Laughlin, Naeser, & Gordon, 1979; Sparks & Holland, 1976; Sparks, Helm, & Albert, 1974) was to provide a systematic hierarchy for development from phrases sung in unison by the aphasic and the therapist, to normal conversational speech production, by gradual withdrawal of support by the therapist, and reduction of the initially highly exaggerated intonation towards more normal patterns and to show that, to some extent at least, it worked. Sparks, Helm and Albert (1974) and Helm-Estabrooks (1983) speculate on the neuroanatomical basis of their therapy method, and propose that it involves using the intact right hemisphere abilities to improve the performance of the damaged left hemisphere. This is reminiscent of the speculations of their classical localisationist predecessors (e.g., Bastian, 1898; Broca, 1865) on the extent to which the right hemisphere can be induced to take over the damaged functions of the left.

Taking the view that:

Language may not be destroyed in global dysphasia, but instead may no longer be accessible by primary pathways. (Albert et al., 1981, p. 143)

The neo-classical school have described a number of methods of treatment in which they attempt to access the intact linguistic abilities of global aphasics by alternative means. Baker, Berry, Gardner, Zurif, Davis, and Veroff (1975) and Gardner, Zurif, Berry, and Baker (1976) report on experiments where eight global aphasics used combinations of visual symbols written on index cards to carry out commands, respond to questions, and describe events (VIC). The symbols were as representational as possible, but as some represented relatively abstract concepts, their reference was not immediately obvious. The patients were trained for four hours a week over three months, and five learnt to perform the tasks described above. Two of them became able, in addition, to use the system to express their feelings, needs, and desires.

The VIC system has the problem that its "sentences" are not immediately comprehensible to normal people. Other more easily comprehensible systems of communication for use in therapy have been developed. Capitalising on the relatively intact gestural abilities of global aphasics, Helm and Benson (1978) proposed the system of Visual Action Therapy (VAT) in which aphasics learn in a hierarchical system to associate representational drawings and later gesture with objects and actions, and then to produce increasingly symbolic gesture. Helm-Estabrooks, Fitzpatrick and Barresi (1981b) report that global aphasics treated in this way show most improvement in auditory comprehension and gestural pantomime, although individual patients improve in other language areas. Schlanger and Freiman (1979) have also described the use of pantomime in therapy.

The use of pantomime and sign languages in combination with speech has often been used as a therapy method, particularly with non-fluent aphasics. Backus (1945) advocated encouraging patients to use pantomime in order to elicit language; Chen (1971) combined finger spelling and American Sign Language (ASL) signs as an adjunct to therapy and found that half his patients learnt to understand the signs. Skelly, Schinsky, Smith, and Fust

(1974) used Amerind because it is a simple sign language that is relatively easily comprehensible, even to those who have not been trained in it. Six months of therapy in Amerind, accompanied by oral speech, for six chronic non-fluent aphasics, resulted in all of them mastering a considerable vocabulary of signs, and improvement in oral speech production for five of them. A number of other therapists who have described the outcome of treatment with Amerind are cited by Skelly (1979); others have used American Sign Language (Bonvillian & Friedman, 1978); Australian National Sign Language (Moody, 1982); Blissymbols (Johannsen-Horbach, Cegla, Mager, Schempp, & Wallesch, 1985); cued speech (Royall & Horner, 1983); or a combination of ASL and Amerind (Guilford, Scheuerle, & Shirek, 1982; Kirshner & Webb, 1981). (See Christopolou & Bonvillian, 1985; Peterson & Krishner, 1981, for reviews).

Skelly et al. (1974) claimed that treatment with Amerind could result in acquisition of both signs and verbal language; however in her study, and most others, signs from the therapist are combined with oral language. Where treatment is by sign alone, aphasic patients only learn in sign and there is no change in oral language; to improve in both sign and language, combined inputs from the therapist are necessary (Hoodin & Thompson, 1983; Kearns, Simmons, & Sisterhen, 1982).

Some doubts on the specific efficacy of gesture as a therapy method have been raised by Cicone, Wapner, Foldi, Zurif, and Gardner (1979). They found that the spontaneous gesture of a group of aphasics showed very similar patterns of impairment to their oral speech production; gesture was not successfully used as a supplement to deficient language. Like Finkeln-burg (1870), they speculate that a central difficulty with symbols of any kind underlies both the problem in gesture and the aphasic deficit. They suggest that the impression that aphasics communicate better in "real life situations," may depend on utilisation and production of other non-gestural pragmatic cues. This, then, leaves open the possibility that it is not gesture or sign language itself that results in therapeutic improvement. Cicone et al.'s results have been questioned; a number of studies have failed to find impressive correspondences between the severity of aphasia and patients' ability to understand or produce meaningful gesture (Behrmann & Penn, 1984; Daniloff, Noll, Fristoe, & Lloyd, 1982; see Feyereisen & Seron, 1982, for a review).

An ingenous method was proposed to utilise global aphasics' involuntary utterances as a basis for treatment. This approach was named "voluntary control of involuntary utterances" (like most of the therapy methods of the neo-classical school this becomes enshrined as an acronym—**VCIU**: Helm & Barresi, 1980; Helm-Estabrooks, 1984). This is based around oral reading—a skill that is often surprisingly well preserved in global aphasics. Patients are given words to read that they have been heard to produce as involuntary utterances; if the word is read correctly it remains in a patient's "vocabulary set"; if the patient makes an error—for example reading TABLE as "chair"—he/she is immediately given CHAIR to read. According to Helm-Estabrooks and Barresi, this will then be read correctly, and CHAIR can be added to the patient's vocabulary set. Thus, by incorporating words produced as errors or involuntary utterances into a patient's vocabulary and producing them as correct responses, considerable reading vocabularies can be built up. Using this approach Helm-Estabrooks and Barresi report that three patients managed to acquire a reading vocabulary of over 200 words and phrases, which included a large proportion of more emotionally-loaded terms. Words brought into the patients' vocabulary in this way can then become the focus for other kinds of treatment activity.

Helm-Estabrooks has also suggested a syntax retraining programme for agrammatic aphasics that she calls, **HELPSS**—the Helm-Elicited Language Program for Syntax Stimulation (Albert et al., 1981; Helm-Estabrooks, Fitzpatrick, & Barresi, 1981a), based on the proposal that their problem is in access to syntax rather than a loss of grammatical knowledge. A hierarchy of constructions that is derived from the performance of aphasics as a *group* is elicited first by repetition of a sentence produced by the therapist as a story completion, and then as a completion by the aphasic alone. Intransitive commands are elicited first because these are in general the easiest constructions for Broca's aphasics to produce (Gleason, Goodglass, Green, Ackerman, & Hyde, 1975; Goodglass, Gleason, Bernholtz, & Hyde, 1972), followed by transitive commands, WH-questions, and transitive and then intransitive declaratives. Treatment of one chronic Broca's aphasic by this method resulted in improved performance in the production of syntax in the North Western Syntax Screening Test (Lee, 1969) as well as the use of a wider range of syntactic constructions in spontaneous speech (Helm-Estabrooks et al., 1981). The particular hierarchy that HELPSS employs was challenged by Salvatore, Trunzo, Holtzapple, & Graham (1983); they showed that none of their individual patients demonstrated the order of difficulty for the constructions that the treatment program assumed. The particular constructions that were difficult varied from patient to patient; as Tissot, Mounin, & Lhermitte (1973) and Howard (1985) argue, "agrammatic" difficulties in sentence production may be of several different kinds.

Shewan and Bandur (1986) provide an unusually comprehensive and detailed description of their approach to aphasia therapy; in the usual style of the neo-classical school, its name is an acronym—**LOT**—Language Oriented Therapy. Shewan and Bandur's account is unusual in that they explain the rationale behind their approach, explain the sources of their treatment hierarchies, and try to demonstrate empirically that the approach is of real use. They consider that in aphasia language processes may be lost or disordered at phonological, semantic, or syntactic levels; there may also be impaired access to (relatively intact) language abilities. Like the therapists of the stimulation school, Shewan and Bandur take the view that patients should practice tasks that are just at the limit of their capacities; treatment should focus on tasks where "the patient makes errors at a rate of 20 to 30% on a formalised test." Shewan and Bandur emphasise that the effect of treatment pitched at this level is not re-learning; instead they suggest that the effects are *physiological*, although unfortunately they cite no evidence to support this claim:

> The method provides opportunities for patients to access and to process language material at a level appropriate to their abilities. This processing provides practice and reorganisational opportunities so that the neuro-physiological mechanism can improve and alter its functioning. This may happen by increasing efficiency, developing alternate pathways and networks, or repairing impaired pathways. (Shewan & Bandur, 1986, p. 14)

Treatment is directed at the four traditional modalities: spoken language comprehension; written language comprehension; and spoken and written language production; to which Shewan and Bandur add a fifth—the comprehension and production of gesture. In striking contrast to the therapists of the stimulation school, who believed that the processes of auditory comprehension were centrally involved on all language performance, Shewan and Bandur state that their five "modalities are considered to be mutually exclusive and non-overlapping (pp. 9–11)." Within each modality they recognise a number of different "areas" (which again are "mutually exclusive and collectively encompass the entire modality"), in which patients' performance might be disturbed. For each "area," Shewan and Bandur suggest a hierarchy of treatment tasks; these hierarchies are based on reviews of most of the available neuropsychological literature (in English) that could give an idea of the relative order of difficulty of different tasks. Where possible in their hierarchies Shewan and Bandur provide different orders of difficulty for patients of different neo-classical "diagnostic groups," but they emphasise that:

> Since these hierarchies are reflective of group performance, the same hier-archy may not hold for all aphasic patients. By gathering baseline data, the clinician can determine each individual's particular hierarchy of difficulty and can select content using this knowledge. (p. 13)

Within each area, therapists should use "cues" to elicit correct responses. Elaborating on an idea from Berman and Peelle (1967), Shewan and Bandur suggest that the therapist should find out the particular types of cue that work for each patient; the patients are then encouraged to generate these cues for themselves, and to incorporate them into their own language performance. Treatment, then, is aimed at providing the patient with cueing strategies to overcome their own aphasic limitations. Laudable as this idea is, there is a problem; therapist-given cues generally work because they provide a patient with information that the patient does not already have (e.g., the first sound of a sought-for word). If the patient does not have this information, there is no way in which he/she can use it in any self-cueing system.

Shewan and Kertesz (1984) attempted to evaluate the effectiveness of their "language oriented therapy." Seventy-seven aphasic patients were assigned at random to one of three treatment regimes: LOT; stimulation therapy based on Schuell and Wepman given by a trained therapist; or general language stimulation from an untrained nurse volunteer. The outcome of these three groups was compared with 23 patients who were unable, or unwilling, to attend for therapy. The results were disappointingly equivocal; taken together, all three treated groups improved significantly more than the untreated patients, but there were no significant differences in outcome between the three treatment approaches. Shewan and Bandur feel that this demonstrates "that LOT is an efficacious type of treatment"; more critical readers will wonder whether the poorer outcome of the untreated group was related to the reasons that they were not treated. Strong conclusions can only be drawn from clinical trials where allocation to groups is randomised and outside the control of patients or physicians (cf. Cochrane, 1972).

Shewan and Bandur feel that:

> Treatment materials and their progression in difficulty should reflect current knowledge about how patients process language. To that end, LOT is based on information and data gathered from the fields of speech-language pathology, linguistics, psycholinguistics and neuropsychology. (pp. 8–9)

The result is that the approach, magpie-like, picks pieces of knowledge from different areas to generate hierarchies, but can never create any kind of coherent theory. Beyond the assumption that practising tasks on the edges of patients' abilities will (somehow) have a beneficial physiological effect on the brain, there is no attempt to generate any theory of therapy. In practice, many of the assumptions built into the theory (e.g., that different modalities are independent) are almost certainly false. Shewan and Bandur's approach represents possibly the best and most coherent atheoretical approach to treatment, but reveals, at the same time, the need for a coherent and motivated theory.

Like the stimulation therapists, the neo-classical school believe that in most cases aphasia results from a failure in access to and use of language, rather than its loss. Their general approach to therapy is stimulation, but is specific to each particular diagnostic group, which is defined in terms both of the *level* of linguistic impairment and the *localisation* of the lesion. The form of stimulation is related to information from performance of groups of aphasics in neurolinguistic tasks. The most original contribution, from Sparks, Helm-Estabrooks, and their colleagues in Boston, has been in the revival and development of a variety of therapy methods in which relatively intact abilities (singing, gesture, involuntary utterances, etc.) are used to *support* language performance, and in accepting as an integral part of the development of new therapy methods the need to demonstrate that they are effective.

THE NEUROLINGUISTIC SCHOOL

In 1969 one of the principal papers presented to a congress devoted to applied linguistics was entitled "*La Neurolinguistique*." Its authors, the neurologist Hécaen and the linguist Dubois, declared the object of this sub-discipline to be, firstly, to analyse neurologically-caused verbal disorders with the aim of establishing a "purely linguistic typology" and, secondly, to achieve an experimentally verifiable neurolinguistic classification correlating topographical sites of lesions with the linguistic types (Hécaen & Dubois, 1971, p. 85). The Hécaen and Dubois paper discussed aphasia in the light of certain linguistic concepts that had been articulated in the previous decade or so, including Chomsky's (1957) distinction between **competence** and **performance**, the multi-level structure of language and the bipolar organisation of language along an axis of syntagmatic relations and an axis of paradigmatic relations (Jakobson, 1956).

Hécaen and Dubois then hazarded a provisional attempt at a truly linguistic classification of the aphasias—aphasia of phonemic realisation; disturbance of syntactic realisation; and so on. No mention was made in this paper of implications of a new, unified, neurolinguistic view for re-education.

We are not sure when or by whom the term "neurolinguistics" was coined, but by the 1970s it was widely used: Lebrun (1976) traces the term back to a thesis title submitted by M. Kendig at Columbia University in 1935. There had, of course, been somewhat isolated application of certain facets of linguistics for a long time: Kussmaul (1876), Steinthal (1871), Finkelnburg (1870), Pick (1913), Isserlin (1922) and others in syntax and morphology; Alajouanine, Ombredane, and Durand (1939) and Goldstein (1942) in phonetics and phonology. Goldstein saw the importance for re-education of Jakobson's (1941) postulated hierarchy of re-acquisition of phonemes and phonemic oppositions. Luria, who with Vygotskii had taken a proper course in linguistics before the Second World War, and whose linguistic theory as a result was based on the Prague school (Trubetzkoy, 1939), was one of the first to use the notion of phonemic distinctions in interpreting certain problems of sensory aphasia. He also drew attention to the importance of syntactic complexity in comprehension and repetition at a time when most investigators were only looking at the dimension of length of utterance.

Jakobson's 1956 paper, describing aphasic disorders in terms of disruption along the syntagmatic axis (contiguity disorders) or the paradigmatic (similarity disorders), had implications for re-education and set some therapists off on a new tack. They began to concentrate on *combination* of linguistic units as a goal for their patients with Broca's aphasia. For a long time emphasis in therapy had been almost exclusively on the *paradigmatic axis* (i.e., on *selection* of the appropriate lexical item in its slot in the sentence). With agrammatic patients, early introduction of simple subject-verb combinations in the language re-education plan has somewhat the same goal as Beyn and Shokhor-Trotskaya's (1966) "preventive method," that is to say, the re-acquisition of some form of "propositional speech" as soon as a modicum of lexical items—verbal forms as well as nouns—became available.

Dividing the commonest forms of aphasia into disorders of combination (or contiguity) and disorders of selection (or similarity) can be seen as an over-simplification, even if Jakobson's other dichotomies are also embraced (Jakobson, 1964); all the same, this system (which Jakobson attempted to map on to Luria's classification) did at least orientate therapists towards a more productive form of re-education than exclusive word-retrieval drills and facilitations.

Around this time, certain researchers were able to show the importance of frequency in word-retrieval (Newcombe, Oldfield, & Wingfield, 1964; Rochford & Williams, 1965). Therapists then had access to one empirically-motivated dimension for ordering items in terms of difficulty on the "paradigmatic axis." In 1966 Marshall and Newcombe claimed to show the operation of semantic features in paraphasic errors; patients were more likely to make errors involving single semantic feature differences than multi-feature errors. In the early 1970s, interest developed in applying phonological principles, and in particular the notion of phonological features, to the analysis of deviations in speech production (Blumstein, 1973; Green, 1970), and in the United States and elsewhere a number of workers began using post-Chomskyan linguistics in the analysis of aphasic deficits in lexicon, morphology, and syntax (e.g., Lecours & Rouillon, 1976; Weigl & Bierwisch, 1970; Whitaker, 1971).

Today the German groups in Bonn (Stachowiak, Kotten, Ohlendorf, Engl) and in Aachen (Poeck, Huber, de Bleser) are some of the best representatives of the neurolinguistic school. Leischner, until recently director of the *Rheinische Landesklinik für Sprachgestörte*, had taken an interest in linguistic facets of aphasia for a considerable time (Leischner, 1955; 1976; Panse, Kandler, & Leischner, 1952) and had also been actively involved in therapy since the 1950s (Leischner, 1959). The academic linguist Peuser, formerly at the same institute as Leischner, later described a therapeutic scheme for a variety of aphasic types (Peuser, 1978). For receptive problems in "total" and "mixed" aphasia he recommends that the therapist should first try to "deblock" (Weigl, 1961) comprehension of linguistic symbols with the help of pictures. Intralinguistic relations are then invoked to reinforce extra-linguistic activities, in the form of repetition of words proffered by the therapist. The progression is from substantives and elementary verbs (lexemic level) to the syntagmatic level by pictorial representations of complex situations. Although grammatical words (**functors**) resist deblocking at this stage, patients of these two groups manage to understand simple sentences. Patients with motor-amnesic aphasia may have difficulty in *understanding* **function words** (articles, prepositions, auxiliaries, etc.) as well as handling them expressively and the receptive aspect has to be worked on before the expressive; and here Peuser uses a model loosely based on Chomsky's (1965) "transformational generative grammar." Peuser is also particularly interested in the relations between the phonic and the graphic codes (Peuser, 1974, 1978).

In the hands of linguists such as Peuser, the "levels" of text, pragmatics and communication are all important. With patients described as mixed aphasics, the therapist aims at deblocking whole sentences and abstract relational words by means of pictures. To expand the lexicon, the paradigmatic relationship to synonyms and antonyms are used. For "motor amnesic aphasia," grammar and lexicon are both treated, the latter by exploiting the resources of semantic fields (Peuser, 1974). Engl, Kotten, Ohlendorf, and Poser (1982) have compiled a detailed linguistic programme leading up to composition of *texts*, a linguistic level which many therapists often stop short of. Questions of re-acquisition of prepositions and use of "order of mention" strategies have been examined by Kotten from the therapeutic standpoint in another study (Kotten, 1977). In a further study, Kotten considered the extent to which actual exchange of information takes place in the various activities of a speech therapy session (Kotten, 1979).

The linguists of the Aachen group—Huber, Stachowiak, de Bleser and, until recently, Weniger—with the collaboration of the logopaedist Springer, have been investigating the possibilities of verbal retraining on a number of linguistic levels for some time and the result has been the development of various useful therapeutic programmes with some evidence for their efficacy. These include descriptions of specific therapy for impaired phonemic organisation (Huber, Mayer, & Kerschensteiner, 1978); therapy for global aphasia (Rohricht, Springer, & Weniger, 1978); reconstruction of syntax (Springer & Weniger, 1980), and transition from systematic practice of syntactic structures to spontaneous speech in dialogue (de Bleser & Weismann, 1981). In a general statement of their approach (Poeck, Huber, Kerschensteiner, Stachowiak, & Weniger, 1977; Weniger, Huber, Stachowiak, & Poeck, 1980) the group stress that in building their remedial programmes on linguistic foundations they do not aim to teach the patient to deal with linguistic segments—phonemes, inflections, sentence patterns, etc.—but at enabling the patient to use the linguistic processes and rules by which words, sentences, and discourse are produced.

Whereas the didactic school emphasises that therapy plans should be designed around the individual patient's deficits and needs, the Aachen group explicitly state that their programmes are constructed to deal with a specific linguistic problem and will consequently be appropriate for a *group* of aphasics who all share the same linguistic deficit (Poeck et al., 1977). While many therapists accept the need for linguistic analysis at patients' difficulties, there remains little agreement between different groups of workers about the precise nature of the deficit in any particular group of patients. As a consequence, different approaches to treatment that are all motivated by a shared aim to incorporate linguistic parameters will often incorporate very different treatment techniques (cf. Hatfield & Shewell, 1983).

THE COGNITIVE NEUROPSYCHOLOGY SCHOOL

Since the mid-1970s a new, and radically different, approach to the study of aphasia has developed, and with it a new school of aphasia therapy is emerging—the cognitive neuropsychology school.

The initial impetus for the development of this school came from Marshall and Newcombe's (1966, 1973) studies of patients with acquired dyslexia. They noticed that one patient (GR, who they called a "deep dyslexic") was unable to read simple non-words (e.g., CAG, BOM). When reading real words, GR appeared to use a specifically *semantic* routine: he made semantic reading errors (e.g., reading LIBERTY as "freedom"; UNCLE as "nephew"), and he was better at reading concrete words than abstract words. Another patient, JC, who they described as a "surface dyslexic," showed a complementary pattern. He could read non-words, but, when reading real words, often failed to use word-specific knowledge of pronunciation; instead, he seemed to use a system of, as Marshall and

Newcombe put it, "grapheme-to-phoneme correspondences" for reading real words, even when this gave incorrect pronunciations. So for example JC read GRIND as "grinned," LISTEN as "Liston," and GUEST as "just."

Marshall and Newcombe realised that these two patterns of reading disability corresponded directly to the dual route theory of word reading, which had been developed by cognitive psychologists who were modelling information processing in reading on the basis of laboratory experiments with normal subjects (see e.g., Coltheart, 1978). Within the dual route theory, there were two ways in which real words could be pronounced. Using the lexical route the whole word was identified in a lexicon of real, known words and then its (word specific) pronunciation could be retrieved, or, alternatively, its meaning accessed. The non-lexical route has to be used when words are unknown, and so have no lexical representation, but could, equally, be applied to real words; this uses knowledge of the correspondences between word spelling and word phonology to generate a pronunciation. The non-lexical route, therefore, had to be used for pronouncing non-words, and when applied to real words would only generate the correct pronunciation for words whose spelling accurately represents their phonology—regular words (e.g., TABLE, KERNEL, FEW), but not words whose spelling is irregular (e.g., YACHT, COLONEL, SEW).

A patient who only had a non-lexical route available in reading would not be able to read irregular words, but would succeed with non-words and would try to apply spelling-to-sound correspondences in reading aloud. A patient who could use only a lexical route would not be able to read non-words, but would have no particular difficulty with irregular words and would be able to access word meaning. These two characterisations, which come from an information-processing theory developed independently from neuropsychological data, apply reasonably well to the two different patients Marshall and Newcombe had described: GR read using the lexical route, and JC read via the non-lexical route.

This earliest work in the cognitive neuropsychology approach to aphasia shows all the methodological features that have become the characteristics of the school. First, patients' difficulties are located within information processing models, which have been developed from laboratory studies with "normal" subjects (who are, in the typical psychological experiment, students). In general, it is assumed that patients operate with a normal information processing system in which one or more of the components are unavailable or defective (the "subtraction hypothesis").

Second, cognitive neuropsychologists assume that, when one or more components of an information processing system are impaired by brain damage, the remaining components will operate normally (although, of course, they may not get their normal inputs). Thus, as far as possible, the components of the system will operate as self-contained information processors; this is the *modularity* assumption (cf. Shallice, 1979). As a consequence, it is possible to get selective lesions affecting only one part of a processing system.

Thirdly, cognitive neuropsychologists operate with data from single subjects. They argue that the purpose is to understand how an individual patient's pattern of intact and impaired language skills can be accounted for in terms of intact and impaired information processing components. Any system that can account for all aspects of language processing has to be reasonably complex (after all producing and understanding language *is* complex). In a system with N components, each of which can be impaired or intact, there are $2^N - 1$ possible patterns of impairment; Marshall and Newcombe (1973) point out that a minimal system of single word reading needs 14 components. This predicts at least 16,383 different kinds of acquired dyslexia. Under such circumstances, any group of patients is bound to be heterogeneous; the mean score of any group is therefore meaningless. What is true of the group scores may or may not be true of each of the individuals of which it is composed (see e.g., Howard, Patterson, Franklin, Morton, & Orchard-Lisle, 1984). In a rigorous approach, cognitive neuropsychologists will never use groups of patients, unless they can show that, for the specific purposes involved, the patients form a qualitatively homogeneous set; more typically, they will analyse a single patient, or contrast the patterns of two different patients.

Fourth, as well as rejecting the notion of aphasic syndromes, members of the cognitive neuropsychological school do not use the localisation of lesions in the brain as explanatory concepts. The accounts of patients are in terms of information-processing models, and the selective impairment of particular components of these models. Lexical processing theories are often expressed in the form of "box and arrow" diagrams. A typical example is shown in Fig. 6.

This particular model is taken from Patterson and Shewell (1987), which is based on the version of the logogen model proposed by Morton and Patterson (1980). Different cognitive neuropsychologists have adopted different variants of these theories, but they hold in common assumptions about the general nature of the theory (compare, for example, Allport & Funnell, 1981; Newcombe & Marshall, 1980; Shallice & Warrington, 1980). While, in form, these models resemble the theories of the nineteenth century diagram makers—Wernicke, Lichtheim, Broadbent, and Bastian—they are, in fact, diagrams of a very different kind. The nineteenth century diagram makers used boxes (or blobs) to represent *centres* in the cerebral cortex, and arrows stood for neural tracts running between these centres; in general they assumed that there was a simple one-to-one correspondence between neural elements and psychological

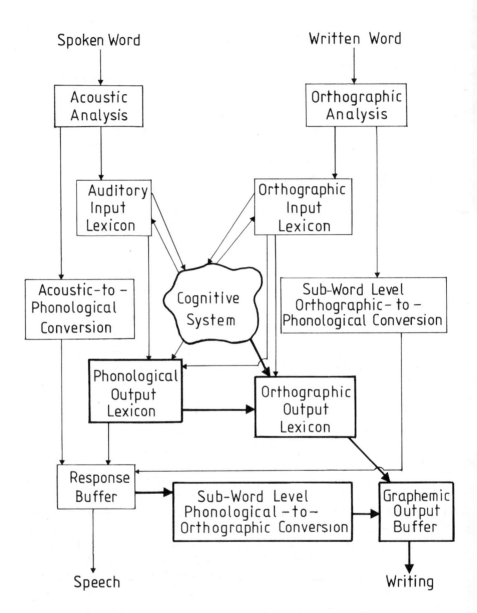

FIG. 6. An information processing model of the lexicon. The auditory input lexicon recognises spoken words, and the visual input lexicon recognises written words; the phonological output lexicon specifies the articulatory form of words, and the orthographic output lexicon their spelling. The other "sub-word level" procedures allow processing of non-words (and words, but by sub-lexical processes).

processes, or, even, in Wernicke's most extreme position, that neural elements were identical with psychological processes (see Wernicke, 1874; p. 143 in 1977 translation).

Cognitive neuropsychological theories, in contrast, are nothing to do with the brain: they are the diagrammatic part of theories that specify how information is processed in language comprehension and production. All that is assumed is that localised brain damage can result in selective impairment of one or more modules; not that information processing modules correspond directly to bits of brain. From this perspective, a theory of language localisation in the brain can only be developed once there is a coherent theory of language comprehension and production; the question of localisation is secondary (Mehler, Morton, & Jusczyk, 1984).

The fifth characteristic of cognitive neuropsychological approaches to aphasia is a concern with the psycholinguistically-defined variables that affect patients' performance, and the kinds of errors which are made in tasks. With JC and GR the comparison between real word and non-word reading was used to establish the routines that they could use in word reading. The comparison between regular and irregular words could have been used to confirm that JC was reading via a non-lexical route; the comparison between reading abstract and concrete words was used to demonstrate that GR relied on a specifically semantic routine in reading. The kinds of errors that the patients made were, similarly, used to draw conclusions about the processing routines they had available: GR's errors reflected the use of (partial) semantic information, while JC's seemed to reflect partial failure in his use of spelling-to-sound correspondence rules.

The initial impetus for the development of a cognitive neuropsychology came from studies of acquired disorders of reading (see Coltheart, 1985; Coltheart, Patterson, & Marshall, 1980; Patterson, Marshall, & Coltheart, 1986). This was, Coltheart (1985) suggests, because cognitive theories of reading were sufficiently well-developed that they could be easily applied to clinical data. The approach, which has achieved most popularity in Britain and Western Europe, has more recently been extended to a variety of other areas. These include disorders of writing (e.g., Hatfield & Patterson, 1983, 1984); disorders of word comprehension (e.g., Butterworth, Howard, & McLoughlin, 1984); disorders of spoken word production (e.g., Butterworth, 1979; Ellis, 1985; Howard et al., 1985a); and disorders of word repetition (e.g., Allport, 1984). Less progress has been made so far in the study of disorders of word production at phonetic and phonological levels, or in "syntactic" difficulties in sentence comprehension and sentence production (but see Butterworth & Howard, 1987). The cognitive neuropsychological approach has been extended to other, non-linguistic areas of processing: for example **short-term memory** (Butterworth, Camp-bell, & Howard, 1986; Shallice & Warrington, 1977; Vallar & Baddeley, 1984) and object recognition (e.g., Humphreys & Riddoch, 1987).

A theoretical approach whose aim is to understand the specific informa-tion processing deficits of individual patients has obvious application to treatment. This is because treatment can be directed precisely at the problems that have been identified, and can utilise the processing abilities that remain intact. The development of treatment approaches from a cognitive neuropsychological perspective is still at its early stages (see Howard & Patterson, 1987, for a review). It is perhaps inevitable that most of the treatment studies currently available concentrate on word reading and word writing—the areas in which cognitive neuropsychology was first established.

An analysis, in information processing terms, of what is wrong with a patient does not uniquely determine what to do about it. Workers within this school have adopted one of three approaches to the problems. Where the problem is one of loss of item-specific information, rules or procedures, therapists have either helped their patients to *re-learn* the missing informa-tion, or they have achieved the same result using different methods of processing (i.e. *reorganisation of function*). Where the problem lies in a failure of access to intact information, approaches have relied on *facilita-tion* of the defective access routines.

Byng and Coltheart (1986) describe an example of re-learning applied to a **surface dyslexic** patient, EE. He had difficulty in reading aloud and understanding irregular words. From the set of the 485 commonest words in English (as identified by the Kucera and Francis, 1967, written word count) Byng and Coltheart identified the 54 words that EE could not read aloud correctly. They allocated these words randomly to two equal sets (A and B). On two pre-tests EE showed no significant differences between reading the two sets. EE was then sent away to re-learn the pronunciations of words in set A; for each of these he had a card that had the written word and a picture mnemonic for its meaning. Each day he had to spend 15 minutes at home reading the words aloud, using the mnemonic cues. After two weeks EE was re-tested twice; he was 100% and 96% correct with the treated words from set A, and significantly worse with words from the untested set B (85% and 74%). There were, therefore, item-specific treatment effects that must be an effect of the treatment routines that Byng and Coltheart employed.

De Partz (1986) describes how, with a deep dyslexic patient, SP, she retaught him the spelling-to-sound correspondences in French. Initially SP could read only 2/30 simple non-words, and in real word reading he managed only 73 in a battery of 238 words of different types; he made semantic errors, and was worse at reading abstract words than matched concrete words. The relearning followed the following sequence of stages: first, for each letter SP selected a code word that began with the letter, and whose first sound was the characteristic sound of that letter in French—so for A SP learned *"Allo"* for B *"Bébé"*, and so on. To learn these 26 code words took 52 half-hour sessions. Then the patient was taught to segment off the first sound from each code word; initially SP was allowed to say the code word but later, as the process became automatic, he had to only imagine it and simply say the sound corresponding to each letter. In the third stage, the patient was taught to read single syllable non-words by sounding out each letter and then blending the sounds together; when he was presented with real words he was instructed to maintain this analytic approach. The fourth stage used the same approach to teach the sounds corresponding to "complex graphemes"—groups of letters that corres- pond to single French phonemes (e.g., AU, OU, CH, etc.). At the end of this fourth period (after nine months of treatment), the patient was reassessed. On the set of non-words where before therapy he had managed 2/30 he was correct on 27/30. On the real word battery he had improved from 73/238 to 204/278. His errors demonstrated that he really was using the rule system that he had been taught: for example he misread CELLE (/sel/) as "/kel/"—he had not been taught the rule that C is pronounced as/s/ when followed by E or I. A further period of treatment was therefore directed towards teaching SP the context sensitive spelling-to-sound rules; at the end of this SP read all but one of the words in the assessment battery correctly.

Two recent studies deal with the treatment of two different patients who were agrammatic in speech comprehension and production. After detailed assessment Byng and Coltheart (1986) and Jones (1986) were able to establish that their patients had specific difficulty with "thematic roles" (cf. Jackendoff, 1972); that is with establishing the mappings between syntactic categories (e.g., subject, object) and semantic roles (e.g., agent, patient). Both of these authors then instituted treatments to teach their patients about these semantic roles; after treatment was completed reassessment was able to demonstrate that both patients had improved, but, because improvement was confined to the aspects treated—assignment of thematic roles—it was therefore a specific effect of treatment.

These two studies of treatment of patients with difficulties with sentence production follow on from earlier work that adopts an approach based on "reorganisation of function." This approach accepts, with Luria, that patients can learn to perform defective functions, using other intact proces- sing abilities. However, this work is not tied to the Pavlovian cortical analyser model; the re-education schemes are based on the conception of restructuring skills on psycholinguistic models that depend on the cognitive processes involved. The aims are also modified; like the pragmatic school, the goal of treatment is seen as improving communication rather than the reacquisition of standard forms of language. Treatment makes use of the patient's own strategies wherever these favour unambiguous communication; and where a patient has not yet developed a specific strategy, or substitute, for a linguistic feature, the therapist endeavours to suggest one, building on the patient's remaining information processing skills. This approach, therefore, differs from Luria's in two ways: first it is reconstitution based on information processing models of language production and comprehension; and secondly by an acceptance that the aim of treatment is effective communication, rather than "normal" language.

An example of this type of compensation is the reconstruction of certain syntactic and morphological features by extra reliance on semantics. Two patients with classical **telegraphic speech** (Tissot, Mounin, & Lhermitte, 1973) but well-retained capacity to use semantics in comprehension of some linguistic structures, were re-trained on a semantic basis (Elvin & Hatfield, 1978; Hatfield & Elvin, 1978). For this group an elementary syntax, or syntax replacement, was created on an essentially semantic basis (concepts such as Actor or Do-er, Action, etc., being substituted for subject of sentence, verb, grammatical object of sentence); similarly, in re-training prepositional phrases the semantic element was emphasised wherever possible. With some patients this trend has been taken much further, and patients have been positively encouraged to have recourse to strategies that they have used spontaneously, such as the use of nouns, verbs, or adverbs to replace prepositions, provided the result is to the benefit of communication and provided some expression of a proposition results (Hatfield, 1979).

Hatfield (1982, 1983) describes a treatment procedure that exploits the greatly superior ability of so-called deep dysgraphic patients (Bub & Kertesz, 1982) to write **content words** compared with **function words**; homophonic or quasi-homophonic content words can be used to access target function words (*inn* for *in*; *bean* for *been*; *hat* for *at*; *witch* for *which*; etc.) A small amount of paired-associate learning has to take place, but this is essentially building on a strong tendency arising spontaneously among this group (Hatfield, 1982).

Beauvois and Derouesné (1982) report a number of further examples of treatment of individual patients, based on an explicit and detailed analysis of their deficits in terms of an information-processing model. Their aim in general, like Luria's, is to use other means to achieve the original ends; their theory of the components of language is entirely different. They describe particular schemes that they used successfully with four different patients. Their methods emphasise the use of a variety of strategies, which may either be normal or unusual ways of doing a task, but which are based on use of the particular component abilities that remain intact.

Word-retrieval problems of aphasic patients are, typically (but not invari-ably), difficulties in access to intact phonological word representations rather than loss of the word forms themselves; this is shown by the fact that word-retrieval problems are not consistently found with specific items (Head, 1926; Howard et al., 1984), and that partial information from a cue can elicit complete word forms from patients (Pease & Goodglass, 1978; Rochford & Williams, 1965). Under these circumstances, it is natural to adopt treatment approaches that try to facilitate the use of access routines. In a series of experiments Patterson, Purell, and Morton (1983) estab-lished that techniques that provide aphasic patients with information about the phonological form of words that they could not find as picture names (phonemic cueing, word repetition) were effective *cues* for word-retrieval (i.e. they had large immediate effects) but half-an-hour later the picture names that had been cued were no more likely to be found as picture names than control items whose names had not been cued; in their terminology, these phonological treatments were effective as cues but not as "facilitators." Howard et al. (1985a) showed that, in contrast, techni-ques that require patients to access the semantic representation correspond-ing to a picture name that cannot be found (e.g., matching written or spoken words to pictures; making semantic judgements), even where the patient never utters the sought-for word, have specific effects that last for at least 24 hours. This contrast, Howard et al. suggest, represents the properties of priming of lexical representations at two levels—the semantic system and the phonological word form. In a therapy experiment with 12 patients using a within-subject design, Howard et al. (1985b) demons-trated that both the phonological and semantic techniques caused item specific improvement in word-retrieval, but the semantic technique resulted in marginally greater improvement. Over the 13 week course of the experiment, 8 of the 12 chronic aphasic patients showed significant improvements in picture-naming.

Treatment from the perspective of the neuropsychological school is still in its early stages. Its characteristics have, however, emerged. Treatment is grounded in analyses of individual patients' problems in terms of explicit and detailed information-processing models. Typically they deal with individual subjects, or where groups of subjects are reported all compari-sons are within-subject. Treatment methods of a variety of different types can be adopted, depending on the analysis of the underlying disorder: direct relearning, reorganisation of function, or facilitation of access routines. Treatment methods have to be both founded in a rational analysis of the patient's problem, and central to the approach is the recognition of the need to demonstrate that a patient's improvement is the specific and identifiable consequence of the treatment offered.

CONTEMPORARY SCHOOLS: CONCLUDING REMARKS

Since the Second World War, a variety of very different schools of treatment have developed. As we have demonstrated, the schools have taken very different views of the nature of aphasia and of the process of treatment. As a result, aphasia therapy is developing a number of competing theories; the option of eclecticism—choosing bits and pieces from different approaches according to what seems useful—becomes increasingly untenable.

The story of modern aphasia therapy is mostly one of a succession of theoretical perspectives from related fields, which have been imported to aphasiology to develop particular positions in relation to language disorders. Luria's ideas were based on Pavlovian neurophysiology and the linguistics of the Prague School; the stimulation school drew upon the psychometric developments of the 1940s and 1950s; behaviour modification was inspired by the Skinnerian behaviourism that dominated much of academic psychology in the 1960s. Different linguistic notions became more and more incorporated into therapy plans by therapists of several schools, not only the one that we have labelled here as the neurolinguistic school. The neo-classical school dependend both on a rediscovery of the nineteenth century Wernicke-Lichtheim theory, and the interest in syntax generated by Chomsky's (1957, 1965) development of transformational grammar. The pragmatic school, in contrast, was developed in response to a growing interest in theoretical pragmatics in the late 1970s. While incorporating ideas from theoretical linguistics, the cognitive neuropsychology school is founded in the theories of modern cognitive psychology. The essential difference among various approaches rests on whether bits of linguistic science are collected piecemeal and *ad hoc*, or whether these are part of a unified system.

While theories from related fields have been incorporated, aphasia therapy has not yet really come to terms with the need to develop a theory of therapy—a way of systematically relating an analysis of the patient's problems to the process of treatment itself. Too often, as we have seen, the relationship between deficit and treatment is based on some implicit idea of how treatment has its effects, which has no good justification or scientific support. In the final part of this book we will offer some suggestions of how this gap might be bridged.

A remedial approach can be too rigid, as we suspect Gutzmann's to have been in the nineteenth century (although we are simply judging by his writings); it can also be too eclectic and atheoretical, with exercises and activities losing their effect because they are introduced at the wrong moment or for the wrong type of patient. If there is one maxim that ought to be written large over the desk of every aphasia therapist it is a quotation from Schuell:

> A good therapist should never be taken unawares by the question, "Why are you doing this?" (Schuell et al., 1964, p. 333).

SECTION 3
CONTEMPORARY ISSUES IN APHASIA
THERAPY

THE EFFECTIVENESS OF APHASIA THERAPY

The Group Study Approach

The Principles and Problems of Group Treatment Studies. In Pharaonic Egypt aphasia was "a condition not to be treated"; to a varying extent this view persists even today. Benson (1979a) notes this and suggests a reason:

> A long standing hindrance to the acceptance of aphasia rehabilitation by neurologists has been a deeply entrenched and widely taught adage that therapy for aphasia is ineffective. Some degree of spontaneous recovery is so frequent that many neurologists sincerely believe that the improvements gained through formal therapy merely represent the anticipated spontaneous recovery. (p. 188)

For the nineteenth- and early twentieth-century neurologists, the demonstration that chronic aphasics, whose condition had remained unchanged for a period of years, could show substantial improvement once therapy was started, was convincing evidence that treatment of aphasia *could* be effective (see Froment & Monod, 1914; Gutzmann, 1896; Mills, 1904; Singer & Low, 1933; Trousseau, 1861). This improvement could not plausibly be attributed to anything other than therapy; recent knowledge about the time course and extent of spontaneous recovery (Kertesz, 1979; Willmes & Poeck, 1984) gives us no grounds for doubting the original interpretation.

There is recent evidence that uses the same approach. Broida (1977) demonstrates that her patients who had been aphasic for between one and nine years could improve substantially when treated. Basso et al. (1979) report on two patients where therapy started eleven years and two years after onset; both improved.

Another convincing form of evidence that therapy can have a direct effect on aphasic language comes from studies of treatment of bilingual patients. Watamori and Sasanuma (1976, 1978) report the results of therapy with two native Japanese patients who spoke both English and

109

Japanese. Early on both patients elected to be treated only in English, and showed substantially greater improvement in English than in Japanese. As the aphasics were native Japanese speakers living in Japan, the only reasonable explanation for the greater improvement in English is that it is a result of therapy.

Given a substantial body of knowledge of this sort, there can be no doubt to anyone who has read any of the literature that aphasia therapy *can* be effective with at least some patients. Single patient studies, though, are done on selected aphasics; their results cannot be generalised to the whole population of aphasics, nor are they intended to be.

The group study approach asks a rather different question; not content with the demonstration that some sorts of therapy work with some sorts of patient, it considers whether aphasia therapy *in general* benefits aphasics *as a group*. This approach is, as Holland (1975) pointed out, culturally specific; group studies of therapy are confined to Western Europe and North America in the years since the Second World War. The era in which they are possible may be coming to an end. Sarno (1981), describing the position in the United States, notes that:

> It is now very difficult, if not impossible, to have a comparable control group of patients since it has become a cultural imperative in many settings that all patients have treatment. (p. 491)

The group study is designed to answer a question of "patient management"; is it worthwhile providing language therapy for aphasics? The method by which a group study attempts to answer this is the *randomised clinical trial* (RCT; Baddeley, Meade, & Newcombe, 1980; Bulpitt, 1983). In concept, the design is extremely straightforward: aphasics are randomly assigned to two groups. One group has therapy, and the other not; if the treated patients show more improvement then treatment was of benefit. Given the simplicity and apparent logic of this approach, it is remarkable that after more than 30 group studies of aphasia therapy have been published, there is so little agreement on the conclusions that can be drawn.

To illustrate this we quote from some recent reviews of the evidence. Darley (1979) concludes that:

> Aphasia therapy works. It works so well that every neurologist, psychiatrist, and speech-language pathologist responsible for patient management should refuse to accede to a plan that abandons the patient to neglect. (p. 629)

Marshall, Holmes, and Newcombe (1975) are extremely tentative:

> Definitive answers to questions about the degree of recovery possible after an aphasia and the role that therapy may play in augmenting such recovery do not, at the moment, exist. (p. 251)

Miller (1984) agrees with them:

> On the face of it there is very little evidence that can be offered in an attempt to argue that any form of therapy for aphasia is of proven value. (p. 108)

Shewan (1986) has no doubts:

> [Efficacy] studies vary considerably in their scientific merit; some are well designed clinical trials; others are clinical descriptions, often arrived at retrospectively. Despite these variations one finds a consistent theme —aphasic patients benefit significantly from language treatment even after the period of spontaneous recovery has passed . . . Some skeptics remain but their numbers are fewer and their fate determined. (p. 42)

We believe that no conclusions are justified; the reason for the confusion is that RCTs, which derive their form and methodology from clinical drug trials, make methodological and empirical assumptions that do not and cannot apply to aphasia therapy (see Howard, 1986, for this argument in more detail). The most important methodological assumptions are that the subjects form a homogeneous group, that treatment is homogeneous, and that differences between the treatment of groups is specifiable. The major empirical problems concern the measurement of outcome, and differentiation of the effects of treatment from other sources of variation, particularly spontaneous recovery.

In order to do a useful clinical trial, it must first be established that the patients have the *same* problem; it can differ in severity but not in kind. So, for example, if a treatment for headache is being studied it is important to establish that all the subjects have the same sorts of headaches; if some have migraines, others cerebral tumours, and the rest tension headaches we would not expect one particular treatment to have the same sort of effect on all the patients.

Aphasics do not form a homogeneous population. The qualitative forms of aphasia are very different from each other. It is hard to imagine that anyone on meeting, say, a Broca's and a Wernicke's aphasic, could suppose that they had the same problem. In any case, if they differed only in severity and not type then, in recovery, one form would evolve into the other—with these two diagnoses this never happens (Kertesz & McCabe, 1977; Leischner, 1976). Furthermore, for example, on measures of word fluency aphasics form a population with a *bimodal* distribution (Benson, 1967; Goodglass, Quadfasel, & Timberlake, 1964). There are in addition a large and increasing number of *double dissociations* described between individual aphasics, as well as groups of patients (Albert et al., 1981; Lesser, 1978); that is, one can find pairs of tasks where one patient performs significantly better than another at one task, while on the other the first patient is significantly worse than the second (Shallice, 1979). No single dimension of severity can accommodate such data. All of these observations are incompatible with the view that aphasics are a homogeneous population; there are a variety of *qualitative* differences between them. This should not surprise us; language is clearly complex and as a result we would expect that brain damage could affect it in many different ways.

Aphasics themselves form a very varied population. It is alleged that a large number of factors may affect the outcome—including, for example, age, handedness, site, extent and aetiology of lesion, and type and severity of aphasia (see Darley, 1982). Between them these factors may cause substantial variation in the outcome. Effects of therapy, however real, may then be undetectable.

Two approaches to this problem have been used: the investigator can take very large numbers of patients and assign them at random to experimental groups, and hope that differences due to all the other variables drop out; the alternative is to compare the performance of groups that are matched, as far as possible, for all relevant variables (e.g., Hagen, 1973), then the methodological assumption of homogeneity is very much more plausible. This, inevitably, requires *selection* of patients; the results of matched studies are then open to the challenge that they do not generalise to aphasics as a group.

In a clinical trial, it is assumed that the treatment is homogeneous. When the effectiveness of a drug is being tested, it is reasonable to assume that a single chemical will act in essentially the same way on the subjects, *if* it has been established that they form a homogeneous population. Aphasia therapy is very different: as we have demonstrated in the previous sections, it is axiomatic to every school of treatment that the tasks a patient is asked to do should be determined by his/her particular aphasic symptom complex. So, for different patients, therapy varies both in the sorts of tasks and in their level of difficulty. The most that can be hoped for is that all the patients in a given trial are treated by methods motivated by a particular philosophy; in multi-centre studies even this degree of uniformity is usually impossible.

To interpret the results of a clinical trial it must be possible to specify the differences in the treatment of the subject groups. In a drug trial where one group of patients takes a placebo and the other an identical pill that contains a biologically active chemical, it is reasonably clear that the only difference between the treatments is that one group gets the drug and the other does not. In trials of aphasia therapy no attempt has ever been made to specify exactly what the difference between the treatments is. As many writers have pointed out, even where patients have no professional therapy, family, friends, and the aphasics themselves often organise more or less formal attempts of treatment (e.g., Froment & Monod, 1914; Weisenburg & McBride, 1935). Aphasia is, after all, a problem that demands a response. So all untreated groups contain aphasics who are being treated. The only realistic sort of untreated group would be aphasics exposed only to a language that they cannot speak—for example English aphasics transported to China. This problem is even more acute in trials that compare treatment by qualified therapists with unqualified volunteers; volunteers are usually given support and ideas by trained therapists. Even if they are not, volunteers and therapists may end up doing very similar things; we certainly have no idea of the way in which the *actual treatment* of the aphasics in the two groups differs.

To measure changes in aphasia during a clinical trial requires testing that is *reliable* enough to give consistent measures; that is *sensitive* enough to measure the improvement that the particular therapy involved is intended to produce; and that is *valid* so that it measures changes that are of real consequence in the patients' lives. All of these requirements present major problems for clinical trials of aphasia therapy.

Aphasia performance is generally rather unreliable; for example, a patient presented with a picture may find the name one day and not the next (Head, 1926). There are two sources of a variability—*extrinsic* from influences external to the aphasia and *intrinsic* variation resulting from the language disturbance itself. A large number of extrinsic factors may cause variation: test performance is worse in the evening (Tompkins, Marshall, & Phillips, 1980); or after exercise (Marshall & King, 1973); if the patient is discouraged verbally (Stoicheff, 1960); non-verbally (Chester & Egolf, 1974); or by the difficulty of the task (Brookshire, 1972, 1976). Item-by-item performance is also intrinsically variable—particular word forms may be accessible one day and not the next, and semantic processes may be affected so that they are unreliable (Allport, 1985). In a recent study, we found that the contingencies between performance on naming a set of pictures twice, two days apart, can be as low as 0.3 (Howard et al., 1984); performance on one item on one day does not reliably predict performance on the same item a couple of days later, even though the overall level of impairment remains unchanged. These sources of variation may be fairly large; they present no insuperable problem, but, by introducing more "noise" to the measurement, they make it harder to uncover effects of therapy.

The need for test routines that are reliable—and therefore not sensitive to day-to-day variability from extrinsic and intrinsic sources—comes into conflict with the need for tests that are senitive to those day-to-day changes that are the result of improvement. In fact, the problem of sensitivity is more acute. Most therapy studies have used more-or-less standardised tests of aphasia that sample performance on a large range of tasks with a small number of items on each. Some abilities may not be tested at all. Therapy, where it is in any way systematic, is intended to produce improvement in a specific function or task. If this improvement is not sampled by the test, or if it is tested with just a small number of items, there will probably be no improvement in overall test scores, however much difference therapy has made to the quality of the patient's life. For example, the Boston Diagnostic Aphasia Examination (BDAE; Goodglass & Kaplan, 1972) tests object picture-naming with only six items. Substantial changes in a patient's word retrieval might make no difference to a patient's overall BDAE scores. Standardised tests that measure a non-specific overall level of deficit cannot be expected to measure specific improvement—particularly when the unreliability of performance is taken into account.

If therapy is to be of any use at all, improvement must make a real difference to aphasics' lives. If a test is a valid measure, there should only be improvement in test scores where there is real improvement in communication, and conversely where in reality the aphasic experiences no change, test scores should not change. One way to avoid the problem of validity is to design therapy purely to improve scores in a test; for example Holland and Sonderman (1974) and Burger, Wertz, and Woods (1983) used programmed learning to improve aphasics' performance on tasks from the Token Test (de Renzi & Vignolo, 1962). This is what Martin (1981b) describes as test-centred therapy. Many therapists, though, have a broader aim: to improve an aphasic's ability to communicate, using linguistic and non-linguistic methods. Most standardised aphasia tests do not consider whether their measures of language performance are valid, but some tests are specifically designed to evaluate how well an aphasic can communicate in conversation (Functional Communication Profile; Sarno, 1969) and in role play situations as well (Communicative Abilities in Daily Living; Holland, 1980; Edinburgh Functional Communication Profile; Skinner et al., 1984). There is some doubt whether these two sorts of tests measure the same thing: Sarno, Sarno, and Levita (1971) found no relationship between improvement on the NCCEA (Neurosensory Centre Comprehensive Examination for Aphasia; Spreen & Benton, 1969), and the FCP; and Helmick, Watamori, and Palmer (1976) found little relationship between spouses' assessments of aphasics' difficulties and therapists' estimations of them with the FCP (cf. Linebaugh & Young-Charles, 1978, 1981).

To demonstrate effects of therapy, they must be differentiated from the effects of all the other sources of variation. This is a straightforward statistical problem, in one sense, but in practice it may be extremely difficult. As we discussed, there are a large number of factors that may have systematic effects on outcome and these may *interact*. For example, it is often alleged that therapy is more effective when it is initiated shortly after the onset of aphasia (Deal & Deal, 1978; Holland, 1969). This will show itself as an interaction between the effects of treatment and the duration of aphasia; but very few studies have examined their results for interactions between variables. Most have investigated each independently (e.g., Vignolo, 1964); although there is no *a priori* reason to suppose that effects are independent. Secondly, the contribution of other variables may be so large that a trial may not be able to differentiate the effects of therapy even where they are substantial. In particular spontaneous recovery may cause so much improvement, that all effects of therapy are swamped. It is therefore essential that investigators who find no effect of treatment also report how large an effect their experiment could have been expected to detect. The only case in which this has been done is instructive: Meikle, Wechsler, Tupper, Benenson, Butler, Mulhall, and Stern (1979) compared the effects of therapy by trained therapists or volunteers. Their measure of improvement was the length of treatment before scores from regular assessment on the PICA (Porch Index of Communicative Ability; Porch, 1971) had plateaued, and on this basis they found no significant difference in outcome between the two groups. But they report that they only had a 76% chance of detecting a difference if improvement by the treated group had been sustained for *four times* as long as in the group treated by volunteers; we have no grounds to expect that therapy by trained staff would have so large an effect.

If a clinical trial finds significant differences between groups treated and untreated patients drawn at random from aphasic patients, then the results are said to be "generalisable." That is, if another set of patients were drawn from the same population, and given the same treatment, we would expect the same outcome. The group results cannot, on the other hand, be generalised to the individual members of the group. Some of the group members will probably have benefitted from the treatment they had, and some will not; what is true for the average of the group is not true for the individual members who comprise it. Nor, in fact, can the results be easily generalised to other groups of patients: if the treatment is undefined (and, in fact, because it varies from patient to patient, undefinable) then it will be impossible to give the "same" treatment to another set of patients. And if, as argued above, the aphasic patients themselves form a heterogeneous population, we cannot be confident that another set of patients are the "same."

Given the heterogeneity of the patients and the therapy involved in a RCT it is likely that only a proportion of patients will actually benefit from the treatment that they are given. Some will be given inappropriate treatment; others will be unable to benefit from treatment because they are too impaired in their general physical state, or are confused or demented. Others might have benefitted from treatment, but the treatment that they received was too intermittent, or did not continue for long enough to have an effect. The result of this is that only a proportion of patients can be expected to benefit. If, at the same time, some, but not all, of the patients are improving due to spontaneous recovery, RCTs may be very unlikely to establish that there are real effects of treatment for some of the patients, because of the accumulated noise in the measurements (Pring, 1983, 1986).

Three Examples of Group Studies of Treatment Effectiveness. In view of these major problems with clinical trials of aphasia therapy we will not review this literature in any detail. In any case there are a variety of recent reviews available, although none of them makes explicit all the assumptions of this approach and the limitations these impose on the interpretation of results (for reviews see Darley, 1982; Holland, 1975; Lincoln, 1985; Miller, 1984; Sarno, 1981; Seron, 1979; Shewan, 1986; for a critique, Howard, 1986). But, we will consider briefly three studies to illustrate our points.

Hagen (1973) followed two groups of ten patients. They were all classified on the Minnesota Test for Differential Diagnosis of Aphasia as suffering from "aphasia with sensorimotor impairment," and were right-handed with a single thrombotic or embolic lesion of the left middle cerebral artery; were native English speakers; showed no dysarthria and no psychiatric disturbance. The two groups were comparable in age and initial severity of aphasia; improvement was measured by testing with the MTDDA 3, 6, 12, and 18 months after onset. All patients were resident in the same hospital and had the same treatment, except the treated group had 18 hours of aphasia therapy a week in the period from 6 to 18 months after onset. The results indicated that there was spontaneous recovery, which in some areas continued for as much as 12 months after onset; but the treated group improved significantly more than the controls in the MTDDA sub-tests measuring "reading comprehension," "language formulation," "speech production," "spelling," and "arithmetic."

This trial makes significant attempts to reduce the heterogeneity in the subject population by choosing to follow a strictly limited group of aphasics. This opens the possibility that treatment could be relatively homogeneous; unfortunately it "varied from patient to patient according to their needs (Hagen, 1973, p. 456)," and we are given little information on the specific tasks and stimuli which were used in treatment. The difference in treatment between the groups is, in one way, closely defined, as apart from aphasia therapy the subjects had a very similar regime. This study, then, provides a demonstration that therapy for one class of patients is effective in particular ways; unfortunately we do not know what therapy consisted of, nor what parts of it were effective. The use of a closely-specified subject group leaves it open to the criticism that its results cannot be generalised to the population of aphasics as a whole; but, as we have seen, no group study can usefully be generalised.

The approach used by Basso, Capitani, and Vignolo (1979) was very different; they compared the outcome in a group of 162 aphasics who were treated in 3–5 sessions a week for at least 5 months, with 119 patients who "were prevented from attending therapy by extraneous factors such as family or transportation problems." They took a stringent criterion of improvement: an aphasic had to improve by at least two points on a four point scale of severity of impairment, which was derived from "objective" test scores. They investigated the effects of four factors and their inter-actions on the outcome: whether the aphasic was fluent or non-fluent; severely or moderately impaired; treated or not treated; and how long after onset the patients entered the study. In all four modalities tested—oral expression, auditory comprehension, reading, and writ-ing—the chances of improvement were greater if the aphasic patient was initially less impaired, seen soon after onset, or rehabilitated. The effects of fluency and all interactions were not significant. As the patients were not assigned at random to the treated and untreated groups the results are open to criticism; the authors counter this to some extent when they show that the groups did not differ in education, handedness, aetiology, or sex distribution. The treated patients were significantly younger, but Basso et al. show that age itself has no effect on outcome, nor does it affect the results of treatment. It is still clearly possible to argue that there may have been other differences between the groups—for example in motivation (Benson, 1979a)—but if so these differences, whatever they may be, are having a remarkably large effect. Basso et al. do, at least, demonstrate that there are no significant differences between their two groups on any of the variables that other studies have shown to affect the outcome. The most plausible interpretation is that treatment had a decisive effect on outcome; those who doubt this have a responsibility to suggest what uncontrolled variable could explain the results.

In interpreting this study there is a more serious problem: treatment varied from patient to patient—all that united it was a philosophy of stimulation therapy where responses are elicited "first in an automatic way and then in more and more voluntary ways (p. 192)." It remains tantalis-ingly unclear which therapy techniques actually were beneficial. But at least Basso et al. do not treat aphasics as a homogeneous population, recognising that fluency, severity, and duration of aphasia could have an effect and that they might *interact* with each other and with the effects of treatment; in this aspect the study is unique.

David, Enderby, and Bainton (1982) compare the outcome in two groups of 48 patients, half of whom were treated by volunteers and the others by trained therapists. Treatment was for a total of 30 hours over 15 to 20 weeks. They found that both groups improved to an equivalent extent, as measured by scores on the FCP; significantly the amount of improvement was not related to how long after onset treatment began. This implies that improvement cannot in any simple way be attributed to spontaneous recovery; presumably both therapists and volunteers were doing something that was useful. Unfortunately it is impossible to interpret the results of this study as no attempt is made to satisfy the methodological assumptions implicit in the approach. The aphasics are treated as a homogeneous population; the only variable within aphasia whose effect is investigated is initial severity. No account is taken of any qualitative differences between patients. No attempt is made to ensure that treatment is homogeneous; patients were treated at 15 different hospitals by therapists using a variety of different approaches. The amount of therapy provided was small; there are indications from the literature that therapy needs to be more intensive (Pizzamiglio & Roberts, 1967; Somerville, 1974) and more prolonged (Smith, 1972; Vignolo, 1964) before any substantial effects can be expected. Finally, there is no attempt to specify what the actual difference between the treatment of the two groups was; therapists and volunteers may have done very similar or very different things—we do not know. All that we can conclude is that patients in both groups improved on the measures used.

As can be seen, group studies of the effects of treatment in aphasia have produced contradictory results. Trials that compare the outcome in aphasic patients who were treated with the outcome in those patients who were unable to attend for treatment because of geographical reasons, or lack of therapy staff, are near unanimous in reporting significant effects of treatment (Basso, Capitani, & Vignolo, 1979; Basso, Faglioni, & Vignolo, 1975; Dordain & Normand, 1981; Leischner, 1976; Smith, 1972). Trials of treatment where the patients are assigned to different groups using experimental procedures are more divided: some find significant effects of treatment (Hagen, 1973; Shewan & Kertesz, 1984; Wertz et al., 1981; Wertz et al., 1986); and some do not (David, Enderby, & Bainton, 1982; Lincoln et al., 1984; Meikle et al., 1979). It is notable that all the treatment studies that fail to find significant effects of treatment involve relatively small durations of treatment. In the Lincoln et al. study, for example, three-quarters of the patients had less than 18 hours of treatment; this is unfortunate when Vignolo (1964) had reported that at least 72 hours of treatment were needed to find significant effects.

Conclusion. Clinical trials of aphasia therapy yield a confused picture. The trials with negative outcomes are exclusively English, and all involve small amounts of treatment. However, we have argued that these trials yield little useful evidence whatever their outcome. This is because they apply heterogeneous and undefined treatments to heterogeneous groups of patients using global and insensitive assessment techniques. Their group results cannot be generalised to any individual aphasic patient, and the treatment procedures involved can never be applied by another therapist because they are never described in detail. In fact the clinical trial approach makes assumptions that are virtually impossible to meet. To the extent to which particular studies have acknowledged and attempted to meet these assumptions, we can draw tentative conclusions from them. So both the Hagen and Basso et al. experiments suggest that therapy of some sort can be effective. At the opposite extreme David et al.'s study cannot be used as evidence for anything at all.

The problem, of course, is that the question asked is too imprecise: does language therapy, in general, benefit aphasics as a whole? A precisely analogous question would be to ask: "Does medicine benefit people with headaches?" No one would expect useful evidence from such a study, where a whole lot of different doctors would be treating many different sorts of headaches in different ways. In the control group some subjects would be medicating themselves, in exactly the same way as the doctors would be, and others not. Measurement of the severity of the headaches would be difficult; and it would not be clear whether the measures were reliable, sensitive, or valid. Many patients in both groups would recover spontaneously to varying extents.

A methodologically valid clinical trial is in theory possible. It requires a group of patients who, in relation to the treatment offered, form a homogenous population. They need to be assigned at random to two treatment groups. The treatment has to be described in sufficient detail for other therapists to apply the same treatments with their patients. The therapy has to be sufficiently intensive and prolonged to give a reasonable expectation of treatment effects. The groups of patients need to be sufficiently large to give reasonable expectation of finding treatment effects when these may not apply to all the patients and may be smaller than the effects of spontaneous recovery. The assessments used need to be sensitive to improvement of the kind that might be expected. No RCT of treatment with aphasic patients has even approached this minimal set of methodological requirements; for this reason no safe conclusions of any kind can be drawn from group studies of treatment in aphasia.

Realistically, these requirements are almost impossible to meet in practice; it will be difficult to do a sound RCT of aphasia therapy. This is because it is unlikely that any particular therapist or group of therapists will have access to sufficient patients for whom treatment of the same kind is appropriate. To study the effects of treatment in aphasia, we will therefore have to adopt rather different experimental designs. These, which will have to involve within-patient comparisons, and, most typically, single patients, can be scientifically rigorous. We can use these treatment designs to ask questions that are specific enough to permit a sensible answer. We turn to a discussion of some of these methods, and the results of studies that have used them, in the next section.

The Effectiveness of Specific Techniques

Treatment Designs. There is no shortage of studies of performance of single patients or groups of aphasics on particular tasks. There is no shortage of generalised studies of groups of aphasics in treatment. There is no shortage of *ex cathedra* pronouncements on how to do treatment. There is very little satisfactory evidence on the progress of specific patients treated according to specific (and motivated) methods. As we will show, since 1975 this has gradually begun to change.

The shortage of specific treatment studies cannot be blamed on methodological difficulties; indeed a variety of different experimental designs of therapy with single patients are available (Albert et al., 1981; Coltheart, 1983; Lapointe, 1977; Seron, 1979; Weniger et al., 1980). All avoid the almost impossible task of "matching" one aphasic to another, by using the patient as his/her own control. The aim of within-subject treatment designs is to show that improvement is not due to spontaneous recovery, and is specific to the treatment method used.

Treatment studies need to differentiate between improvement from three different sources: improvement that would have happened in the absence of any intervention (i.e., "spontaneous recovery"); improvement that is due to non-specific aspects of treatment (e.g., support, interest, or encouragement from the therapist); or improvement that is a specific consequence of the treatment given (see Howard, 1986; Howard & Patterson, 1987).

The improvement shown in Fig. 7A is uninformative; it is possible that the score would have improved at that rate with no intervention. But if there is improvement at a known and predictable rate, or, more simply, performance is static before therapy starts (a "baseline"; Fig. 7B), the results are more convincing. This is sometimes called a "time series design" (McReynolds & Kearns, 1982), and is generally suitable for treatment when the effects are likely to be global—that is, improvement is anticipated in all aspects of language. If a third phase of the study without treatment is added, and improvement is confined to the second phase when the patient was being treated, then the improvement can be confidently attributed to the treatment. This "time series" design is the weakest test of treatment effects; it is probably unsuitable for use when spontaneous recovery is continuing and some improvement can be anticipated in the no-treatment phases. Pring (1986) suggests some modifications which may be used to overcome this.

If the effects of treatment are likely to be confined to one modality and task then one can use a "crossover design" (Coltheart, 1983). Here performance is measured in two different tasks (A and B). After a period of treatment directed at task A, performance in A and B is assessed. Then a period of treatment directed at task B follows, and treatment is again measured. If A improves and B does not when A is treated, and B improves and A does not when B is treated (see Fig. 7C), we can be confident that both treatment approaches were successful. The difficulties in interpretation of this design will emerge if performance on both tasks changes when only one is the focus of treatment, or if only one treatment is effective. Under such circumstances it can be difficult to come to any firm conclusions (Howard, 1986).

The most powerful design ("multiple baseline") can be used where it is anticipated that treatment effects will be item-specific. Here items (e.g., words, sentences, phonemes) can be allocated at random to two sets. One set is the focus of treatment, and the other acts as control items. If improvement is confined to "treated" items, then therapy has been effective and specific (Fig. 7D). But if both treated and untreated items improve (Fig. 7E) the results can be interpreted either as evidence of *generalisation* of the effects of treatment to untreated items (e.g., Seron et al., 1979; Wiegel-Crump & Koenigsknecht, 1973); or that this reflects spontaneous recovery or non-specific effects of treatment (Newcombe et al., 1975); in this case the interpretation is ambiguous.

More complex designs involving alternating varieties of therapy are potentially more revealing; two different methods of treating the same task can be alternated using different items for each method (Fig. 7F; cf. Helmick & Wipplinger, 1975). Or, combined designs can be used to compare different kinds of treatment, and examine whether treatment effects are item-specific (e.g., Howard et al., 1985b).

The *stability* of the effects of treatment can be measured by testing the patient(s) again some time after therapy is over.

We are not suggesting that experimental designs of this class are without their difficulties, either of construction or interpretation; but that they are a potential, and largely unexploited, source of sound empirical data on the effectiveness of therapeutic techniques.

Early studies of the effects of specific treatment techniques are scattered and, on the whole, methodologically inadequate. Since the mid-1970s, however, an increasing number of studies have reported on the outcome of specific treatments. As we noted in our discussion of the contemporary schools, studies of this kind are often inspired by the methodology developed by the behaviour modification school; most of the satisfactory

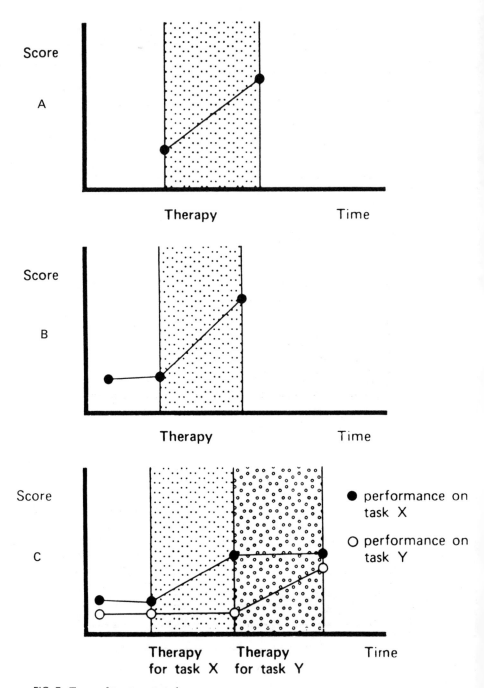

FIG. 7. Types of treatment study.

A. Treatment with no baseline: improvement may be due to spontaneous recovery.

B. Performance shown to be static before treatment starts: the basic "time series" design.

C. Alternating treatments for different tasks: a "cross-over" design. In this case both are effective and their effects are task specific.

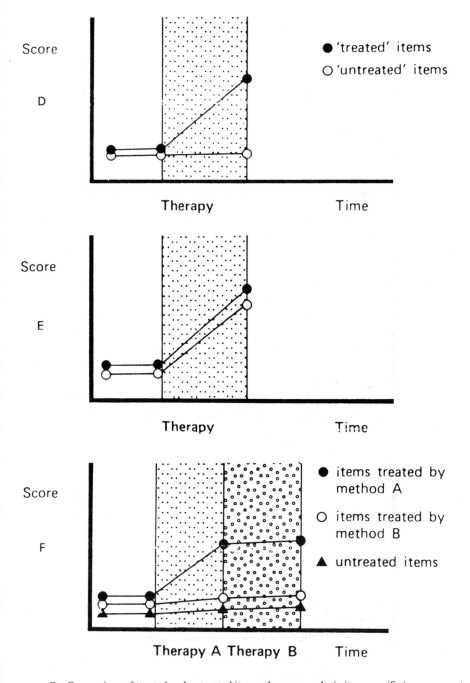

D. Comparison of treated and untreated items: therapy results in item-specific improvement.

E. Parallel improvement in treated and untreated items: compatible either with generalisation or with non-specific effects of therapy.

F. Comparing two therapy methods for one function: in this case only therapy A works and its effects are item specific.

reports come from therapists who represent the neo-classical, neurolinguistic, and cognitive neuropsychology schools. It is beyond the scope of this book to provide a comprehensive review of this literature. We will confine ourselves to a sketch of some studies of specific treatments aimed at three areas of impairment: agrammatism, speech production, and word retrieval.

Treatments of Grammatical Impairment. A variety of techniques for the treatment of agrammatism have been tested. Beyn and her various colleagues have described the technique of preventive therapy for potentially agrammatic patients. It emphasises the early use of verbs, function words, phrases, and sentences, with nouns introduced only later on and then in the oblique case. Beyn and Shokhor-Trotskaya (1966) describe the outcome of treatment by this method in 25 cases of motor aphasia; in none did a telegraphic style of speech develop. Unfortunately, as there is no control group, it is not possible to verify their statement that "it is inevitable that telegraphic speech would have appeared with any other method"; but the fact that 64% of the subjects showed marked agrammatism makes the claim fairly credible. They do provide data comparing the proportions of different parts of speech produced in picture description by two patients treated by the preventive method, two aphasics treated "with the aid of the usual methods" and two normal subjects. The differences are most obvious in the number of nouns produced: conventionally-treated patients produced them as 80–82% of their output; those treated by the preventive method 44–45%; normals 36–37%. This provides at least some evidence that the preventive method may be effective.

Other workers have described methods for the *remediation* of agrammatism. Holland and Levy (1971) trained subjects to produce active declarative sentences to describe pictures; the particular sentences that were trained improved and there was transfer of improvement to question forms of those sentences. The negative and passive forms did not improve, nor did the production of other active declarative sentences. Naeser (1974) gave four patients therapy in producing three sorts of sentences; they were, however, initially very good at producing the basic syntactic patterns (88% correct) so they had little opportunity to get much better. She reports that the patients did improve in their ability to produce exactly the same verb form and tense as they had in the examples (52% to 88%), and in producing a verb that agreed in number with the subject (61% to 91%).

The production of correct sentences by six "expressive" aphasics was treated by Wiegel-Crump (1976) by extensive repetition of the correct form (up to 10 times until repeated correctly twice in succession). The subjects could not initially produce any correct sentences, and still could not after 20 therapy sessions of social conversation; but after 20 hours of sentence repetition they were able to produce 30% of the drilled sentences correctly. And, interestingly, they were equally successful, though slower, at producing sentences that had not been drilled.

Generalisation to untrained sentences was not found by Shewan (1976) in the production of active declarative sentence by a Broca's aphasic. Therapy was either by selecting and ordering written constituents, or just providing the appropriate verb form, written and spoken, for the aphasic to construct the sentence around. Both methods resulted in improvement in the production of syntactically appropriate sentences, but only for the sentences which had actually been worked on. In their study, Thompson, McReynolds, and Vance (1982) did find evidence for limited generalisation. They trained two agrammatic patients, by repetition and sentence completion, to produce a limited set of sentences as picture descriptions: for example "the bike is behind the tent," "the tree is behind the house." They then tested generalisation to description of pictures where all the elements had been trained, but never as a complete sentence—i.e., "the bike is behind the house," and "the tree is behind the tent." Improvement in describing the treatment pictures generalised to these (closely) related untreated pictures, demonstrating that the patients were not learning to produce sentences as unanalysed wholes, but had gained some ability to recombine their component constituents. Using the same kind of treatment based on sentence repetition, Kearns and Salmon (1984) demonstrated that training two Broca's aphasics to produce *is* as an auxiliary (as in "she is cutting the string"), resulted in improvement that generalised to the production of *is* as an auxiliary with other untrained sentences, and to the production of *is* as a copular (as in "the house is large").

Weniger et al. (1980) trained a Broca's aphasic to produce sentences to describe pictures, but used a rather more "multi-modality" approach. He had to order written constituents, read the sentence aloud, copy it, then write it from memory, read it aloud again, and then say the sentence aloud from memory. After he had done this five times for each sentence, he needed no help to describe all of the pictures; and his performance on other similar and dissimilar sentences was unanimously judged in blind ratings to be improved as a result of therapy.

The progress of one Broca's aphasic during a course of syntax stimulation therapy is described by Helm-Estabrooks et al. (1981a) (see p. 91). He showed substantial improvement that was also apparent in his spontaneous speech.

When discussing the approaches to treatment of the cognitive neuropsychology school, we described the methods used by Jones (1986) and Byng and Coltheart (1986) in treating two aphasic patients who they show to have specific difficulty in relating syntactic structures to thematic roles. With BB, Jones restricted treatment to identification of different semantic roles in sentences of increasing syntactic complexity; speech production was not involved, and was in fact specifically discouraged. But BB improved in sentence comprehension and sentence production. With BRB, Byng confined treatment to teaching him about thematic roles in prepositional phrases, with written word presentation. His improvement generalised to other sentences where comprehension depends on thematic roles, with both auditory and visual presentation, and his ability to produce spoken sentences with complex argument structures also improved. Byng is, however, able to show that BRB's performances did not change in fields unrelated to the treatment—abstract word comprehension, non-word reading; his improvement cannot, therefore, be attributed to across-the-board spontaneous recovery.

Aphasic difficulties in sentence comprehension and production have received increasing attention since Goodglass reawakened interest in the area in the late 1950s. Greater understanding of sentence processing systems allowed some very specific approaches to be developed; Byng's and Jones' studies represent a new departure in treatment of grammatical disturbances. Previous approaches had simply tried, using massive sentence repetition, to increase patients' ability to produce these sentences unaided. Byng and Jones identify for their patients the underlying deficit, and aim treatment specifically at that area. Both investigators are able to show, not only improvement in the treatment tasks, but also improvement with other sentence types and in other modalities that involve functions at which treatment is targeted.

Treatment of Disorders of Speech Production. The neo-classical school have tested the effects of several methods to help speech production. The use of melodic intonation therapy (MIT) to improve speech production is particularly noteworthy because of the relatively rigorous way in which its usefulness has been demonstrated. Sparks, Helm, and Albert (1974) studied eight aphasics who followed a course of MIT; all the patients had had therapy and none had improved in the previous six months. They had severely impaired speech output but fairly good auditory comprehension. After treatment BDAE results showed significant improvement in naming and in phrase length, but no effects in auditory or reading comprehension; the authors judged the outcome good in four aphasics, moderate for two, and poor for two. They offer speculation on what defines an aphasic who will benefit from MIT, suggesting that good auditory comprehension, self-criticism of errors, poor repetition, and good motivation, as well as very restricted and possibly stereotypic speech output are necessary.

Using a similar approach Skelly et al. (1974) followed the improvement of six "oral verbal apraxics," five of whom were at least two years post-onset and had had at least six months of speech therapy, when treated with Amerind signs accompanied by speech. After six months of therapy, reassessment on the PICA showed that verbal scores had made good improvement but there was little change in "gestural" or "graphic" scores.

Although many severe, non-fluent aphasics experience major impairments in speech production, there has been little experimental work directed at these problems. The principal exception is those workers (e.g., Darley, Aronson, & Brown, 1975; Wertz, Lapointe, & Rosenbek, 1984) who have viewed these speech production problems as, primarily, disorders in the *control* of articulation—that is, as an "apraxia of speech"—rather than as a linguistic impairment (see Blumstein, 1981). From this perspective treatment should be aimed at increasing articulatory control; Wertz, Lapointe, and Rosenbek (1984) argue that patients should be treated primarily by repetition, to teach contrasts between phonemes. They give several case studies demonstrating that, with this kind of therapy, patients can improve their articulation even long after the onset of the disorder, when spontaneous recovery can be presumed to be over.

Treatment of Disturbances of Word Retrieval. For many aphasics word retrieval is a significant problem, and often poses the major residual difficulty for those that have had good spontaneous recovery (Kertesz & McCabe, 1977). The use of a wide variety of techniques of eliciting picture names to treat picture-naming difficulties following the methods of Schuell was investigated by Wiegel-Crump and Koenigsknecht (1973). Four anomic aphasics were trained in 18 sessions to produce the names of 20 pictures they could not find in the pre-test; after this they were able to name 96% of these pictures, and there was generalisation to other pictures whose names had not been worked on (70% correct). (Unfortunately these patients were only "at least three months" post-onset, and it is certainly possible that the generalisation effect is only evidence of spontaneous improvement.) Seron et al. (1979) compared two approaches to treatment of word retrieval problems with chronic aphasic patients. With one group of four patients, treatment was based on only a small number of names which the patients had been unable to find in a pre-test, and concentrated on teaching the patients strategies for word retrieval. The second group of patients were taught the names of a much larger set of items. In 20 therapy sessions spread over two months, one of the four patients in the second group improved significantly, compared with three of the subjects in the first group. On the basis of these findings Seron et al. suggest that, for some patients at least, therapy aimed at access strategies which focusses on a small number of lexical items will be most effective.

In these experiments, using a wide variety of different treatment techniques, patients show improved word retrieval. But which of all these techniques are useful?

Aphasics can be helped to retrieve picture names in response to a wide variety of cues (Love & Webb, 1977; Pease & Goodglass, 1978; Podraza & Darley, 1977; Rochford & Williams, 1962); phonemic cues, repetition, and sentence completion appear particularly effective. Naming is also better when pictures are exposed for longer (Brookshire, 1971); when aphasics are relaxed (Marshall & Watts, 1976); in the morning (Tompkins, Marshall, & Phillips, 1980); when they hear laughter (Potter & Goodman, 1983); when they have not just had exercise (Marshall & King, 1973); and when pictures are presented with others they can name successfully (Brookshire, 1972). Similarly comprehension is better when instructions are single words, slow or redundant sentences (Gardner, Albert, & Weintraub, 1975; Liles & Brookshire, 1975; Weidner & Lasky, 1976); when mixed with easier sentences (Brookshire, 1976); when sentences are spoken by a variety of speakers (Heilman, Gold, & Tucker, 1975); and when they are spoken rather than tape-recorded (Green & Boller, 1974).

All of these techniques could provide a basis for aphasia therapy *if* we assume (as Schuell did) that production of a successful and correct response is itself a therapeutic event. No therapist would normally argue that relaxation, for example, could be specifically effective as a treatment method; while a relaxed aphasic may be more able to make use of the linguistic abilities he/she may have, we would not expect relaxation itself to *change* the aphasia. We claim, therefore, that only *some* techniques that help patients to produce correct responses will be useful as therapy techniques, in that they cause long-term change in a patient's level of performance; other techniques might temporarily improve a patient's performance, but will have no possibility of changing it. This claim is, of course, open to experimental test; and there is some recent evidence on this.

Howard et al. (1985a) drew a distinction between "prompts," "facilitators." and "therapy techniques." If a patient cannot find a word, and a cue has a significantly greater effect on word retrieval than provision of extra time, then that cue is a successful *prompt*. If production of a name in response to a prompt significantly increases the chance of finding that name again unaided, compared to items that have not been cued, say 20 minutes or 24 hours later, then there has been *facilitation*. If a prompt is a facilitator, then it is possible that when used many times over a longer period it will be a useful *therapy* technique. It would be harder to argue that a cue that did not facilitate was actually effective in therapy. Studies of facilitation, then, have the advantage that one can test experimentally for the effect of a single prompting event hours, or even days, after it has happened.

Using this approach, Patterson, Purell, and Morton (1983) showed that both repetition and phonemic cueing, although very effective as prompts, made no difference to aphasics' picture naming half-an-hour later; neither technique was a facilitator. Cohen, Engel, Kelter, and List (1979) compared completion of clichés (from songs, nursery rhymes, and so on) with relatively open-ended sentences. While the clichés were more effective as prompts, the aphasics were more likely 24 hours later to name pictures whose names had been elicited by open-ended sentence completion—this was then the better facilitator. In a series of experiments, Howard et al. (1985a) were able to demonstrate that pointing to a picture out of a choice of four to spoken command resulted in substantial facilitation of name retrieval that was still present 24 hours later, even though the aphasics did not even say the name. They showed that similar long-term facilitation effects can be found after a variety of techniques that require the aphasics to access a verbal semantic representation corresponding to the name they could not find—for example, written word-to-picture matching, and auditory semantic judgements. In a therapy experiment with 12 chronic aphasic patients, Howard et al. (1985b) compared the effects of repeated use of techniques that provided patients with phonological information about picture names, with those that required the patients to access the corresponding semantic representations; both techniques resulted in day-by-day improvement, and the semantic techniques had a significantly better outcome due to greater generalisation to untreated items. The techniques that are the better facilitators when used once only are also more effective when used repeatedly over a series of days.

These results cast doubt on a number of assumptions that have been held by a variety of therapists. First, they demonstrate significant improvement in picture naming as a result of treatment by word comprehension tasks that do not directly involve speech production; contrary to Shewan and Bandur's (1986) assumption of the independence of modalities, production and comprehension processes clearly interact. Secondly, the treatment tasks—auditory word-to-picture matching, etc.—were well within the patients' capabilities; it is clearly not necessary for therapy to rely exclusively on tasks that are at the edge of a patient's current performance abilities.

Third, as we saw in the previous section, many of the contemporary schools of aphasia therapy assume that simply eliciting a response from an aphasic, by whatever means are available, is itself therapeutic. This assumption is clearly no longer tenable. Indeed, in name retrieval the most effective prompts have the shortest-lasting effects. Effects depend on *how* a word is elicited. As aphasia therapists, we urgently need to accumulate empirical evidence about which particular techniques are effective for patients with different types of disorder, so that we can distinguish between the techniques that have real therapeutic effects and those that serve simply to salve the clinician's and aphasic's morale.

ON THE LOGIC OF APHASIA THERAPY

When a therapist begins to work with an aphasic patient, the initial objective is to find out what is going wrong and how. This is the basis for therapy. As Schuell (1970) puts it:

> 1. The clinician must know which cerebral processes are impaired and which are intact.
> 2. The clinician must know the level at which performance breaks down in each language modality.
> 3. The clinician must know the reason that performance breaks down when it does. (p. 69)

The purpose of an assessment is to enable the therapist to formulate a hypothesis about the underlying deficits, which are responsible for the patient's impaired performance. To do this both standardised and non-standardised but systematic tests are necessary; in general published aphasia assessments sample a wide range of tasks with little depth. In order to understand why performance in a particular task breaks down it is usually necessary to investigate it further (Coltheart, 1983).

This sounds like a complex task and in practice it often is. But to plan treatment, it is not essential to demonstrate beyond all doubt what the underlying impairment is. All that is required is a hypothesis of what is wrong, sufficiently detailed to be able to *motivate* therapy. A hypothesis should be able to predict the patient's response to therapy and the pattern of errors that will occur in it. Treatment then is a *test* of the hypothesis; if it does not run as predicted, the hypothesis will need to be changed. A therapists must know what changes he/she is trying to effect, and how; to decide what they should be requires an idea of what is wrong.

The problem that has dogged aphasia therapy is the relationship between a hypothesis of the form of impairment and the actual process of therapy. Knowing what is wrong does not in any simple way determine what to do about it. We want to argue that if the steps involved are specified, then we can start to develop a metatheory of the relationship. Without this, treatment will remain an arbitrary hit and miss affair.

The first step is to decide the strategy of therapy. Broadly speaking, there are three options available: restoration, reconstitution, or compensation. *Restoration* is aimed at the direct improvement of the impaired abilities. If an aphasic cannot read because visual letter identification is impossible, then the patient is given taks to improve letter identification. By contrast reconstitution and compensation assume that if a cognitive process is impaired it remains impaired. *Reconstitution* avoids an impaired process by getting a patient to do the task in another way using intact abilities to avoid the problem. So if our patient cannot recognise letters visually, but can gesturally, he/she could be taught so recognise them by tracing them out. The reconstitution approach must then be based on a detailed analysis of the patterns of impaired and intact processes. *Compensation* is the least specific approach; the aim is get the aphasic to function as well as possible by using whatever abilities remain intact. So, for example, a patient who is agrammatic in comprehension could be taught to derive meaning from the content words and their order alone; it is a rough strategy that will work on the whole. Alternatively, after a serious attempt at improving word-retrieval, a patient might be allowed, or positively encouraged, to use his/her habitual **circumlocutions** where these are seen to be effective communication devices.

Restoration therefore is intended to enable the patient to operate normally by normal means; reconstitution that the aphasic performs normally using unusual methods. Compensation is aimed at the patient performing abnormally but optimally.

The choice between these strategies is not necessarily simple. Much may depend on the particular patients involved. It is traditionally supposed that improvement will be greatest when the most impaired functions are the focus of treatment. This is not surprising, but not necessarily universally true. Wapner and Gardner (1979) found that global aphasics made more improvement in tasks where their initial performance was better and suggest "it may be more efficient to focus attention on those areas of performance where some signs of spared capacity is already evident, than to tackle the most vitiated lingusitic capacities (p. 770)." This question is related to what the aims of therapy are. In the case of a chronic global aphasic it is probably unrealistic to aim for anything related to normal language; instead it may be appropriate to maximise the aphasic's communication abilities utilising whatever cognitive functions remain. On the other hand, with a residual aphasic who has circumscribed problems, it would be sensible to try to eliminate these.

Once this decision has been made we have to select the therapeutic approach: direct, indirect, or support. The *direct* method is the traditional one. In the case of a patient with a receptive agrammatism, where you believe that a short-term memory deficit underlies this (Caramazza, Basili, Koller, & Berndt, 1981), you would practise auditory-verbal memory tasks; for the speech reduction difficulties of a Broca's aphasic you would practise articulation; with an anomic patient you would practise name retrieval with whatever cues you think appropriate. The *indirect* method would be more subtle: for a dysarthric patient you might use **PNF** (Proprioceptive Neural Facilitation) to improve oral proprioception; if, like Howard et al. (1985a), you believe that an aphasic's word retrieval problem reflects an underlying impairment in using a full semantic representation, then you could do comprehension tasks that require the aphasic to access the semantics in order to make the representation easier to use in naming. With indirect therapy it is, then, especially necessary to specify *how* you hypothesise that this task actually affects the target performance. In *support* therapy you use an intact ability to help organise/elicit the disrupted performance. Examples would be using pieces of paper to facilitate sentence formation in dynamic aphasia (Luria, 1973); musical and rhythmical abilities to facilitate output in MIT; gesture and whole body movement for comprehension in VAT; or sign language to improve comprehension and output.

With the defect to be treated decided, and the strategy and approach to therapy selected, we then need to decide what steps to use to get from the aphasic's present abilities to the target performance—we need a treatment hierarchy, but where should it come from?

Many therapists have produced treatment hierarchies whose source is obscure; there is no explicit argument about what makes a task more complex, or why practice in one task is necessary before the next can be attempted. Darley (1982), for example, manages to eleborate an extensive hierarchy based tenuously on Schuell's claim that "auditory stimulation is crucial in control of language processes (Schuell et al., 1964, p. 338)." The trouble with essentially unmotivated orders of difficulty is that they may bear no relation to the difficulties real aphasics have. Darley presents as his first task in therapy for reading, pointing to letters when they are named by the examiner; this he misleadingly calls recognising letters (it is possible, of course, for aphasics to recognise letters without knowing anything about their names). Once this is mastered the patient can proceeed to reading single words. Implicit in this is the assumption that the ability to point to letters on command is a necessary component of word reading; there is no evidence that this is true for either normal people (Henderson, 1982) or aphasics (Coltheart, Patterson, & Marshall, 1980), with the possible exception of **letter-by-letter readers** (Patterson & Kay, 1982). Clearly explicit justification is necessary; *ex cathedra* pronouncements on the hierarchy of tasks to be used in therapy may contain truths reflecting years of imaginative and effective clinical practice, or they may depend on prejudices based on outmoded psychological theories, or even total ignorance. If therapy is to progress hierarchies need more detailed and more tenable justification.

Some therapists have tried to derive hierarchies from intuition (e.g., Keenan, 1966, on picture-naming) or "logic"; this applies to most of the therapists of the behaviour modification school. Sarno, Silverman, and Sands (1970), for example, used a hierarchy that they "thought representative of the order of acquisition of skills in the recovery process (p. 615)"; they comment, though, that "some patients demonstrated their poorest performance in what we had considered the simplest tasks and did best in tasks we considered more difficult." Holland (1970) created her hierarchies:

> Either by requiring the patient to produce more words, by requiring [. . .] selections among previously taught simple responses, or by using progressively more complex (or subtle) stimulus material (items) or by some combination or sequencing of all these. (p. 379)

Which, it would appear, can be translated into "the tasks become more difficult by making them more difficult."

Logic then, as Sarno, Silverman, and Sands found out, may not provide an appropriate hierarchy. Alternatively one can be derived from a theory; Holland and Levy (1971) gleaned the idea from early transformational grammar (Chomsky, 1957), that a "kernel" sentence (simple declarative) represented the simplest grammatical construction. Therapy for agrammatism, then, involved first treaching some kernel sentences, and then eliciting transformationally derived forms (questions, commands, passives, relative clauses) from them.

Another approach to the same problem was used by Helm-Estabrooks, Fitzpatrick, and Barresi (1981a); they quote evidence that particular constructions are easier for non-fluent aphasics *as a group* to produce (Goodglass et al., 1972; Gleason et al., 1975), and argues that therapy for agrammatism of speech should therefore start with imperatives and work up via WH-questions and intransitives, to active transitive sentences. In a similar vein Gardner, Albert, and Weintraub (1975) found that for a *group* of aphasics comprehension was worse on neutral or semantically anomalous sentences than single words and slowed or redundant sentences; on this basis they suggest that an appropriate therapeutic hierarchy for auditory comprehension would be "begin with the word alone, move next to the word in a slowly enunciated, semantically redundant utterance, then gradually eliminate redundant semantic cues and increase the rate of speaking (p. 160)."

The average performance of a group of patients may not reflect the performance of any individuals in the group; Salvatore et al. (1983) found that none of their individual patients found the same order of difficulty of grammatical constructions that Helm-Estabrooks' hierarchy suggests. Shewan and Bandur (1986) recognise this conflict between mean group performance and individual hierarchies of difficulty; they suggest, therefore, that the clinician should "gather baseline data [to] determine each individuals' particular hierarchy of difficulty (p. 13)."

The individual patient's performance can be used as a basis for a hierarchy. For example, with deep dyslexics, who can read concrete words better than abstract words, it would be sensible to start with the concrete words for which reading is more likely to be successful and then, as these are learned, to introduce increasingly abstract words. Here the strategy is to discover empirically for each patient what determines what they find difficult, and to base the treatment hierarchy on that. Or, as Croskey and Adams (1969) suggest, therapy at naming should be directed at the items that the patient can sometimes but not always retrieve correctly, rather than those that are never available.

A historically popular source for hierarchies has been the order of development in children. This was the basis of much early German theory, and was, for example, advocated by Jakobson (1941) in the treatment of articulation; and it is the origin of the emphasis on auditory stimulation particularly with nouns (Froment & Monod, 1914; Wepman, 1951). Since the demonstration that aphasias are not related to stages in language development (Dennis & Wiegel-Crump, 1979), developmental orders are no longer much used as sources of hierarchies, although they may provide a crude measure of linguistic complexity.

Finally, the therapist must decide how to implement this treatment hierarchy. What criteria are used to decide when one step is finished and it is appropriate to move onto the next one? Or should several be worked on at once? How are the patients' errors to be dealt with—particularly when different sorts of errors will reflect failure in different ways? When, how, and why is the hierarchy to be modified? Presumably there are no "correct" answers to these, but it is necessary that the decisions taken are at least motivated and coherent rather than *ad hoc* or intuitive.

In the practice of therapy, there is no obvious connection between what has been identified as the underlying problem and the *process* of treatment. It is conspicuous how the vast bulk of aphasiological work has been devoted to debate about underlying problems, and remarkably little to therapy for them. This is surprising, as therapy can clearly provide an experimental *test* of hypothesised disorders; if deficit X is thought to cause problems A, B, and C, and therapy for X results in its improvement, then A, B, and C must improve correspondingly. If they are unchanged then the hypothesis needs changing. Beauvois and Derouesné (1982) and Byng and Coltheart (1986) provide the only good examples of the use of treatment studies to test theoretical claims.

In this section we have argued that theory can be systematically related to therapy by breaking the problem down into a series of decisions:

1. Decide *what* is the problem to be treated:
   — specify what the original aphasic condition is, in terms of performance in both standardised and non-standardised tests;
   — specify what are the proposed underlying defect(s);
   — decide what language performance therapy is intended to improve.

2. Decide *how* to conduct the treatment:
   — decide what strategy to use: restoration, reconstitution, or compensation;
   — decide how this is to be implemented: by direct, indirect, or facilitation therapy;
   — specify the hierarchy, its motivation and its implementation; and exactly what is done.
3. Explain *why* these methods have been chosen:
   — specify how, in theory, therapeutic tasks are meant to change the target performance.
4. Then find out, measure, and record what actually happens.
5. And, fundamental to the whole process, specify why improving this performance is of use to the individual patient.

We are not suggesting that there are "correct" answers to all (or indeed, any) of these; much will depend on the particular therapist's theory. Earlier we discussed various experimental designs that can be used to investigate the effectiveness of particular therapeutic procedures with individual patients. If therapy is organised in this way it can be made both *rational* and *specific* (Hatfield & Shewell, 1983); then we can develop theory that relates to therapy and therapy that relates to theory. If we motivate, specify, and test our therapy it will get better; it needs to.

Glossary

Terms are listed alphabetically. Important cross-references in the glossary are in bold type; for each reference, where appropriate, we refer to one source (or occasionally more) where the question is dealt with in more detail.

Abstract attitude. Goldstein (1948) considered that some aphasic patients had an impairment in abstract reasoning. Initially this theory was inspired by his observations that patients might, even in non-verbal tasks, group objects in curious ways—they did not seem to appreciate the (abstract) categories into which they fell. Patients can be absorbed by the concrete details of a task and be unable to distinguish its elements. Goldstein's concept has been criticised for not being precise, and has received little attention from contemporary researchers, even where they have been concerned with aphasic categorisation.

Agrammatism. The grammatical disturbance in the speech of non-fluent aphasic patients. Speech consists mostly of content words, and there are few attempts at syntactic structures; many function words and inflections are missing, and there are few verbs. In **inflecting languages** such as German or Russian verbs mostly appear in the infinitive and nouns in the nominative. Some (but not all) patients who are agrammatic in speech production also have difficulties in sentence comprehension, where understanding the sentences requires knowledge of their syntactic structures. A variety of very different kinds of difficulties in sentence comprehension and production may have been categorised together as agrammatism (see Howard, 1985; Kean, 1985; Tissot, Mounin, & Lhermitte, 1973).

Anomia. A difficulty in word finding; most often demonstrated in picture-naming tasks, but often also evident in **circumlocutions** in spontaneous speech. Some degree of anomia is found in virtually all aphasic patients; where it is the most prominent problem, a patient is said to show **anomic aphasia**.

Anomic aphasia (also called **amnesic aphasia**). A type of aphasia in which a difficulty in retrieving content words, and sometimes particularly nouns, is the most obvious problem. The difficulty may be confined to speech production, but some patients also have problems in word comprehension. Other aspects of language are relatively well-preserved; repetition is good and spoken language is grammatically well-formed, although there may be many circumlocutions.

Aphasia. This refers to a disorder of language following some kind of acquired brain damage. This book considers only aphasia in adults who had learned to speak normally before the brain damage. The term excludes disorders in language comprehension or expression that are primarily due to mental disorders, including psychosis, dementia, and confusion. It also excludes disorders that are due to difficulties in sensation (e.g., deafness), or due to difficulties in articulation or its control (dysarthrias). The term is thus intended to include all disorders of language that are primarily due to impairment to the linguistic system itself. The boundaries of this have not been easy to determine in practice; there is, for example, debate on whether a difficulty in organising the movements of articulation (**articulatory apraxia**) should be considered a primarily motor disorder (and therefore non-aphasic), or a primarily linguistic one (and therefore aphasic).

Aphasia classification. An area of extraordinary terminological and conceptual confusion. Most modern workers, including the neo-classical school and the neurolinguistic school would adopt a classification system that is closely based on the nineteenth century **Wernicke–Lichtheim schema**. Patients are classified on (1) the relative impairment in different modalities—auditory comprehension, repetition, and naming; and (2) on whether their speech can be classified as fluent or non-fluent. This yields eight aphasia types as shown in Table 1. The commonest types are global, Broca's, Wernicke's, conduction, and anomic. This classification is the basis of many of the modern standard aphasia tests including the BDAE, WAB, and the Aachen Aphasia Test (Huber, Poeck, & Willmes, 1984). The status of these aphasia types is a matter of dispute; some workers have treated them as syndromes (qualitatively homogeneous groups of patients), while others have considered them, at best, crude short-hand descriptions of patient behaviour (see Marshall, 1982b, 1986). See Weisenburg and McBride (1935), Lesser (1978) or Lecours et al. (1983) for comparisons of the aphasia classifications of different authors.

TABLE 1
The Neo-classical Categories of Aphasia

Aphasia Type	Spontaneous Speech	Auditory Comprehension	Repetition	Naming
Global	Non-fluent	Poor	Poor	Poor
Broca's	Non-fluent	Good	Poor	Poor
Isolation	Non-fluent	Poor	Good	Poor
Transcortical motor	Non-fluent	Good	Good	Poor
Wernicke's	Fluent	Poor	Poor	Poor
Conduction	Fluent	Good	Poor	Poor
Transcortical sensory	Fluent	Poor	Good	Poor
Anomic	Fluent	Good	Good	Poor

Aphasic alexia. A term used by Lhermitte and Ducarne (1965); equivalent to **dysphasic dyslexia**—see **dyslexia**.

Aphemia. A term that Broca (1861, 1869) attempted to introduce to describe "loss of the faculty of articulated language." In aphemia there is very much reduced vocabulary or even speechlessness except for some oaths and neologisms. Ideas, as shown by gestures, are intact, and comprehension is good even for words and sentences that the patient cannot repeat. Broca wanted to distinguish this from "verbal amnesia" in which there is no longer a connection between words and the ideas that they represent. Trousseau (1864) objected to the term "aphemia," believing, according to Head (1926), that in Greek it meant "infamous"; he introduced his own coining—"aphasia"—which gained general acceptance.

Apoplexy. A term used by Hippocrates to refer to any sudden attack of paralysis or loss of sensation as a result of cerebral disease. Equivalent to the modern term **stroke**.

Apraxia. Any disorder of the organisation of movement; the concept was developed by Liepmann (1900). Involuntary movements may be relatively normal, but more deliberate or symbolic acts are disturbed. Apraxia is, most typically, confined to movements of one kind, or one part of the body; hence the sub-categories. A range of different types of apraxia have been proposed: limb apraxia, ideomotor apraxia, ideational apraxia, constructional apraxia, dressing apraxia, etc.

Articulatory apraxia (also called **apraxia of speech**). A difficulty in the *organisation* of movements of the articulators for the production of speech sounds. There should be no motor difficulty, and speech sounds may be produced correctly in relatively automatic ways (e.g., swearing, counting, singing), but impossible when produced deliberately. Articulatory apraxia is often accompanied by oral apraxia—a defect in the organisation of non-speech mouth movements—and aphasia. There is much debate about whether **articulatory apraxia** should be considered a language disorder (and therefore a symptom of aphasia), or a disorder of motor control. In many patients, the articulatory disorder is affected by linguistic factors (e.g., syntactic category, word frequency, real word vs non-word); in these cases it would seem unprofitable to ignore the linguistic dimension. The term has been used in many different ways; many authors now would avoid using it at all, while others use it to describe any articulatory difficulties of a non-fluent aphasic patient (see Wertz et al., 1984).

Associationism. A psychological theory, which can be traced back to Aristotle, but which was first fully developed by the English Empiricists, particularly Hume. Association is the fundamental principle of mental life. Sensations or images can become associated by one of three relations: similarity, contrast, and contiguity. Complex ideas are built up from simple sensations by these laws of association; the early empiricists hoped to reduce these three laws to one—the law of contiguity—and to create a mental mechanics that would rival the physical mechanics that Newton had developed.

Associationism remained the dominating perspective on psychology throughout the nineteenth century (e.g., James Mill, Herbert Spencer, Ebbinghaus) and in the twentieth century was developed into **behaviourism**, which aimed to explain all behaviour in terms of associations between stimuli and responses.

Automatic speech. Speech where the process is initiated by the clinician and completed "automatically" by the patient. This includes all **serial speech** (i.e., counting, months, etc.) as well as songs, poetry, and cliché completion (as when a patient says "dogs" after the clinician says "It's raining cats and . . ."). According to Jackson, this is non-propositional, and therefore not real speech. Automatic speech is often the only speech that very severe global aphasics can produce.

BDAE—Boston Diagnostic Aphasia Examination. A comprehensive aphasia test developed in Boston by Goodglass and Kaplan (1972). It samples a very wide range of language performance with small numbers of items testing each function. Patients' spontaneous speech (partly elicited by description of the famous "cookie theft picture") is rated for fluency, error types, word finding, etc.; at the time that it was introduced, emphasis on the properties of speech was an innovation. On the basis of BDAE scores, around 40% of patients can be assigned to neo-classical categories of aphasia; the remainder represent mixtures of different types.

Behaviourism. An approach to psychology developed by J.B. Watson (1914) that asserts that psychology should only be concerned with observable behaviour, and should not consider mental events —thoughts, feelings, concepts. It became the dominant approach to psychology in the United States following the Second World War. In its most extreme examples, no internal state of an organism could be discussed. It lead to a largely sterile psychology, which avoided theory; it was strongly concerned with the behaviour of laboratory rats, hoping that investigation of lower animals in controlled situations would yield general principles that could explain the behaviour of humans. Now largely abandoned.

Blister. Application of substances to the skin with the aim of causing either reddening and peeling of the skin, or the collection of fluid beneath it. This is intended to relieve congestion (accumulation of fluid) in the organs lying beneath the blister.

Bright's disease. An infection or inflammation of the kidneys —glomerulonephritis. In the chronic stage, the kidneys are damaged, so the blood pressure rises. This can lead to cerebral thrombosis or haemorrhage, which can result in aphasia.

Broca's aphasia. A neo-classical category of aphasia. Spontaneous speech is non-fluent, and sometimes there is a degree of dysarthria and/or articulatory apraxia. Function words and grammatical affixes may be omitted, and syntactic structure simplified or even absent; verbs are often rare and nouns relatively common. Language comprehension is by comparison relatively good, although there may be difficulty with grammatically complex sentences. There are almost always word retrieval problems, evident in both picture-naming and spontaneous speech; repetition is disturbed in line with the disruption of spontaneous speech (see e.g., Albert et al., 1981; Goodglass & Kaplan, 1972).

CADL—Communicative Activities in Daily Living. A test by Holland (1980) intended to sample how effectively an aphasic patient can communicate, using language, mime, gesture, etc., in real life situations. On the basis of an interview and a role play of the patient going to see the doctor, performance is assessed on a variety of functions. These include ability to perform certain speech acts (e.g., greeting, requesting, informing), reading, writing, and the use of verbal context, but also tasks that are more unusual in aphasia examinations—e.g., ability to dial a telephone number, recognition of facial expression, and ability to appreciate the humour of cartoons.

Cantharides. A preparation of dried blister beetles (Spanish flies). It can be applied to the skin to cause blistering; this relieves underlying congestion. Taken orally it acts as a stimulant and diuretic.

Catastrophic reaction. A term used by Goldstein (1948) to describe the emotional collapse of an aphasic patient faced with a situation with which he/she cannot cope. It provokes anxiety, sweating, tears, and rage. Goldstein suggests that much of aphasic patients' behaviour can be understood as attempts to avoid situations that provoke catastrophic reactions; as a result patients may appear excessively orderly and rigid.

Cautery. Application of a hot instrument or other irritant to the skin or a wound. Now used for sealing and sterilising wounds; in the mediaeval period cauteries were often used to blister and irritate parts of the body.

Cerebral congestion. A term used up to the twentieth century for accumulation of fluid in the brain; this causes raised intracranial pressure (due usually to blocked circulation of cerebrospinal fluid, or haemorrhage within the skull). Often, in the past, treated by bleeding which, by lowering the blood pressure, may have caused temporary relief.

Cerebrovascular accident (CVA). A failure of the system of blood supply to the brain that causes destruction of some brain tissue. Three different types are normally distinguished: thrombotic CVA, where a blood clot develops in one of the cerebral arteries until it blocks the circulation; embolic CVA, where a blood clot, or other material from elsewhere in the body, gets into the circulation and lodges in one of the cerebral vessels, blocking it. The third cause is **haemorrhage** caused by rupture of a blood vessel. CVAs are commonly referred to as **strokes**. A CVA usually causes localised damage. The effect of the CVA depends entirely on the size and location of the damaged cerebral tissue. About half of stroke sufferers survive for more than 30 days after the onset; up to 10% of the survivors may experience some degree of language impairment (see Wade et al., 1985).

Chronic endocarditis. Chronic inflammation of the endocardium—the membrane lining the interior of the heart. The membrane becomes ulcerated and, particularly where it covers the valves, fragments can break off as emboli. These can cause an embolic CVA.

Circumlocution. Attempt to explain a word in a roundabout way, or finding a way to avoid using a word. It usually reflects an underlying difficulty in word retrieval.

Competence and **performance.** Chomsky (1957) argued that the subject matter of linguistics should not be the actual speech performance of people in the language community, but rather the set of sentences that native speakers would accept (on the basis of their intuition) as well-formed sentences of the language. Linguists should aim to describe the native speakers' linguistic competence. Speakers' actual performance, in contrast, deviates from this because of various non-linguistic limitations—speech errors, short-term memory span, etc. The study of the factors that explain why speakers' performance deviates from their competence is not part of linguistics. This distinction led to a rather fruitless debate on whether aphasia should be considered a disorder of linguistic performance or competence (e.g., Weigl & Bierwisch, 1970; Whitaker, 1971; see Lesser, 1978, pp. 46–53); this turns out to be substantially the same as the question of whether aphasia should be considered a defect in access to (intact) language, or a deficit in language itself. Almost certainly some aphasics have central difficulties in language, and others in access processes; there is no general answer that will inevitably apply to all patients (cf. Shallice, 1987).

Content words. Many researchers have wanted to distinguish between **content** words and **function** words (or functors). Content words are those in open grammatical categories—nouns, adjectives, verbs, and (some) adverbs—to which new words can potentially be added. Function words, which come from closed grammatical categories (determiners, prepositions, conjunctions, pronouns, etc.), tend to carry much of the information on the syntactic structure of sentences. The distinction has often been criticised because no clear-cut dividing line can be drawn on the basis of any one feature; but, nevertheless, the distinction has been of practical value to clinicians.

Conduction aphasia. A category of aphasia in which repetition is disturbed more severely than other functions. Auditory comprehension is reasonably good, although there may be a subtle difficulty with grammatically complex sentences. Speech production is fluent, but there are often phonemic paraphasias; these are usually more prominent in repetition tasks. Shallice and Warrington (1977) argue that there are (at least) two varieties of conduction aphasia: a reproduction disorder causing phonological errors in all speech production tasks; and a limitation in auditory-verbal short-term memory.

Deblocking. A method used by Weigl to allow patients to produce words or sentences in a modality in which they would usually be unavailable. If a word that cannot be used in (impaired) task A, is used in (relatively intact) task B, it will be successfully produced in task A if presented within about ten minutes. The word will then remain available in task A for much longer—for days, months, or even years. Task A is called the deblocking task and task B the deblocked task. Any task—oral word reading, copying, auditory comprehension, picture-naming—can be used, although they may vary in their effectiveness as deblockers. Weigl insists that deblocking should be (1) successive; and (2) the patient should remain unaware of the relationship between the deblocking task and the task to be deblocked (see Weigl, 1980).

Deep dyslexia. A disorder of oral word reading in which (1) the patient cannot read non-words (e.g., GOCK); (2) concrete words are read better than abstract words; (3) function words are read worse than content words; (4) words with grammatical inflections are hard; (5) semantic errors (e.g., CAT → "dog," AVERAGE → "bad"), morphological errors (e.g., WALKING → "walks") and visual errors (e.g., WIRE → "wine") occur. Many, but not all deep dyslexics are also Broca's aphasics and deep dysgraphics. These patients are thought to read aloud using only a route that involves access to central semantic representations (see Coltheart et al., 1980).

Deep dysgraphia. An acquired writing difficulty, used to describe a pattern of difficulties in writing words to dictation. Deep dysgraphic patients (1) cannot write non-words to dictation; (2) write concrete words better than abstract words; (3) write function words worse than content words; (4) have difficulty with words with grammatical inflections, and (5) make semantic errors, morphological errors, and visual errors (see Bub & Kertesz, 1982).

Deposited rhythm. Used by Goldstein (1948); we think he intends to describe an emphatic rhythm learned with a sentence as an aid to its recall.

Diagram makers. A term used by Head (1926) to describe the localisationist neurologists of the nineteenth century—Wernicke, Lichtheim, Broadbent, Bastian etc.—because of their tendency to propose theories that were expressed as diagrams (see **Wernicke-Lichtheim model**). Head intended the term as an insult.

Dialectical materialism. A term describing a Marxist approach to reasoning, although the term was never used by Marx himself. The dialectic was a method advanced by Hegel for developing a new view (synthesis) out of two contradictory positions (thesis and antithesis); the synthesis goes beyond both thesis and antithesis, but at the same time incorporates them. Thus, for example, Luria reconciled the localisationist and antilocalisationist positions by developing his theory of functional networks based on cortical analysers, in which functions are both localised and not localised in the brain (Luria, 1966). The materialism indicates opposition to nineteenth century idealism, which held that matter was a product of mind; dialectical materialists hold that mind is the highest product of matter, but are not necessarily reductionist.

Direct method. An approach to aphasia treatment advocated by Kussmaul, Gutzmann, and Froeschels, in which language is reconstituted by dint of repetition. First the patient has to learn to repeat sounds, then words and later phrases. Patients were typically encouraged to use words multimodally; a patient might, for example, hear a word, repeat it, see the written word and copy it; repetition, though, remains the central method of the approach.

Direct speech training. Another phrase for the **direct method**.

Dualism. The view that there are two fundamental types of substances. All substances are either material or mental, and neither can be reduced to the other. In this it is opposed to **reductionism**, which holds that all mental events can be reduced to material events, and **idealism**, which holds that all material events are in fact mental.

Dynamic aphasia. A term used by Luria to describe aphasic patients who have difficulty in converting internal speech into spoken narrative, because of, in Luria's words, "a disturbance in the linear scheme of the sentence (Luria, 1973, p. 320)." Comprehension, word retrieval, and repetition are undisturbed, but the patient is at a loss when required to turn his thoughts into language. There is no category that corresponds to dynamic aphasia in other classification systems.

Dysarthria. A disorder of articulation. This can be due to either a defect in the organs of articulation (i.e., mouth, tongue, larynx, etc.) or, more commonly in aphasic patients, by impairment to the nerves supplying the organs of articulation (Darley, Aronson, & Brown, 1975). A number of different types of dysarthria are recognised, including spastic dysarthria (characterised by raised tone in the muscles controlling articulation), flaccid dysarthria (in which there is reduced tone and weakness), dystonic dysarthria (where poorly-controlled writhing movements may occur), and ataxic dysarthria (where there is poor coordination of muscle movements). There is no deficit of language. There is debate on whether **articulatory apraxia** should be described as a variety of dysarthria.

Dyslexia. A disorder of reading. The traditional classification of disorders of reading, developed by Dejerine (1892), recognises three kinds of dyslexia, which are distinguished by their accompanying disorders. In **dyslexia without dysgraphia** (or pure dyslexia), writing is unaffected but reading is disturbed; in **dyslexia with dysgraphia**, both reading and writing are disturbed, but there is, by comparison, little or no aphasia. In **dysphasic dyslexia**, reading, writing, and other language modalities are impaired. This classification schema is (broadly) accepted by the neo-classical school (cf. Albert et al., 1981). (See also **deep dyslexia, surface dyslexia**, and **letter-by-letter reading**.)

Dysprosody. Impairment in (one or more of) the prosodic aspects of speech: rhythm, intonation, or stress.

Echolalia. The involuntary repetition (by a patient) of other people's speech. It is rare in aphasic patients, although it is said to be a feature of "isolation syndrome," where repetition is the only function which remains (relatively) intact.

EFCP—Edinburgh Functional Communication Profile. An assessment of the communication abilities of elderly patients by Skinner et al. (1984), which is designed to accommodate patients who are aphasic and/or demented. It assesses the effectiveness of communication and indicates the most useful strategies in a variety of modalities including speech, gesture, writing, and facial expression, based on an interview with the patient and information from relatives or professional carers involved with the patient.

Efferent motor aphasia. A category of aphasia proposed by Luria (1947), approximately equivalent to **Broca's aphasia.** In this type of motor aphasia there is a defect in the "serial organisation of the spoken word" and phones are not modified according to their phonological context. As patients improve, agrammatism becomes apparent. Efferent motor aphasia (where the problem is a disorder in output) is distinguished from **afferent motor aphasia**, where articulatory organisation breaks down because of a failure in the use of kinaesthetic feedback for the control of articulation.

Expressive aphasia. See **receptive aphasia**.

FCP—Functional Communication Profile. A language test developed by Taylor (1965) that is intended to sample how aphasic patients communicate in "real-life" situations. It is based on ratings judged from an informal interview with the patient; then performance in 45 different areas is rated on a 9-point scale. The areas covered are intended to sample the normal range of language use—for example, the clinician has to rate the patient's understanding of conversation, television, and films.

Figure. In Gestalt psychology, a figure can only be perceived against its **ground**. That is, in general, mental events need to be considered in their context. This follows directly from the Gestalt thesis that the whole is greater than its parts.

Fluency. In aphasia classification the neo-classical school makes its primary distinction between **fluent** and **non-fluent** aphasias. This distinction is based on a number of characteristics of patients' spontaneous speech. Fluent aphasic have normal or near normal speech rates, and use a variety of different grammatical constructions; function words and grammatical inflections are present, and usually syntactically appropriate. Intonation patterns are present and usually appropriate. Non-fluent aphasics have slow and often laboured speech. The variety of grammatical constructions is often restricted and intonation may be reduced or absent; function words and grammatical affixes may be omitted, and patients may rely a lot on nouns.

Function words (or **functors**). See **content words**.

Gestalt psychology. An approach to psychology developed in Germany in the first quarter of the twentieth century that emphasises that mental events and experience cannot be completely analysed into a series of elements; the whole is more than the sum of the parts. This led to an interest in the way mental events interacted. Goldstein developed a form of gestalt psychology, which he called organismic psychology, which saw the behaviour of an organism as a concerted effort towards particular ends, and saw the importance of maintaining equilibrium. This was reflected in his view of the (damaged or undamaged) brain acting as a whole interacting unit.

Global aphasia. An aphasia in which language is very severely affected in all modalities. In the most extreme cases there may be no evidence of any real knowledge of language remaining. Auditory comprehension is usually the least severely impaired modality.

Ground. See **figure**.

Hand, ear and eye test. A test devised by Head (1926) intended to involve complex symbolic processes; it achieved fame, but was never popular as a clinical instrument. It involves 16 movements (e.g., put left hand to left eye; put right hand to left ear). The patient has to imitate these movements when performed by the examiner, and then when seen in a mirror. Then the patient has to do them in imitation of a drawing, and then the drawings reflected in a mirror. Then the same set of movements have to be done in response to spoken and written commands, and the patient has to describe the movements in speech and in writing when performed by the examiner and when seen in a mirror. Weisenburg and McBride (1935) comment that:

> The tests undoubtedly call for complex processes . . . (and have) aroused the greatest interest among students of aphasia . . . The chief difficulty with these tests lies in their interpretation; when the patient fails the reason for his failure is largely a matter for speculation. (p. 88)

HELPSS—Helm-Elicited Language Program for Syntax Stimulation. An approach to the treatment of agrammatic speech production that Helm developed and named after herself (Helm-Estabrooks, Fitzpatrick & Barresi, 1981a). A hierarchy of syntactic structures are elicited by story completion; the patient first practices repeating the sentences. Later he/she is allowed to attempt them alone.

Hemiplegia. Paralysis of one side of the body. When caused by damage above the level of the brain stem, the paralysis is on the opposite side of the body from the lesion that causes it. Aphasia, which usually follows damage to the left hemisphere (at least in right-handed people), may be accompanied by a right hemiplegia.

Holism. The view that a system is more than the sum of its parts. Applied especially to the opponents of localisationism (e.g., Jackson, Goldstein, and Lashley) who emphasised that the parts of the brain must be considered to be interacting, and that as a result the action of an individual part cannot be separated off.

Indurated chancre. A venereal ulcer; specifically the initial lesion of syphilis.

Inflecting language. A language in which many words have inflectional suffixes that carry several different grammatical distinctions simultaneously. In the Latin word *domus*, for example, the *-us* suffix indicates both nominative and singular. Examples of inflecting languages are Latin, German, and Russian. They can be distinguished from analytic languages (e.g., Chinese or, less strongly, English) where words tend to be single morphemes, and agglutinating languages (e.g., Turkish, Hungarian) where each grammatical distinction is signalled by an individually identifiable morpheme.

Jargon aphasia. A fluent aphasia where the speech production has enough paraphasias and/or neologisms to make it very hard to understand. Asemantic jargon consists mostly of real words but few have any recognisable relation to a target; in neologistic jargon there are many non-existent words (neologisms). In undifferentiated jargon there are few (or no) real words but strings of phonemes in word-like sequences. All three varieties are found in Wernicke's aphasia, particularly soon after onset. In phonemic jargon there are many phonemic paraphasias; this is characteristic of severe conduction aphasia (see Brown, 1981).

Kinaesthesis. The sensation caused by movements; kinaesthetic feedback is important in the control of many movements, especially fine or skilled ones.

Lecture verticale. A method of treatment for reading disorders, invented by Gheorghita (1981) in Romania, in which words are presented with their letters written vertically. Later, sentences are presented with the individual words presented left-to-right but written in a vertical column. Gheorghita believes that presentation in this way can improve reading by forcing the patients to pay deliberate attention to the parts of words (letters), or the parts of sentences (the individual words).

Letter-by-letter readers. Dyslexic patients who, when reading aloud, (1) sometimes name the letters one-by-one as they identify them; and (2) show a linear relationship between word length and reading latencies. Many of these patients make reading errors where letters are mistaken for other visually-similar letters (e.g., reading SORT as "soft"). Some of these patients have good writing and so are, in Dejerine's classification, "pure alexics" (see Patterson & Kay, 1982).

Localisationism. The doctrine that specific mental events are localised in specific parts of cerebral tissue. Most usually "faculties" (e.g., acoustic images of words) have been located in particular centres. Many localisationists were also reductionists; Wernicke, for example, believed that "central nerve endings are invested with the role of psychic elements," and associations were represented by nerve fibres. The nineteenth century localisationists were almost all reductionists.

Logopaedics. A term used in many European countries (including Germany, Poland, Romania, Italy, and the Soviet Union) for speech therapy.

LOT–Lanugage Oriented Therapy. An approach to aphasia treatment adopted by Shewan and Bandur (1986). Treatment, which is suitable for any aphasic patient, is by language stimulation, adopting hierarchies derived from group studies of aphasic patients.

Mentalist. Concerning mental events, thought. Behaviourists felt that mental concepts, including, for example, meaning, were unobservable and therefore could not be part of the concerns of science.

Meninges. A collective term for the membranes surrounding the brain, lying beneath the skull—in fact made up of three membranes: dura mater on the outside, then arachnoid mater and, lying next to the cortex, the pia mater.

Modelling. A term used in behaviour therapy to describe giving the patient an example of how to do something that they can imitate.

Motor aphasia. A term used to describe aphasia in which speech production is much more impaired than comprehension. Patients have non-fluent speech, and often a degree of dysarthria. Although broadly equivalent to the neo-classical **Broca's aphasia**, it has often been used to include all kinds of non-fluent aphasia.

Mnestic. An adjective meaning related to memory.

MTTDA–Minnesota Test for the Differential Diagnosis of Aphasia. A comprehensive formal aphasia test developed by Schuell (1965); it allows patients to be classified into Schuell et al.'s (1964) categories of

aphasia. The sub-tests are grouped into the areas of auditory disturbances, visual and reading disturbances, speech and language disturbances, visuomotor and writing disturbances and numerical relations
and arithmetic processes.

Neologisms. The production of non-existent words in spontaneous
speech; most authors distinguish between phonemic paraphasias (which
bear a clear phonological relationship to the target word) and neologisms (which do not). Where neologisms are frequent, the patient is said
to show neologistic **jargon aphasia** (see Butterworth, 1979).

Neoplasm. A malignant tumour.

Non-fluent. See **fluency.**

Operant conditioning. A term from Skinner (1938) used to describe the
control of behaviour by manipulation of its consequences (the reinforcement). Thus in the classic example, a rat can be conditioned to
press a bar on the side of its cage if this gives it a food pellet (the
reinforcer). Behaviour patterns can be **shaped** by building them up
gradually from their component parts, and reinforcing each part; thus a
rat might first be reinforced for approaching the bar, then for touching
it, and finally reinforcement would only be given for pressing the bar. A
reinforcer is, technically, any consequence of behaviour that tends to
increase the frequency of that behaviour (typically food, drink, or
something else that satisfies).

PACE–Promoting Aphasics' Communicative Efficiency. An approach to
the treatment of aphasia that emphasises that patients should learn to
use whatever means remain available to them to communicate, rather
than trying to treat the language disability itself (see Davis & Wilcox,
1985).

Paedogogics. Teaching of children.

Paragrammatism. A term introduced by Kleist (1916) to refer to the
grammatical errors of fluent aphasics. In general these errors appear to
reflect misselection of function words or grammatical affixes, or confusion of syntactic structures; in contrast to agrammatism, omission of
function words and affixes is comparatively rare (see Butterworth &
Howard, 1977).

Paraphasia. The use of an inappropriate word in speech—a word erroneously used—traditionally divided into semantic paraphasias (e.g., naming a CAT as "a dog"), and phonological paraphasias (or phonemic paraphasias, or literal paraphasias), where the error sounds like the target (e.g., naming a CAT as "a cap"). Phonological paraphasias may either be real words, or non-words (see Ellis, 1985).

Performance. See **competence**.

Perseveration. The production, as an error, of a response that had been produced earlier in a session. The response that is perseverated may have originally occurred either as a correct response or as an error. Perseveration is more common when patients are tired and when they are presented with difficult material. Most commonly the material perseverated has been produced immediately before, but sometimes quite large amounts of material can intervene.

Phoneme. The minimal distinctive sound units of a language. The phonemes /p/ and /b/ can be shown to be contrastive because they distinguish minimal pairs—for example, "pin" and "bin." The phoneme itself is an abstraction; the actual sounds (which are instances of a phoneme) are called phones. In Southern British English there are approximately 20 vowel and 24 consonant phonemes (see e.g., Gimson, 1970).

Phonemic cueing (also called **phonological cueing**). Provision of the first phoneme, or first few phonemes, or first syllable, by the therapist to help an aphasic patient produce a word that he/she would otherwise be unable to find. These are, in general, the most effective cues to word retrieval that a therapist can provide, although not all patients find them useful.

PICA–the Porch Index of Communicative Ability. An aphasia test devised by Porch (1971), which despite some serious weaknesses is still in widespread use in the United States. An overall rating of the severity of aphasia is derived from a series of 18 sub-tests on a set of 10 objects. The sub-tests are grouped into three areas according to the variety of response: verbal (spoken response); gestural (mimed or pointing response); and graphic (written response). Scores are on a scale of 1–16, where 15 is "accurate and complete," 10 is "accurate after self-correction of an error," 5 is "intelligible but not related to test item," and 1 is "no awareness of test item." This scale is, at best, ordinal. Unfortunately the scores are based on averages of these, which yields meaningless results. The results of experiments that rely upon the PICA should therefore be treated with caution.

PNF–Proprioceptive Neural Facilitation. A technique for improving the movement of (partially) paralysed muscles by sensory stimulation of that area (e.g., brushing, application of ice, or heat).

Preventive method. An approach to the treatment of non-fluent aphasics in the early stages of recovery devised by Beyn and Shokhor-Trotskaya (1966), whose aim is to prevent the appearance of agrammatism.

Propositional speech. Hughlings Jackson in opposing the localisationists of the mid-nineteenth century protested that language did not consist of sequences of single words, but of the expression of relationships between concepts; that is, using Herbert Spencer's term, "propositions."

> To speak is not to utter words, it is to propositionise. A proposition is such a relation of words that it makes one new meaning; not by the mere addition of what we call the separate meanings of the several words; the terms in a proposition are modified by each other. Single words are meaningless and so is any unrelated succession of words. The unit of speech is a proposition . . . Loss of speech is therefore the loss of power to propositionise. (Jackson, 1932, p. 159–160)

Jackson went on to argue that aphasic patients may not only have lost the power to *express* propositions, but that they may also fail to generate propositions internally; from this viewpoint aphasia is a problem of both language and thought. Following on from this Head (1926) claimed that (some) aphasic patients had a general problem in symbolic thought; he abandoned the term "propositionise" because he felt it was too imprecise.

Emphasis on the propositional aspect of language therefore stresses the use of language to communicate ideas, and the idea that sentences have conceptual structure.

Pragmatics. The use of language and communication in context. Semantics deals with the meaning conveyed by words or sentences divorced from their context; pragmatics considers the way in which the context affects the meaning conveyed.

Receptive aphasia. Weisenburg and McBride (1935) used the term "predominantly receptive aphasia" to describe any aphasia where the language comprehension problem was more obvious than the difficulty in language production. "Predominantly" is used to show that they recognise that both comprehension and production are usually affected. In "predominantly expressive aphasia," production is rather more severely affected than comprehension. They also recognise "expressive–receptive aphasia," where both comprehension and production are severely disturbed (basically the same as **global aphasia**), and "amnesic aphasia" (**anomic aphasia**).

Reconstitution of function. A term used by Luria to describe his therapy approach, where an impaired function is performed in a different, roundabout way. Initially the patient has to learn to use the new approach deliberately, but with practice it should become increasingly unconscious and automatic (see Luria, 1948).

Reductionism. The doctrine that all mental events can be completely explained as physical events.

Reflex Arc Theory. In a spinal relex, stimulation from a sensory nerve to the spinal cord directly activates a motor nerve from the spinal cord; this simple relex involves only two neurones. For example, touching something very hot causes withdrawal of the hand via a simple spinal reflex. The discovery, in the nineteenth century, of these simple connections between sensory and motor events provided a model for neurological theorising. In the **Wernicke–Lichtheim model**, speech is seen as a (rather more complex) reflex arc, in which a series of centres mediate the reflex. Word repetition, in this view, is another form of reflex. The "psychological school" of Pick, Goldstein, Head, etc. rejected this view, arguing that language was a much more complex kind of activity.

Reinforcement. See **operant conditioning.**

Sensory aphasia. A term used to describe aphasia where language comprehension problems are especially prominent; speech production is fluent, and uses a variety of grammatical constructions. Some authors have used the term to describe all fluent aphasias other than anomic aphasia, but Luria uses it much as the neo-classical Wernicke's aphasia.

Serial speech. Any well-known sequence, particularly counting, the alphabet, days of the week, and months of the year. Any sequence known to a patient might be included, e.g., dates of the kings of England, the cranial nerves, or familiar poetry or songs. Even severely affected aphasics may be able to produce a surprising amount of serial speech if started off by the examiner.

Short-term Memory (STM). A term used by psychologists to refer to the memory system that can be used to hold information for a minute or two. Repeating digit lists, and holding telephone numbers will usually involve STM; the capacity of the auditory-verbal STM is around 7 items in normal people. There is controversy over whether the STM system used for list repetition is also involved in other tasks such as language comprehension.

Signifiant and **signifié.** De Saussure (1916) claimed that in order to communicate ideas they had to be part of a system of signs. The sign is the union of a form that signifies (the *signifiant*—e.g., the spoken or written word) and the signified (the *signifié*—e.g., the concept a word represents). Language is a system of signs, each of which is an inseparable union of *signifiant* and *signifié*.

Spanish flies. See **cantharides.**

Spontaneous recovery. Most aphasic patients have relatively severe language deficits immediately after onset, which gradually improve over the next three months, even when there is no formal language therapy. The extent of spontaneous recovery is very variable, and although all commentators agree that most improvement occurs in the first three months, more sensitive tests may show improvement at an ever-decreasing rate continuing over six months or even a year. The causes of spontaneous recovery are not well understood; the physiological improvement (subsidence of swelling, etc.) after a CVA is mostly complete within the first month. Von Monakow (1914) suggested that after this point the improvement is due to recovery from "diaschisis," where the brain accommodates to changed patterns of activation within it (see Kertesz, 1979).

Stroke. See **cerebrovascular accident.**

Surface dyslexia. A disorder of oral word reading in which (1) words with regular spelling (e.g., FEW, KERNEL) are read much more accurately than words with irregular spelling (e.g., SEW, COLONEL); (2) nonwords are read with reasonable accuracy; and (3) many of the errors are phonologically plausible renderings of the letter string (e.g., BEAR → "beer," YACHT → "/jætʃt/"). This is usually interpreted as an impairment in lexical reading, so that the patient is forced to rely on some kind of sub-lexical reading routine, using for example "grapheme-to-phoneme conversion rules." Many (but not all) surface dyslexics are also surface dysgraphic (see Patterson, Marshall, & Coltheart, 1986).

Surface dysgraphia. A pattern of impairment in writing words to dictation in which a patient (1) writes more accurately words whose spelling is uniquely determined by their phonology (e.g., BANK, RIDGE); (2) writes non-words with reasonable accuracy; and (3) makes errors that are orthographically plausible renderings of the words (e.g., "blue" → BLOO, "yacht" → YOT). These patients are thought to be relying on a sub-lexical routine for word writing as lexical access to specifications of spellings is impaired.

Synthesis. See **dialectical materialism.**

Telegraphic style. The speech of some agrammatic patients—omitting function words and affixes—is said to resemble the style used in telegrammes.

Total aphasia. A synonym for **global aphasia.**

VAT—Visual Action Therapy. A system developed by Helm and Benson (1975) in which global aphasics are taught to appreciate line drawings and then to produce some symbolic gesture.

VCIU—Voluntary Control of Involuntary Utterances. An approach to treatment with severe aphasics that aims to elicit responses that have initially been produced as errors or involuntary utterances as correct reading responses (Helm & Barresi, 1980).

Venesection. The act of blood letting by opening a vein, commonly used up to the nineteenth century in the treatment of a wide range of disorders. In most cases it probably did the patient more harm than good, but venesection can be temporarily effective in lowering blood pressure.

VIC—Visual Communication. A system of written symbols developed by Baker et al. (1975) and Gardner et al. (1976) to allow global aphasics to express themselves with a non-verbal system.

Vichy water. A still bottled spring water from the town of Vichy in central France; very widely drunk in France.

WAB—The Western Aphasia Battery. An aphasic test devised by Kertesz and Poole (1974). Based closely on the BDAE, it assigns patients to the neo-classical aphasic syndromes on the basis of a rating of spontaneous speech, and the scores in tests of auditory comprehension, repetition, and naming. It also gives a figure for the degree of overall language impairment—a "language quotient." There is an associated set of tests of reading, writing, apraxia, etc. that yields another index—the "cortical quotient."

Wernicke–Lichtheim model (or **schema**). A model of the speech centres in the cerebral cortex developed by Lichtheim (1885) on the basis of Wernicke's (1874) proposals. The aim was to provide a theory of the localisation of language centres in the brain, from which it would be possible to *deduce* all the forms of aphasia that were actually observed. In its full form there are five centres: A the centre for auditory word images lies in Wernicke's area in the temporal lobe: M the centre for motor word images lies in Broca's area in the frontal lobe; B the centre of word concepts lies in the inferior part of the parietal lobe. As shown in the diagram these three centres are joined by tracts. Broca's aphasia is caused by a lesion of M; Wernicke's aphasia by a lesion of W; conduction aphasia by a lesion of the A–M tract, and anomic aphasia by a lesion to the B–M tract or, where comprehension is also disturbed, a lesion of B. The other neo-classical syndromes all have their corresponding lesions on the diagram: transcortical motor aphasia is due to a lesion in B–M; transcortical sensory aphasia to a lesion in A–B; and isolation syndrome to a lesion in A–B and B–M; global aphasia is due to multiple lesions involving both A and M. To account for reading and writing there is a centre O for visual word images, and E, the centre for

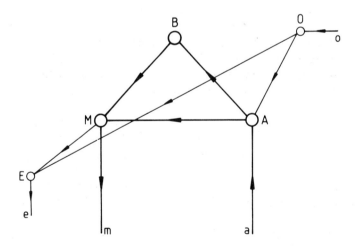

FIG. 8. The Wernicke–Lichtheim model. A = centre of auditory word images; M = centre of motor word images; B = centre of word concepts; O = centre of visual word images; E = centre of writing images; a = auditory input; o = visual input; m = articulatory output; e = written output.

controlling spelling. The reading and writing centres cannot access word concepts directly but only via the corresponding speech centres A and M. Bastian's (1898) model was a variant of this, but he did not recognise a centre for word concepts separate from auditory word images. The schema enjoyed considerable success in describing patterns of impairment with single words, although in Head's (1926) view it made researchers try to fit the performances of their patients to the schema, rather than paying attention to their actual behaviour.

Wernicke's aphasia. A neo-classical category of aphasia. Wernicke's aphasics have fluent spontaneous speech in which there are a variety of grammatical constructions; where there are frequent paraphasias and/or neologisms, the speech may be described as **jargon**. Word comprehension is poor, and repetition is also disturbed (see e.g., Albert et al., 1981; Goodglass & Kaplan, 1972).

Word blindness. A word used in the nineteenth and early twentieth century to describe **dyslexia**; use of the term is often intended to emphasise a similarity with **word deafness**. Some authors have used the term to describe only **dyslexia without disgraphia**.

Word deafness. A difficulty in word comprehension despite good hearing, at least of non-speech sounds. A relatively rare disorder, it was classically sub-divided into two types (see e.g., von Monakow, 1914; cf. Friedman & Kohn, 1986): word-sound deafness where there is a primary difficulty in phoneme identification; patients should be able to discriminate non-speech sounds, but are unable to determine whether or not something is a real word. In word-meaning deafness the patient knows that he/she has heard a familiar real word but has no idea of its significance. While many patients describe occasional episodes of word deafness, it is probably very rare as an isolated symptom

References

Abercrombie, D. (1965) *Studies in phonetics and linguistics*. Oxford: Oxford University Press.

Akhutina, T. V. (1978) O ponimanii i postroenii aktivnykh/passivnykh konstruktsii bol' nymi s afaziei. (Comprehension and production of active/passive constructions by aphasic patients.) In H. Mierzejewska (Ed.) *Badania Lingwistyczne nad afazja*. Warsaw: Ossolineum.

Alajouanine, T., Ombredane, A., & Durand, M. (1939) *Le syndrome de désintégration phonétique dans l'aphasie*. Paris: Masson.

Albert, M. L., Goodglass, H., Helm, N. A., Rubens. A. B., & Alexander, M. P. (1981) *Clinical aspects of dysphasia*. Vienna: Springer.

Albert, M. L., Sparks, R., & Helm, N. A. (1973) Melodic intonation therapy for aphasia. *Archives of Neurology, 29*, 130–131.

Allport, D. A. (1984) Auditory-verbal short term memory and conduction aphasia. In H. Bouma & D. G. Bouwhuis (Eds.), *Attention and performance X: control of language processes*. Hillsdale, New Jersey: Lawrence Erlbaum Associates Inc.

Allport, D. A. (1985) Distributed memory, modular subsystems and dysphasia. In S. K. Newman & R. Epstein (Eds.), *Current perspectives in dysphasia*. Edinburgh: Churchill Livingstone.

Allport, D. A., & Funnell, E. (1981) Components of the mental lexicon. *Proceedings of The Royal Society of London, B295*, 397–410.

Anokhin, P. K. (1935) *Problemy tsentra i periferii v fiziologii nervnoi deyatel 'nosti*. (Problems of centre and periphery in the physiology of nervous activity.) Gorkii: Gosizdat.

Anokhin, P. K. (1974) *Biology and neurophysiology of conditioned reflex*. Translated and edited by S. Corson. Oxford: Pergamon.

Arceus, F. (Arceo) (1658) *De recta curandorum vulnerum ratione*. Amsterdam. (First published Antwerp, 1574).

Aten, J. L., Cagliuri, M. P. & Holland, A. L (1982) The efficacy of functional communication therapy for chronic aphasic patients. *Journal of Speech and Hearing Disorders, 47*, 93–96.

Ayres, S. K. B., Potter, R. E. & MacDearmon, J. R. (1975) Using reinforcement therapy and precision teaching techniques with adult aphasics. *Journal of Behaviour Therapy and Experimental Psychiatry, 6*, 301–305.

Backus, O. L. (1945) The rehabilitation of aphasic veterans. *Journal of Speech and Hearing Disorders, 10*, 149–153.

Baddeley, A., Meade, T., & Newcombe, F. (1980) Design problems in research on rehabilitation after brain damage. *International Rehabilitation Medicine, 2*, 138–142.

Baldi, F. (1936) Il canto negli afasici, i riflessi condizionati e la rieducazione del linguaggio. *Rivista di Neurologia, 9*, 217–232.

Baker, E., Berry, T., Gardner, H., Zurif, E., Davis, L., & Veroff, A. (1975) Can linguistic function be dissociated from natural language? *Nature, 254*, 509–510.

Basso, A., Capitani, E., & Vignolo, L. (1979) Influence of rehabilitation on language skills in aphasic patients: a controlled study. *Archives of Neurology, 36*, 190–196.

Basso, A., Faglioni, P., & Vignolo, L. A. (1975) Etude controlée de la rééducation du langage dans l'aphasie: comparaison entre aphasiques traités et non-traités. *Revue Neurologique, 131*, 607–614

Bastian, H. C. (1869) On the various forms of loss of speech in cerebral disease. *British and Foreign Medical–Chirurgical Review, 43*, 209–236, 470–492.

Bastian, H. C. (1898) *A treatise on aphasia and other speech defects.* London: Lewis.

Bay, E. (1973) Der gegenwärtige Stand der Aphasieforschung. *Nervenartzt, 44*, 57–64.

Beauvois, M.-F., & Derouesné, J. (1982) Recherche en neuropsychologie et reéducation: quels rapports? In X. Seron & C. Laterre (Eds.), *Reéduquer le cerveau.* Brussels: Mardaga.

Behrmann, M., & Penn, C. (1984) Non-verbal communication of aphasic patients. *British Journal of Disorders of Communication, 19*, 155–168.

Benson, D. F. (1967) Fluency in aphasia: correlation with radioactive scan localisation. *Cortex, 3*, 373–392.

Benson, D. F. (1979a) Aphasia rehabilitation. *Archives of Neurology, 36*, 187–189.

Benson, D. F. (1979b) Aphasia, alexia and agraphia. New York: Churchill Livingstone.

Benton, A. L. (1964) Contributions to aphasia before Broca. *Cortex, 1*, 314–327.

Benton, A. L. (1965) Johann A. P. Gesner on aphasia. *Medical History, 9*, 54–60.

Benton, A. L., & Joynt, R. J. (1960) Early descriptions of aphasia. *Archives of Neurology, 3*, 205–222.

Berman, M., & Peelle, L. (1967) Self generated cues. *Journal of Speech and Hearing Disorders, 32*, 372–376.

Bernard, D. (1885) *De l'aphasie et de ses diverses formes.* Paris: Progrès Medicale, Delahaye et Lecrosnier.

Beyn, E. S. (1947) *Vosstanovlenie rechevykh protsessor pri sensornoi afazii.* (Restoration of speech processes in sensory aphasia.) Moscow: Uch. zap. Univ. Mosk., III.

Beyn, E. S. (1957) Osnovnye zakony struktury slova i grammaticheskogo stroeniya rechi pri afazii. (Fundamental laws of the structure of words and of the grammatical construction of speech in aphasia.) *Voprosy psikhologii, 4.*

Beyn, E. S. (1964) *Afazia i puti ee preodolenia.* (Aphasia and ways of overcoming it.) Leningrad: Izd. Med.

Beyn, E. S., & Shokhor-Trotskaya, M. K. (1966) The preventive method of speech rehabilitation in aphasia. *Cortex, 2*, 96–108.

Beyn, E. S., & Vizel', T. G. (1979) Zur Therapie der grammatischen Stoerungen bei Aphasie. In G. Peuser (Ed.), *Studien zur Sprachtherapie.* Munich: Fink.

Beyn, E. S., Gertzenshtein, E. N., Rudenko, E. Y., & Shiaptanova, S. L. (1962) *Posobie po vosstanovlenii u bol nykh s afaziei.* (Methods of restoring speech in aphasia.) Moscow: Gos. Izd. Med. Lit.

Beyn, E. S., Vizel', T. G., & Hatfield, F. M. (1979) Aspects of agrammatism in aphasia. *Language and Speech, 22*, 327–346.

Blackman, N., & Tureen, L. L. (1948) A psychosomatic approach to rehabilitation. *Transactions of the American Neurological Association, 73*, 193–196.

Blumstein, S. E. (1973) *A phonological investigation of aphasic speech.* The Hague: Mouton.

Blumstein, S. E. (1981) Phonological aspects of aphasia. In M. T. Sarno (Ed.) *Acquired aphasia.* New York: Academic Press.

Blumstein, S. E., Baker, E., & Goodglass, H. (1977) Phonological factors in auditory comprehension in aphasia. *Neuropsychologia, 15*, 19–30.

Bollinger, R. L., & Stout, C. E. (1976) Response-contigent small-step treatment: performance-based communication intervention. *Journal of Speech and Hearing Disorders, 41*, 40–51.

Bonvillian, J., & Friedman, R. (1978) Language development in another mode: the acquisition of signs by a brain damaged adult. *Sign Language Studies, 19*, 111–120.

Boswell, J. (1791) *The life of Samuel Johnson*. London: Dilly. (Reprinted, 1901. London: Everyman, Dent.)

Bouillaud, J. (1825) Recherches clinique propres a démontrer que la perte de la parole correspond à la lésion des lobules antérieurs du cerveau. *Archives Générales de la Médecine, 8*, 25–45.

Braun, R. (1973) *Vorschlage zur Therapie von Aphasien. No. 3 Die Sprachheilarbeit.* Deutsche Gesellschaft für Sprachheilpädagogik. Hamburg: Wartenburg.

Breasted, J. H. (1930) *The Edwin Smith Surgical Papyrus.* (Translator and editor.) Chicago: Chicago University Press.

Bristowe, J. S. (1880) *The physiological and pathological relations of the voice and speech.* London: Bogue.

Broca, P. (1861) Perte de la parole. *Bulletin de la Société d'Anthropologie de Paris, 2*, 219–237.

Broca, P. (1865) Remarques sur le siège de la faculté du langage articulé. *Bulletin de la Société d'Anthropologie de Paris, 6*, 330–357. Edited version reprinted in H. Hecaen & J. Dubois (Eds.) (1969) *La naissance de la neuropsychologie du langage 1825—1865.* Paris: Flammarion.

Broca, P. (1869) Sur le siège de la faculté du langage articulé. *Tribune Médicale, 74*, 254–256; *75*, 265–269.

Broida, H. (1977) Language therapy effects in long term aphasia. *Archives of Physical Medicine and Rehabilitation, 58*, 248–253.

Brookshire, R. H. (1969) Probability learning by aphasic subjects. *Journal of Speech and Hearing Research, 12*, 857–864.

Brookshire, R. H. (1971) Effects of trial time and inter-trial interval on naming by aphasic subjects. *Journal of Communication Disorders, 3*, 289–301.

Brookshire, R. H. (1972) Effects of task difficulty on naming performance of aphasic subjects. *Journal of Speech and Hearing Disorders, 27*, 11–16.

Brookshire, R. H. (1976) Effects of task difficulty on sentence comprehension performance of aphasic subjects. *Journal of Communication Disorders, 9*, 167–173.

Brown, J. W. (1972) *Aphasia, apraxia and agnosia: clinical and theoretical aspects.* Springfield, Illinois: Thomas.

Brown, J. W. (Ed.) (1981) *Jargonaphasia.* New York: Academic Press.

Brown, R. (1973) *A first language: the early stages.* Cambridge, Massachussetts: Harvard University Press.

Bruce, C., & Howard, D. (1987) Why don't Broca's aphasics cue themselves? An investigation of phonemic cueing and tip-of-the-tongue information. *Neuropsychologia*, in press.

Bub, D., & Kertesz, A. (1982) Deep agraphia. *Brain and Language, 17*, 146–165.

Bulpitt, C. J. (1983) *Randomised clinical trials.* The Hague: Nijhoff.

Burger, L. H., & Wertz, R. T. (1984) The effect of a token training program on auditory comprehension in a case of Wernicke's aphasia. In R. H. Brookshire (Ed.), *Clinical aphasiology conference proceedings, 1984.* Minneapolis: BRK.

Burger, L. H., Wertz, R. T., & Woods, D. (1983) A response to treatment in a case of cortical deafness. In R. H. Brookshire (Ed.), *Clinical aphasiology conference proceedings, 1983.* Minneapolis: BRK.

Butfield, E. (1958) Rehabilitation of the dysphasic patient. *Speech Pathology and Therapy, 1*, 9–17.

Butfield, E. (1960) Acquired receptive dysphasia. *Speech Pathology and Therapy, 3*, 8–12.

Butfield, E., & Zangwill, O. L. (1946) Re-education in aphasia; a review of 70 cases. *Journal of Neurology, Neurosurgery and Psychiatry, 9*, 75–79.

Butterworth, B. L. (1979) Hesitation and the production of verbal paraphasias and neologisms in jagon aphasia. *Brain and Language, 8*, 133–161.

Butterworth, B. L., & Howard, D. (1987) Paragrammatisms. *Cognition.*, in press.

Butterworth, B. L., Campbell, R., & Howard, D. (1986) The uses of short term memory: a case study. *Quarterly Journal of Experimental Psychology*, in press.

Butterworth, B. L., Howard, D., & McLoughlin, P. J. (1984) The semantic deficit in aphasia: the relationship between semantic errors in auditory comprehension and picture naming. *Neuropsychologia, 22*, 409–426.

Byng, S., & Coltheart, M. (1986) Aphasia therapy research: methodological requirements and illustrative results. In E. Hjelmquist & L. B. Nilsson (Eds.), *Communication and handicap*. Amsterdam: North-Holland, Elsevier.

Caramazza, A., & Zurif, E. B. (1976) Dissociation of algorithmic and heuristic processes in language comprehension: evidence from aphasia. *Brain and Language, 3*, 572–582.

Caramazza, A., Basili, A. G., Koller, J. J., & Berndt, R. S. (1981) An investigation of repetition and language processing in a case of conduction aphasia. *Brain and Language, 14*, 235–271.

Carson, D. H., Carson, F. E., & Tikovsky, R. S. (1968) On learning characteristics of the adult aphasic. *Cortex, 4*, 92–112.

Castiglioni, A. (1947) *A history of medicine*. 2nd edition, translated and edited by E. B. Krumbhaar. London: Routledge & Kegan Paul.

Chanet, P. (1649) *Traité de l'esprit de l'homme et de ses fonctions*. Paris: Veuve Jean Camusat et Pierre le Petit.

Chen, L. C. Y. (1971) Manual communication by combined alphabet and gestures. *Archives of Physical Medicine and Rehabilitation, 52*, 381–384.

Chester, S. L., & Egolf, D. B. (1974) Non-verbal communication and aphasia therapy. *Rehabilitation Literature, 8*, 231–233.

Chomsky, N. (1957) *Syntactic structures*. The Hague: Mouton.

Chomsky, N. (1959) A review of Skinner's Verbal Behaviour. *Language, 35*, 26–58.

Chomsky, N. (1965) *Aspects of the theory of syntax*. Cambridge, Massachussetts: MIT Press.

Christopolou, C., & Bonvillian, J. D. (1985) Sign language, pantomime and gestural processing in aphasic persons. *Journal of Communication Disorders, 18*, 1–20.

Cicone, M., Wapner, W., Foldi, N., Zurif, E., & Gardner, H. (1979) The relation between gesture and language in aphasic communication. *Brain and Language, 8*, 324–349.

Cochrane, A. L. (1972) *Effectiveness and efficiency: random reflections on health services*. London: Nuffield Provincial Hospitals Trust.

Cohen, R., Engel, D., Kelter, S., & List, G. (1979) Kurz- und Langzeiteffekte von Bennenhilfen bei Aphatikern. In G. Peuser (Ed.), *Studien zur Sprachtherapie*. Munich: Wilhelm Fink.

Colby, K. M., Christinaz, D., Parkinson, R. C., Graham, S., & Karpf, C. (1981) A word finding computer program with dynamic lexical–semantic memory for patients with anomia using an intelligent prosthesis. *Brain and Language, 14*, 272–281.

Coltheart, M. (1978) Lexical access in simple reading tasks. In G. Underwood (Ed.) *Strategies of information processing*. London: Academic Press.

Coltheart, M. (1983) Investigating the efficacy of speech therapy. In C. Code & D. J. Muller (Eds.), *Aphasia Therapy*. London: Edward Arnold.

Coltheart, M. (1985) Cognitive neuropsychology and the study of reading. In M. I. Posner & O. S. M. Marin (Eds.), *Attention and performance, XI*. Hillsdale, New Jersey: Lawrence Erlbaum Associates Inc.

Coltheart, M., Patterson, K. E., & Marshall, J. C. (Eds.) (1980) *Deep dyslexia*. London: Routledge & Kegan Paul.

Costello, J. M. (1977) Programmed instruction. *Journal of Speech and Hearing Disorders, 42*, 3–28.

Critchley, M. (1970) *Aphasiology and other aspects of language*. London: Edward Arnold.

Croskey, C. S., & Adams, M. R. (1969) A rationale and clinical methodology for selecting vocabulary stimulus material for individual aphasic patients. *Journal of Communication Disorders, 2*, 340–343.

Culton, G., & Ferguson, P. A. (1979) Comprehension training with aphasic subjects: the development and application of five automated language programs. *Journal of Communication Disorders, 12*, 69–82.

Dalin, O. (1745) Berattelse om en dumbe, som kan sinnga. *Kungliga Svenska Vetenskapsakadamien, Handinglar, 6*, 114–115. (Cited by Benton & Joynt, 1960).

Daniloff, J. K., Noll, J. D., Fristoe, M., & Lloyd, L. L. (1982) Gesture recognition in patients with aphasia. *Journal of Speech and Hearing Disorders, 47*, 43–49.

Darley, F. L. (1979) Treat or neglect? *A.S.H.A., 21*, 628–631.

Darley, F. L. (1982) *Aphasia*. Philadelphia: W. B. Saunders.

Darley, F. L., Aronson, A. E., & Brown, J. R. (1975) *Motor speech disorders*. Philadelphia: W. B. Saunders.

David, R. M., Enderby, P., & Bainton, D. (1982) Treatment of acquired aphasia: speech therapists and volunteers compared. *Journal of Neurology, Neurosurgery and Psychiatry, 45*, 957–961.

Davis, G. A. (1980) A critical look at PACE therapy. In R. H. Brookshire (Ed.) *Clinical Aphasiology Conference Proceedings, 1980*. Minneapolis: BRK.

Davis, G. A., & Wilcox, M. J. (1981) Incorporating parameters of natural conversation in aphasia treatment. In R. Chapey (Ed.), *Language intervention strategies in adult aphasia*. 1st edition. Baltimore: Williams and Wilkins.

Davis, G. A., & Wilcox, M. J. (1985) *Adult aphasia rehabilitation: applied pragmatics*. Windsor: NFER-Nelson.

Deal, J. L., & Deal, L. A. (1978) Efficacy of aphasia rehabilitation: preliminary results. In R. H. Brookshire (Ed.), *Clinical Aphasiology Conference Proceedings, 1978*. Minneapolis: BRK.

De Bleser, R., & Weismann, H. (1981) Uebergang von Struktürübungen zum spontänen Dialog in der Therapie von Aphasikern. *Sprache-Stimme-Gehör, 5*, 74–79.

Déjerine, J. (1892) Contribution a l'étude anatomoclinique et clinique des différentes variétés de cécité verbale. *Mémoires de la Société de Biologie, 4*, 61–90.

Dennis, M., & Wiegel-Crump, C. A. (1979) Aphasic dissolution and language acquisition. In H. Whitaker & H. A. Whitaker (Eds.), *Studies in neurolinguistics, volume 4*. New York: Academic Press.

de Partz, M. P. (1986) Reeducation of a deep dyslexic patient: rationale of the method and results. *Cognitive Neuropsychology, 3*, 149–177.

de Renzi, E., & Vignolo, L. A. (1962) The token test: a sensitive test to detect receptive disturbances in aphasia. *Brain, 85*, 665–678.

de Saussure, F. (1916) *Cours de linguistique générale*. Lausanne.

Devor, M. (1982) Plasticity in the adult nervous system. In I. S. Illis, E. M. Sedgewick, & H. J. Glanville (Eds.), *Rehabilitation of the neurological patient*. London: Blackwell.

DiCarlo, L. M. (1980) Language recovery in aphasia; effect of systematic filmed programmed instruction. *Archives of Physical Medicine and Rehabilitation, 61*, 41–44.

Doms, M. C., & Bourlard, A. (1982) La méthode roumaine de la lecture verticale dans la therapie de l'aphasie. In X. Seron & C. Laterre (Eds.), *Rééduquer le cerveau; logopédie, psychologie, neurologie*. Brussels: Mardaga.

Dordain, B., & Normand, B. (1981) Comparative study of the oral language of aphasics with and without treatment. *Folia Phoniatrica, 33*, 369–379.

Edwards, A. E. (1965) Automated training for a "matching-to-sample" task in aphasia. *Journal of Speech and Hearing Research, 8*, 39–42.

Eisenson, J. (1973) *Adult aphasia: assessment and treatment.* Englewood Cliffs, New Jersey: Prentice Hall.

Eisenson, J. (1977) Language rehabilitation of aphasic adults: some observations on the state of the art. *Folia Phoniatrica, 29*, 61–83.

Eldridge, M. (1968) *A history of the treatment of speech disorders.* Edinburgh: Livingstone.

Eliasberg, W. A. (1950) A contribution to the prehistory of aphasia. *Journal of the History of Medicine, 5*, 96–101.

Ellis, A. W. (1985) The production of spoken words: a cognitive neuropsychological perspective. In A. W. Ellis (Ed.), *Progress in the psychology of language, volume 2.* London: Lawrence Erlbaum Associates Ltd.

Elvin, M. D., & Hatfield, F. M. (1978) Comprehension by agrammatic patients of prepositions and prepositional phrases. In B. Ege (Ed.), *IALP Congress proceedings volume 2.* Copenhagen: Special-Pedagogisk Forlag.

Elvin, M. D., & Oldfield, R. C. (1951) Disabilities and progress in a dysphasic university student. *Journal of Neurology, Neurosurgery and Psychiatry, 14*, 118–128.

Engl, E., Kotten, A., Ohlendorf, I., & Poser, E. (1982) *Sprachübungen zur Aphasiebehandlung: ein linguistisches Übungsprogramm mit Bildern.* Berlin: Marhold.

Farmer, A. (1977) Self-correctional strategies in the conversational speech of aphasic and non-aphasic brain-damaged adults. *Cortex, 13*, 327–334.

Feuchtwanger, E. (1935) Zu den problemen der Restitution von Aphasien und Amusien. In *Proceedings of the Second International Congress of Phonetic Sciences*, 82–84. Cambridge: Cambridge University Press.

Feyereisen, P., & Seron, X. (1982) Nonverbal communication and aphasia: a review. *Brain and Language, 16*, 191–236.

Filby, Y., & Edwards, A. E. (1963) An application of automated teaching methods to test and teach form discrimination to aphasics. *Journal of Programmed Instruction, 2*, 24–33.

Finkelnburg, F. C. (1870) Asymbolie und Aphasie. *Berliner Klinisches Wochenschrift, 7*, 449–450, 460–462.

Flourens, P. (1824) Recherches expérimentales sur les propriétés et les fonctions du système nerveux. Paris: Baillière.

Franz, S. I. (1906) The reeducation of an aphasic. *Journal of Philosophy, Psychology and Scientific Method, 2*, 589–597.

Franz, S. I. (1924) Studies in re-education: the aphasias. *Journal of Comparative Psychology, 4*, 349–429.

Frazier, C. H., & Ingham, S. D. (1920) A review of the effects of gunshot wounds of the head: based on the observation of two hundred cases at U.S. General Hospital No. 11, Cape May, N.J. *Archives of Neurology, 3*, 17–40.

Freud, S. (1891) *Zur Auffassung der Aphasien.* Vienna: Deuticke. Translated by E. Stengel (1953) *On aphasia.* New York: International Universities Press.

Froeschels, E. (1914) Ueber die Behandlung der Aphasien. *Archiv für Psychiatrie und Nervenkrankheiten, 53*, 221–261.

Froeschels, E. (1916) Zur Behandlung der motorischen Aphasie. *Archiv für Psychiatrie und Nervenkrankheiten, 56*, 1–19.

Froment, J. (1921) La rééducation des aphasiques moteurs: principes, procédés et résultats. *Paris Médical, 41*, 267–273.

Froment, J., & Monod, O. (1914) La rééducation des aphasiques moteurs. *Lyon Médical, 122*, 157–175, 211–231, 283–288, 327–342.

Gans, A. (1914) Ueber einen im Anfang des 18. Jahrhunderts von Dr. Peter Rommel klassisch beschrieben. Fall von transkortikaler motorischer Aphasie. *Zeitschrift für die gesamte Neurologie und Psychiatrie, 24*, 480–482.

Gardner, H. (1977) *The shattered mind: the person after brain damage.* London: Routledge & Kegan Paul.

Gardner, H., Albert, M. L. & Weintraub, S. (1975) Comprehending a word: the influence of speed and redundancy on auditory comprehension in aphasia. *Cortex, 11*, 155–162.

Gardner, H., Zurif, E. B., Berry, T., & Baker, E. (1976) Visual communication in aphasia. *Neuropsychologia, 14*, 275–292.

Gerstman, H. L. (1964) A case of aphasia. *Journal of Speech and Hearing Disorders, 29*, 89–91.

Geschwind, N. (1965) Disconnexion syndromes in animals and man. *Brain, 88*, 237–294, 585–644.

Gesner, J. A. P. (1769) *Samlung von Beobachtungen auf der Artzneigelahrtheit und Naturkunde.* Beck. Cited by Benton (1965).

Gheorgita, N. (1981) Vertical reading: a new method of therapy for reading disturbances in aphasics. *Journal of Clinical Neuropsychology, 3*, 161–165.

Gheorgita, N., & Fradis, A. (1979) Rehabilitations-methoden des Lesens und Schreibens bei Aphatikern. In G. Peuser (Ed.), *Studien zur Sprachtherapie.* Munich: Wilhelm Fink.

Gielewski, E. (1983) Acoustic analysis and auditory retraining in the remediation of sensory aphasia. In C. Code & D. J. Muller (Eds.), *Aphasia therapy.* London: Edward Arnold.

Gimson, A. (1970) *An introduction to the pronunciation of English.* London: Arnold.

Gleason, J. B., Goodglass, H., Green, H., Ackerman, N., & Hyde, M. R. (1975) The retrieval of syntax in Broca's aphasia. *Brain and Language, 2*, 451–471.

Glozman, J. M. (1981) On increasing motivation to communication in aphasics' rehabilitation. *International Journal of Rehabilitation Research, 4*, 78–81.

Goldfarb, R. (1981) Operant conditioning and programmed instruction in aphasia rehabilitation. In R. Chapey (Ed.), *Language intervention strategies in adult aphasia.* Baltimore: Williams & Wilkins.

Goldscheider, A. (1902) *Handbuch der physikalischen Therapie.* Leipzig.

Goldstein, K. (1916) Uebungsschulen für Hirnverletzte. *Zeitschrift für Krüppelfürsorge, 9*, 17–21.

Goldstein, K. (1919) *Die Behandlung, Fürsorge und Begutachtung der Hirnverletzten.* Leipzig: Vogel.

Goldstein, K. (1924) Das Wesen der amnestischen Aphasie. *Schweizer Archiv für Neurologie und Psychiatrie, 15*, 163–175.

Goldstein, K. (1925) Zur Theorie der Funktion des Nervensystems. *Archiv für Psychiatrie und Nervenkrankheiten, 74*, 370–405.

Goldstein, K. (1942) *After effects of brain injuries in war.* London: Heinemann.

Goldstein, K. (1948) *Language and language distrubances.* New York: Grune & Stratton.

Goodglass, H., & Kaplan, E. (1972) *Assessment of aphasia and related disorders.* Philadelphia: Lea & Febiger.

Goodglass, H., Quadfasel, F. A., & Timberlake, W. H. (1964) Phrase length and the type and severity of aphasia. *Cortex, 1*, 133–153.

Goodglass, H., Gleason, J. B., Bernholtz, N. D., & Hyde, M. R. (1972) Some linguistic structures in the speech of a Broca's aphasic. *Cortex, 8*, 191–212.

Goodkin, R. (1969) Changes in word production, sentence production and relevance in an aphasic through verbal conditioning. *Behaviour Research and Therapy, 7*, 93–99.

Goodkin, R., Diller, L., & Shah, N. (1973) Training spouses to improve the functional speech of aphasic patients. In B. Lahey, (Ed.), *The modification of language behaviour.* Springfield, Illinois: C. C. Thomas.

Granich, L. (1947) *Aphasia: a guide to retraining*. New York: Grune & Stratton.

Gratiolet, P. (1861) Contribution to Discussion sur le volume et la forme du cerveau. *Bulletin de la Société d'Anthropologie de Paris, 2*, 66–81.

Green, E. (1970) On the contribution of studies of aphasia to psycholinguistics. *Cortex, 6*, 216–235.

Green E. & Boller, F. (1974) Features of auditory comprehension in severely impaired aphasics. *Cortex, 10*, 133–145.

Green, G. (1982) Assessment and treatment of the adult with severe aphasia: aiming for functional generalisation. *Australian Journal of Communication Disorders, 10*, 11–23.

Green, G. (1984) Communication in aphasia therapy; some of the procedures and issues involved. *British Journal of Disorders of Communication, 19*, 35–46.

Grice, H. P. (1975) Logic and conversation. In P. Cole & J. Morgan (Eds.), *Syntax and semantics 3: speech acts*. New York: Academic Press.

Guilford, A. M., & O'Connor, J. K. (1982) Pragmatic functions in aphasia. *Journal of Communication Disorders, 15*, 337–346.

Guildford, A. M., Scheuerle, J., & Shirek, P. G. (1982) Manual communication skills in aphasia. *Archives of Physical Medicine and Rehabilitation, 63*, 601–604.

Gutzmann, H. (1896) Heilungsversuche bei centromotorischer und centrosensorischer Aphasia. *Archiv für Psychiatrie und Nervenkrankheiten, 28*, 354–378.

Gutzmann, H. (1916) Stimm- und Sprachstoerungen im Kriege und ihre Behandlung. *Berliner klinische Wochenschrift, 53*, 154–158.

Hagen, C. (1973) Communication abilities in hemiplegia: effect of speech therapy. *Archives of Physical Medicine and rehabilitation, 54*, 454–463.

Hatfield, F. M. (1979) Aphasiebehandlung: Annäherungen und Anschauungen. In G. Peuser (Ed.), *Studien zur Sprachtherapie*. Munich: Wilhelm Fink.

Hatfield, F. M. (1981) Analysis and remediation of aphasia in the USSR; the contribution of A. R. Luria. *Journal of Speech and Hearing Disorders, 46*, 338–347.

Hatfield, F. M. (1982) Diverses formes de désintégration du langage écrit et implications pour la rééducation. In X. Seron & C. Laterre (Eds.), *Rééduquer le cerveau: logopédie, psychologie, neurologie*. Brussels: Pierre Mardaga.

Hatfield, F. M. (1983) Aspects of acquired dysgraphia and implications for re-reduction. In C. Code & D. J. Muller (Eds.), *Aphasia therapy*. London: Arnold.

Hatfield, F. M., & Elvin, M. D. (1978) Die Behandlung des Agrammatismus bei Aphasikern. *Sprache-Stimme-Gehör, 4*, 127–172.

Hatfield, F. M., & Patterson, K. E. (1983) Phonological spelling. *Quarterly Journal of Experimental Psychology, 35A*, 451–468.

Hatfield, F. M. & Patterson, K. E. (1984) Interpretation of spelling in aphasia: the impact of recent developments in cognitive psychology. In F. C. Rose (Ed.), *Recent advances in neurology, 42; progress in aphasiology*. New York: Raven.

Hatfield, F. M., & Shewell, C. (1983) Some applications of linguistics to aphasia therapy. In C. Code & D.J. Muller (Eds.), *Aphasia therapy*. London: Edward Arnold.

Hatfield, F. M., & Weddell, R. (1976) Retraining of writing in severe aphasia. In Y. Lebrun & R. Hoops (Eds.), *Recovery in aphasics*. Amsterdam: Swets & Zeitlinger.

Hatfield, F. M. & Zangwill, O. L. (1975) Occupational resettlement in aphasia. *Scandinavian Journal of Rehabilitation Medicine, 7*, 57–60.

Head, H. (1926) *Aphasia and kindred disorders of speech*. Cambridge: Cambridge University Press.

Hécaen, H., & Angelergues, R. (1965) *Pathologie du Langage*. Paris: Larousse.

Hécaen, H., & Dubois, J. (1969) *La naissance de la neuropsychologie du langage 1825—1865*. Paris: Flammarion.

Hécaen, H., & Dubois, J. (1971) La neurolinguistique. In G. E. Perren & J. L. M. Trim (Eds.), *Applications of linguistics*. Cambridge: Cambridge University Press.

Heeschen, C. (1980) Strategies of decoding actor-object relations by aphasic patients. *Cortex, 16*, 5–20.

Heilman, K. M., Gold, M. S., & Tucker, D. M. (1975). Improvement of aphasics' comprehension by use of novel stimuli. *Transactions of the American Neurological Association, 100*, 201–202.

Helm, N. A., & Barresi, B. (1980) Voluntary control of involuntary utterances: a treatment approach for severe aphasia. In R. H. Brookshire (Ed.), *Clinical Aphasiology Conference Proceedings, 1980*. Minneapolis: BRK.

Helm, N. A., & Benson, D. F. (1978) Visual action therapy for global aphasia. Paper presented at Academy of Aphasia, Chicago.

Helm-Estabrooks, N. A. (1983) Exploiting the right hemisphere for language rehabilitation: melodic intonation therapy. In E. Perecman (Ed.), *Cognitive processing in the right hemisphere*. New York: Academic Press.

Helm-Estabrooks, N. A. (1984) Severe aphasia. In A. L. Holland (Ed.), *Language disorders in adults: recent advances*. San Diego, California: College-Hill.

Helm-Estabrooks, N. A., Fitzpatrick, P. M., & Barresi, B. (1981a) Response of an agrammatic patient to a syntax stimulation program for aphasia. *Journal of Speech and Hearing Disorders, 46*, 422–427.

Helm-Estabrooks, N. A., Fitzpatrick, P. M., & Barresi, B. (1981b) Visual action therapy for global aphasia. *Journal of Speech and Hearing Disorders, 47*, 385–389.

Helmick, J. W., & Wipplinger, M. (1975) Effects of stimulus repetition on the naming behaviour of an aphasic adult: a clinical report. *Journal of Communication Disorders, 8*, 23–29.

Helmick, J. W., Watamori, T., & Palmer, J. (1976) Spouses' understanding of the communication disabilities of aphasic patients. *Journal of Speech and Hearing Disorders, 41*, 238–243.

Henderson, L. (1982) *Orthography and word recognition in reading*. London: Academic Press.

Hippocrates (1923) *Volume 1. Epidemics*. Translated by W. H. S. Jones, Reprinted 1972. London: Loeb Classical Library, Heinemann.

Hippocrates (1928) *Volume 3. On wounds in the head*. Translated by E. T. Withington. Reprinted 1968. London: Loeb Classical Library. Heinemann.

Holland, A. L. (1967) Some clinical applications of behavioural principles to clinical speech problems. *Journal of Speech and Hearing Disorders, 32*, 11–16.

Holland, A. L. (1969) Some current trends in aphasia rehabilitation. *A.S.H.A, 11*, 3–7.

Holland, A. L. (1970) Case studies in aphasia rehabilitation using programmed instruction. *Journal of Speech and Hearing Disorders, 35*, 377–390.

Holland, A. L. (1975) The effectiveness of treatment in aphasia. In R. H. Brookshire (Ed.), *Clinical Aphasiology Conference Proceedings, 1975*. Minneapolis: BRK.

Holland, A. L. (1980) *Communicative abilities in daily living*. Baltimore: University Park Press.

Holland, A. L. (1982) Observing functional communication of aphasic patients. *Journal of Speech and Hearing Disorders, 47*, 50–56.

Holland, A. L., & Harris, A. B. (1968) Aphasia rehabilitation using programmed instruction: an intensive case history. In H. N. Sloane & B. D. Macauley (Eds.), *Operant procedures in remedial speech and language training*. Boston: Houghton, Mifflin.

Holland, A. L., & Levy, C. (1971) Syntactic generalisation in aphasics as a function of relearning an active sentence. *Acta Symbolica, 2*, 34–41.

Holland, A. L., & Sonderman, J. C. (1974) Effects of a program based on the Token Test for teaching comprehension skills to aphasics. *Journal of Speech and Hearing Research, 17*, 589–598.

Holland, A. L., Swindell, C. S., & Fromm, D. (1983) A model treatment approach for the acutely aphasic patient. In R. H. Brookshire (Ed.), *Clinical Aphasiology Conference Proceedings, 1983*. Minneapolis: BRK.

Hoodin, R. B., & Thompson, C. K. (1983) Facilitation of verbal labelling in adult aphasia by gestural, verbal or verbal plus gestural training. In R. H. Brookshire (Ed.), *Clinical Aphasiology Conference Proceedings, 1983*. Minneapolis: BRK.

Hopkins, A. (1984) Does speech therapy influence the course of recovery in aphasia after stroke? In C. Warlow & J. Garfield (Eds.), *Dilemmas in the management of the neurological patient*. Edinburgh: Churchill Livingstone.

Howard, D. (1985) Agrammatism. In S. K. Newman & R. Epstein (Eds.), *Current perspectives in dysphasia*. Edinburgh: Churchill Livingstone.

Howard, D. (1986) Beyond randomised controlled trials: the case for effective case studies of the effects of treatment in aphasia. *British Journal of Disorders of Communication, 21*, 89–102.

Howard, D., & Patterson, K. E. (1987) Methodological issues in neuropsychological therapy. In X. Seron & G. Deloche (Eds.), *Cognitive approaches in neuropsychological rehabilitation*. London: Lawrence Erlbaum Associates Ltd.

Howard, D., Patterson, K. E., Franklin, S., Morton, J., & Orchard-Lisle, V. M. (1984) Variability and consistency in picture naming by aphasic patients. In F. C. Rose (Ed.), *Recent advances in neurology, 42; progress in aphasiology*. New York: Raven.

Howard, D., Patterson, K. E., Franklin, S., Orchard-Lisle, V. M., & Morton, J. (1985a) The facilitation of picture naming in aphasia. *Cognitive Neuropsychology, 2*, 49–80.

Howard, D., Patterson, K. E., Franklin, S., Orchard-Lisle, V. M., & Morton, J. (1985b) The treatment of word retrieval deficits in aphasia: a comparison of two therapy methods. *Brain, 108*, 817–829.

Huber, M. (1942) Re-education of aphasics. *Journal of Speech and Hearing Disorders, 7*, 289–292.

Huber, W., Mayer, I., & Kerschensteiner, M. (1978) Phonematischer Jargon bei Wernicker-Aphasie: Untersuchung zur Methode und zum Verlauf der Therapie. *Folia Phoniatrica, 30*, 119–135.

Huber, W., Poeck, K., & Willmes, K. (1984) The Aachen Aphasia Test. In F. C. Rose (Ed.), *Recent advances in neurology, 42; progress in aphasiology*. New York: Raven.

Humphreys, G. W., & Riddoch, M. J. (Eds.), (1987) *Visual object processing: a cognitive neuropsychological approach*. London: Lawrence Erlbaum Associates Ltd.

Isserlin, M. (1922) Ueber Agrammatismus. *Zeitschrift für die gesamte Neurologie und Psychiatrie, 75*, 332–416. Translated and edited by H. Droller, D. Howard, & R. Campbell (1985). On agrammatism. *Cognitive Neuropsychology, 2*, 303–345.

Jackendoff, R. S. (1972) *Semantic interpretation in generative grammar*. Cambridge, Massachussetts: MIT Press.

Jackson, J. Hughlings (1878) On affections of speech from disease of the brain. *Brain, 1*, 304–330.

Jackson, J. Hughlings (1932) *Selected writings*. Edited by J. Taylor. London: Hodder, & Stoughton.

Jakobson, R. (1941) *Kindersprache, Aphasie und allgemeine Lautgesetze*. Uppsala: Universitets Arsskrift.

Jakobson, R. (1956) Two aspects of language and two types of aphasic disturbances. In R.

Jakobson & M. Halle (Eds.), *Fundamentals of language*. The Hague: Mouton.

Jakobson, R. (1964) Towards a linguistic typology of aphasic impairments. In A. V. S. de Rueck & M. O'Connor (Eds.), *Disorders of language*. C.I.B.A. Symposium, London: Churchill.

Johannsen-Horbach, H., Cegla, B., Mager, U., Schempp, B., & Wallesch, C. W. (1985) Treatment of chronic global aphasia with a non-verbal communication system. *Brain and Language, 24*, 74–82.

Johnson, W. (1937) Aphasia. *Speech, 2*, 8–12.

Jones, E. V. (1986) Building the foundations for sentence production in a non-fluent aphasic. *British Journal of Disorders of Communication, 21*, 63–82.

Katz, R. C., & Nagy, V. T. (1982) A computerised treatment system for chronic aphasic patients. In R. H. Brookshire (Ed.), *Clinical Aphasiology Conference Proceedings, 1982*. Minneapolis: BRK.

Katz, R. C., & Nagy, V. T. (1983) A computerised approach for improving word recognition in chronic aphasic patients. In R. H. Brookshire (Ed.), *Clinical Aphasiology Conference Proceedings, 1983*. Minneapolis: BRK.

Kean, M-L. (1985) *Agrammatism*. New York: Academic Press.

Kearns, K. P., & Salmon, S. J. (1984) An experimental analysis of auxiliary and copular verb generalisation in aphasia. *Journal of Speech and Hearing Disorders, 49*, 152–163.

Kearns, K. P., Simmons, N. N., & Sisterhen, C. (1982) Gestural sign (Amer-Ind) as a facilitator of verbalisation in patients with aphasia. In R. H. Brookshire (Ed.), *Clinical Aphasiology Conference Proceedings, 1982*. Minneapolis: BRK.

Keenan, J. (1966) A method for eliciting naming behaviour from aphasic patients. *Journal of Speech and Hearing Disorders, 31*, 261–266.

Keith, R. L., & Aronson, A. E. (1975) Singing as therapy for apraxia of speech and aphasia: report of a case. *Brain and Language, 2*, 483–488.

Keith, R. L., & Darley, F. L. (1967) The use of a specific electric board in rehabilitation of the aphasic patient. *Journal of Speech and Hearing Disorders, 32*, 148–153.

Kertesz, A. (1979) *Aphasia and associated disorders: taxonomy, localisation and recovery*. New York: Grune & Stratton.

Kertesz, A., & McCabe, P. (1977) Recovery patterns and prognosis in aphasia. *Brain, 100*, 1–18.

Kertesz, A., & Poole, E. (1974) The aphasia quotient: the taxonomic approach to the measurement of aphasic disability. *Canadian Journal of Neurological Science, 1*, 7–16.

Kirshner, H., & Webb, W. G. (1981) Selective impairment of the auditory–verbal modality in an acquired communication disorder: benefit from sign language therapy. *Brain and Language, 13*, 161–170.

Kleist, K. (1916) Ueber Leitungsaphasie und die grammatischen Stoerungen. *Monatsschrift für Psychiatrie und Neurologie, 40*, 118–199.

Klimkovski, M. (1966) *Disturbances of audio-verbal memory in left temporal lobe lesions*. Candidate dissertation, Moscow. (Russian).

Kogan, V. M. (1947) *Vosstanovlenie smyslovoi storony rechi pri afazii*. (Restoration of the conceptual aspect of speech in aphasia.) Moscow: Uch. zap Mosk. Univ. III. (Russian).

Kogan, V. M. (1969) *Psikhologicheskie issledovania v praktike vrachebno-trudovoi ekspertizy*. (Psychological investigations in medical rehabilitation). Moscow: Tsen. nauchn.-issled. inst. Eks. Trud. (Russian).

Kohn, S. E., & Friedman, R. B. (1986) Word-meaning deafness: a phonological-semantic dissociation. *Cognitive Neuropsychology, 3*, 291–308.

Kotten, A. (1977) Unterschiede im Beachten örtlicher und zeitlicher Präpositionen bei Aphasikern. *Folia Phoniatrica, 29*, 270–278.

Kotten, A. (1979) Sprachtherapie als Kommunikationssituation. In G. Peuser (Ed.), *Studien zur Sprachtherapie*. Munich: Fink.

Kreindler, A., & Fradis, A. (1968) *Performances in aphasia*. Paris: Gauthier-Villar.

Kucera, H., & Francis, W. N. (1967) *A computational analysis of present-day American English*. Providence, Rhode Island: Brown University Press.

Kuhn, T. S. (1962) *The structure of scientific revolutions*. Chicago: University of Chicago Press.

Kussmaul, A. (1876) *Die Stoerungen der Sprache*. 4th edition edited by H. Gutzmann, 1910. Leipzig: Vogel.

Lapointe, L. L. (1977) Base-10 programmed stimulation: task specification, scoring and plotting performance in aphasia therapy. *Journal of Speech and Hearing Disorders, 42*, 90–105.

Lashley, K. D. (1950) In search of the engram. *Symposia of the Society for Experimental Biology, 4*, 454–482.

Laughlin, S. A., Naeser, M. A., & Gordon, W. P. (1979) Effects of three syllable durations using the melodic intonation therapy technique. *Journal of Speech and Hearing Research, 22*, 311–320.

Lebrun, Y. (1976) Neurolinguistic models of language and speech. In H. Whitaker & H. A. Whitaker (Eds.), *Studies in neurolinguistics: volume 1*. New York: Academic Press.

Lecours, A. R., & Lhermitte, F. (Eds.) (1979) *L'aphasie*. Paris: Flammarion. Translated as A. R. Lecours, F. Lhermitte, & B. Bryans (Eds.) (1983) *Aphasiology*. London: Baillière Tindall.

Lecours, A. R., & Rouillon, F. (1976) Neurolinguistic analysis of jargonaphasia and jargonagraphia. In H. Whitaker & H. A. Whitaker (Eds.), *Studies in neurolinguistics II*. New York: Academic Press.

Lecours, A. R., Coderre, L., Lafond, D., Bergeron, M. & Bryans, B. (1979) Rééducation des aphasiques. In A. R. Lecours & F. Lhermitte (Eds.), *L'aphasie*. Paris: Flammarion. Translated as Aphasia therapy in A. R. Lecours, F. Lhermitte, & B. Bryans (Eds.) (1983) *Aphasiology*. London: Baillière Tindall.

Lecours, A. R., Poncet, M., Ponzio, J., & Ramade-Poncet, M. (1983) Classification of the aphasias. In A. R. Lecours, F. Lhermitte, & B. Bryans (Eds.), *Aphasiology*. London: Baillière Tindall.

Lee, L. L. (1969) *Northwestern syntax screening test*. Evanston, Illinois: Northwestern University Press.

Leischner, A. (1955) Beziehungen der Aphasie-Forschung zur Linguistik. *Sprachforum, 1*, 283–287.

Leischner, A. (1959) Behandlung der Aphasie. *Schweizierisches Medizinisches Wochenschrift, 89*, 242–269.

Leischner, A. (1960) Zur Symptomatologie und Therapie der Aphasien. *Nervenartzt, 31*, 60–67.

Leischner, A. (1972) Über den Verlauf und die Einteilung der aphasischen Syndrome. *Archiv für Psychiatrie und Nervenkrankheiten, 216*, 219–231.

Leischner, A. (1976) Aptitude of aphasics for language treatment. In Y. Lebrun & R. Hoops (Eds.), *Recovery in aphasics*. Amsterdam: Swets & Zeitlinger.

Lesser, R. (1978) *Linguistic investigations of aphasia*. London: Arnold.

Levelt, W. M. (1983) Monitoring and self-repair in speech. *Cognition, 14*, 41–104.

Lhermitte, F., & Ducarne, B. (1965) La rééducation des aphasiques. *Revue du Practicien, 15*, 2345–2363.

Lichtheim, L. (1885) Ueber Aphasie. *Deutsches Archiv für klinischer Medizin, 36*, 204–268. Translated as On aphasia. (1885) *Brain, 7*, 433–485.

Liepmann, H. (1900) *Das Krankheitsbild der Apraxie ("motorischen Asymbolie")*. Berlin: Karger.

Liles, B. Z., & Brookshire, R. H. (1975) The effects of pause time on auditory comprehension of aphasic subjects. *Journal of Communication Disorders, 8*, 221–235.

Lincoln, N. B. (1985) Recovery from dysphasia. In S. K. Newman & R. Epstein (Eds.), *Current perspectives in dysphasia*. Edinburgh: Churchill Livingstone.

Lincoln, N. B., McGuirk, E., Mulley, G. P., Lendrem, W., Jones, A. C., & Mitchell, J. R.A. (1984) Effectiveness of speech therapy for aphasic stroke patients: a randomised controlled trial. *Lancet, 1*, 1197–1200.

Linebaugh, C. W., & Young-Charles, H. Y. (1978) Counseling needs of aphasic patients. In R. H. Brookshire (Ed.), *Clinical Aphasiology Conference Proceedings 1978*. Minneapolis: BRK.

Linebaugh, C. W., & Young-Charles, H. Y. (1981) Confidence ratings in aphasic patients' functional communication: spouses and speech-language pathologists. In R. H. Brookshire (Ed.), *Clinical Aphasiology Conference Proceedings 1981*. Minneapolis: BRK.

Love, R.. J., & Webb, W. G. (1977) The efficacy of cueing techniques in Broca's aphasia. *Journal of Speech and Hearing Disorders, 42*, 170–178.

Luria, A. R. (1947) *Travmaticheskaya afazia*. Moscow: Izd. Akad. Ped. Nauk. RSFSR. English translation by D. Bowden (1970) *Traumatic aphasia*. The Hague: Mouton.

Luria, A. R. (1948) *Vosstanovlenie funktsii mozga posle traumy*. Moscow: Medgiz. Translated by B. Haigh (1963) *Restoration of function after brain injury*. Oxford: Pergamon.

Luria, A. R. (1962) *Vysshie korkovye funktsii cheloveka*. Moscow: Izd. Univ. English Translation by B. Haigh (1966) *Higher cortical functions in man*. London: Tavistock.

Luria, A. R. (1966) L. S. Vygotsky and the problem of functional localisation (Russian). *Voprosy Psikhologii, 12*, 56–61. Translated in M. Cole (Ed.) (1978) *The selected writings of A. R. Luria*. White Plains, Nebraska: Merle Sharpe.

Luria, A. R. (1973) *The working brain*. Translated by B. Haigh. Harmondsworth: Penguin.

Luria, A. R. (1975) *Osnovnye Problemy Neirolingvistiki*. Moscow: Izd. Univ. English translation by B. Haigh (1976) *Basic problems of neurolinguistics*. The Hague: Mouton.

Luria, A. R. (1979) *The making of mind: a personal account of Soviet psychology*. Edited by M. Cole & S. Cole. Cambridge, Massachussetts: Harvard University Press.

MacLeod, E. (1945) Speech therapy in England and America. *Speech, 9*, 10–12.

Marie, P. (1888) De l'aphasie en général et de l'agraphie en particulier, d'après l'enseignement de M. le Professeur Charcot. *Progrès Medicale, 7*, 81–84.

Marie, P. (1906) La troisième circonvolution frontale gauche ne joue aucun rôle spécial dans la fonction du langage. *Semaine Médicale 26*, 241–247.

Marshall, J. C. (1982a) Models of the mind in health and disease. In A. W. Ellis (Ed.) *Normality and pathology in cognitive functions*. London: Academic Press.

Marshall, J. C. (1982b) What is a symptom-complex? In M. A. Arbib, D. Caplan, & J. C. Marshall (Eds.), *Neural models of language processes*. New York: Academic Press.

Marshall, J. C. (1986) The description and interpretation of aphasic language disorder. *Neuropsychologia, 24*, 5–24.

Marshall, J. C., & Newcombe, F. (1966) Syntactic and semantic errors in paralexia. *Neuropsychologia, 4*, 169–176.

Marshall, J. C., & Newcombe, F. (1973) Patterns of paralexia. *Journal of Psycholinguistic Research, 2*, 175–199.

Marshall, J. C., Holmes, J. M., & Newcombe, F. (1975) Fact and theory in recovery from the aphasias. In CIBA Foundation Symposium 34. *Outcome of severe damage to the nervous system*. Amsterdam: Elsevier.

Marshall, R. C. (1976) Word retrieval behaviour of aphasic adults. *Journal of Speech and Hearing Disorders, 41*, 444–451.

Marshall, R. C., & King, P. S. (1973) Effects of fatigue produced by isokinetic exercise on the communicative ability of aphasic adults. *Journal of Speech and Hearing Research, 16*, 222–230.

Marshall, R. C., & Tompkins, C. (1981) Identifying behaviour associated with verbal self-corrections of aphasic adults. *Journal of Speech and Hearing Disorders, 46*, 168–173.

Marshall, R. C., & Tompkins, C. (1982) Verbal self-correction behaviours of fluent and non-fluent aphasic subjects. *Brain and Language, 15*, 292–306.

Marshall, R. C., & Watts, M. (1976) Relaxation training: effects on the communicative ability of aphasic adults. *Archives of Physical Medicine and Rehabilitation, 57*, 464–467.

Martin, A. D. (1981a) An examination of Wepman's thought centred therapy. In R. Chapey (Ed.), *Language intervention strategies in adult aphasia*. Baltimore: Williams & Wilkins.

Martin, A. D. (1981b) Therapy with the jargon aphasic. In J. W. Brown (Ed.), *Jargonaphasia*. New York: Academic Press.

Maruszewski, M. (1975) *Language, communication and the brain*. The Hague: Mouton.

Massa, N. (1558) *Epistolarum medicinalium. Volume II*. Venice.

McReynolds, L. V., & Kearns, K. P. (1982) *Single subject experimental designs in communicative disorders*. Baltimore: University Park Press.

Mehler, J., Morton, J., & Jusczyk, P. W. (1984) On reducing language to biology. *Cognitive Neuropsychology, 1*, 83–116.

Meikle, M., Wechsler, E., Tupper, A., Benenson, M., Butler, J., Mulhall, D., & Stern, G. (1979) Comparative trial of volunteer and professional treatments of dysphasia after stroke. *British Medical Journal, 2*, 87–89.

Meuse, S., & Marquardt, T. P. (1985) Communicative effectiveness in Broca's aphasia. *Journal of Communication Disorders, 18*, 21–34.

Miceli, G., Silveri, M. C., Villa, G., & Caramazza, A. (1984) On the basis of the agrammatic's difficulty in producing main verbs. *Cortex, 20*, 207–220.

Michel, F. (1979) Préservation du langage écrit malgré un déficit majeur du langage oral. *Lyon Médical, 241*, 141–149.

Mierzejewska, H. (Ed.) (1978) *Badania lingwistyczne nad afazja*. Warsaw: Ossolineum.

Miller, E. (1984) *Recovery and management of neuropsychological impairments*. Chichester: Wiley.

Mills, C. K. (1904) Treatment of aphasia by training. *Journal of the American Medical Association, 43*, 1940–1949.

Mills, R. H. (1982) Microcomputerised auditory comprehension training. In R. H. Brookshire (Ed.), *Clinical Aphasiology Conference Proceedings 1982*. Minneapolis: BRK.

Moody, E. J. (1982) Sign language acquisition by a global aphasic. *Journal of Nervous and Mental Disorders, 170*, 113–116.

Morton, J., & Patterson, K. E. (1980) A new attempt at an interpretation, or, an attempt at a new interpretation. In M. Coltheart, K. E. Patterson, & J. C. Marshall (Eds.), *Deep dyslexia*. London: Routledge & Kegan Paul.

Moyer, S. B. (1979) Rehabilitation of alexia: a case study. *Cortex, 15*, 139–144.

Moutier, F. (1908) *L'aphasie de Broca*. Paris: Steinheil.

Myerson, R., & Goodglass, H. (1972) Transformational grammars of three agrammatic patients. *Language and Speech, 15*, 40–50.

Naeser, M. A. (1974) A structured approach to teaching aphasics basic sentence types. *British Journal of Disorders of Communication, 9*, 70–76.

Newcombe, F., & Marshall, J. C. (1980) Transcoding and lexical stabilisation in deep dyslexia. In M. Coltheart, K. E. Patterson, & J. C. Marshall (Eds.), *Deep dyslexia*. London: Routledge & Kegan Paul.

Newcombe, F., Oldfield, R. C., & Wingfield, A. (1964) Object naming by dysphasic patients. *Nature, 207*, 1217–1218.

Newcombe, F., Hiorns, R. W., Marshall, J. C., & Adams, C. B. T. (1975) Acquired dyslexia: patterns of deficit and recovery. In CIBA Foundation Symposium 34, *Outcome of severe damage to the nervous system*. Amsterdam: Elsevier.

Nielson, J. (1946) *Agnosia, apraxia, aphasia*. New York: Hoeber.

Packman, A., & Ingham, R. J. (1977) Contingency management in the treatment of adult aphasia: a review. *Australian Journal of Human Communication Disorders, 5*, 110–118.

Panse, F., Kandler, G., & Leischner, A. (1952) *Klinische und sprachwissenschäftliche Untersuchungen zum Agrammatismus*. Stuttgart: Thieme.

Paré, A. (1628) *Oevres*. Paris. First edition 1585.

Patterson, K. E., & Kay, J. (1982) Letter-by-letter reading: Psychological descriptions of a neurological syndrome. *Quarterly Journal of Experimental Psychology, 34A*, 411–442.

Patterson, K. E., & Shewell, C. (1987) Speak and spell: dissociations and word class effects. In M. Coltheart, R. Job, & G. Sartori (Eds.), *The cognitive neuropsychology of language*. London: Lawrence Erlbaum Associates Ltd.

Patterson, K. E., Marshall, J. C., & Coltheart, M. (1986) *Surface dyslexia: neuropsychological and cognitive analyses of phonological reading*. London: Lawrence Erlbaum Associates Ltd.

Patterson, K. E., Purell, C., & Morton, J. (1983) The facilitation of naming in aphasia. In C. Code & D. J. Muller (Eds.), *Aphasia therapy*. London: Edward Arnold.

Pavlov, I. P. (1949) *Complete collected works, vols 1—6*. Moscow: Izd. Akad. Nauk. (Russian).

Peacher, W. G., & Peacher, G. M. (1948) Management of speech disorders in a hospital clinic. *Disorders of the Nervous System, 9*, 3–9.

Pease, D. M., & Goodglass, H. (1978) The effects of cueing on picture naming in aphasia. *Cortex, 14*, 178–189.

Perello, J. (1976) *The history of the International Association of Logopaedics and Phoniatrics 1924–1976*. Barcelona: Editorial Augusta.

Peterson, L. N., & Kirshner, H. S. (1981) Gestural impairment and gestural ability in aphasia: a review. *Brain and Language, 14*, 333–348.

Peuser, G. (1974) Le role du linguiste dans une clinique d'aphasiologie. *Le Langage et L'Homme, 24*, 24–29.

Peuser, G. (1978) *Aphasie: eine Einführung in die Patholinguistik*. Munich: Fink.

Pick, A. (1898) *Beitrage zur Pathologie und pathologischen Anatomie des Zentralnervensystems, mit Bemerkungen zur normalen Anatomie desselben*. Berlin: Karger.

Pick, A. (1913) *Die agrammatischen Sprachstoerungen*. Berlin: Springer.

Pizzamiglio, L., & Roberts, M. M. (1967) Writing in aphasia: a learning study. *Cortex, 3*, 250–257.

Plinius Secundus Caius (Pliny the Elder) (no date) *Historia Naturalis*. Translated by H. Rackham (1942) *Natural history*. Cambridge, Massachussetts: Loeb.

Podraza, B. L., & Darley, F. L. (1977) Effect of auditory pre-stimulation on naming in aphasia. *Journal of Speech and Hearing Research, 20*, 669–683.

Poeck, K., Huber, W., Kerschensteiner, M., Stachowiak, F-J., & Weniger, D. (1977) Therapie der Aphasien. *Nervenartzt, 48*, 119–126.

Poppelreuter, W. (1917) *Die psychischen Schaedigungen durch Kopfschuss*. Leipzig: Voss.

Porch, B. E. (1971) *Porch Index of Communicative Ability*. Palo Alto, California: Consulting Psychologists Press.

Potter, R. E., & Goodman, N. J. (1983) The implementation of laughter as a therapy facilitator with adult aphasics. *Journal of Communication Disorders, 16*, 41–48.

Pring, T. R. (1983) Speech therapists and volunteers: some comments on recent investigations of their effectiveness in the treatment of aphasia. *British Journal of Disorders of Communication, 18*, 65–73.

Pring, T. R. (1986) Evaluating the effects of speech therapy for aphasics and volunteers: developing the single case methodology. *British Journal of Disorders of Communication, 21*, 103–115.

Prinz, P. M. (1980) A note on requesting strategies in adult aphasics. *Journal of Communication Disorders, 13*, 65–73.

Reason, J., & Lucas, D. (1984) Using cognitive diaries to investigate naturally occurring memory blocks. In J. E. Harris & P. E. Morris (Eds.), *Everyday memory, actions and absent-mindedness*. London: Academic Press.

Rieger, C. (1888) *Bieschriebung der Intelligenzstoerungen in Folge Hirnverletztung*. Wurzburg: Stahel'sche Universitäts Buch- und Kunsthandlung.

Rochford, G., & Williams, M. (1962) Studies in the development and breakdown of the use of names. I: The relationship between nominal dysphasia and the acquisition of vocabulary in childhood. *Journal of Neurology, Neurosurgery and Psychiatry, 25*, 222–227.

Rochford, G., & Williams, M. (1965) Studies in the development and breakdown of the use of names. IV: The effects of word frequency. *Journal of Neurology, Neurosurgery and Psychiatry, 28*, 407–413.

Rohricht, J., Springer, L., & Weniger, D. (1978) Therapie der globalen Aphasie. *Sprache-Stimme-Gehör, 3*, 96–98.

Rommel, P. (1683) *De aphonia rara*. Cited by Gans, 1914.

Rosenburg, B. (1965) The performance of aphasics on automated visuo-perceptual discrimination training and transfer tasks. *Journal of Speech and Hearing Research, 8*, 165–181.

Rosenburg, B., & Edwards, A. E. (1964) The performance of aphasics on three automated perceptual discrimination programmes. *Journal of Speech and Hearing Research, 7*, 295–298.

Rosenburg, B., & Edwards, A. E. (1965) An automated multiple response alternative training programme for use with aphasics. *Journal of Speech and Hearing Research, 8*, 415–419.

Royall, J. B., & Horner, J. (1983) Acquisition and generalisation of cued speech by a chronically aphasic patient. In R. H. Brookshire (Ed.), *Clinical aphasiology conference proceedings 1983*. Minneapolis: BRK.

Saffran, E. M., Schwartz, M. F., & Marin, O. S. M. (1980) The word order problem in agrammatism. II: Production. *Brain and Language, 10*, 263–280.

Salvatore, A. P., Trunzo, M. J., Holtzapple, P., & Graham, L. (1983) Investigating the sentence hierarchy of the Helm Elicited Language Program for Syntax Stimulation. In R. H. Brookshire (Ed.), *Clinical aphasiology conference proceedings 1983*. Minneapolis: BRK.

Sarno, J., Sarno, M. T., & Levita, E. (1971) Evaluating language improvement after completed stroke. *Archives of Physical Medicine and Rehabilitation, 52*, 73–78.

Sarno, M. T. (1969) *The functional communication profile*. New York: Institute of Rehabilitation Medicine, New York University Medical Centre.

Sarno, M. T. (1981) Recovery and rehabilitation in aphasia. In M. T. Sarno (Ed.), *Acquired aphasia*. New York: Academic Press.

Sarno, M. T., & Sands, E. (1970) An objective method for the evaluation of speech therapy in aphasia. *Archives of Physical Medicine and Rehabilitation, 51*, 49–54.

Sarno, M. T., Silverman, M., & Sands, E. (1970) Speech therapy and language recovery in severe aphasia. *Journal of Speech and Hearing Research, 13*, 607–623.

Schenk von Grafenberg, J. (Schenkius) (1644) *Observationum medicarum rariorum. Book VII.* Lugduni. First edition 1585.

Schlanger, P., & Freiman, R. (1979) Pantomime therapy with aphasics. *Aphasia, Apraxia and Agnosia, 1*, 34–39.

Schmidt, J. (Schmidtius) (1676) Observatio CLIV: de oblivione lectionis ex apoplexia salva scriptione. *Miscellanea curiose medico-physica academiae naturae curiosum. Vol IV/IX.* Cited by Bernard, 1885.

Schuell, H. M. (1953) Aphasic difficulties in understanding spoken language. *Neurology, 3*, 176–184.

Schuell, H. M. (1965) *Differential diagnosis of aphasia with the Minnesota Test.* Minneapolis: University of Minnesota Press.

Schuell, H. M. (1970) Aphasia in adults. In NINDS Monographs 10, *Human communication and its disorders.* Washington: US Department of Health, Education and Welfare. (Quoted by Eisenson, 1977).

Schuell, H. M., & Jenkins, J. J. (1961) Reduction of vocabulary in aphasia. *Brain, 84*, 243–261.

Schuell, H. M., Caroll, V. B., & Street, B. S. (1955) Clinical treatment of aphasia. *Journal of Speech and Hearing Disorders, 20*, 43–53.

Schuell, H. M., Jenkins, J. J., & Caroll, J. B. (1962) A factor analysis of the Minnesota Test for differential diagnosis of aphasia. *Journal of Speech and Hearing Research, 5*, 349–369.

Schuell, H. M., Jenkins, J. J., & Jimenez-Pabon, E. (1964) *Aphasia in adults: diagnosis, prognosis and treatment.* New York: Harper & Row.

Schwartz, L., Nemeroff, S., & Reiss, M. (1974) An investigation of writing therapy for the adult aphasic: the word level. *Cortex, 10*, 278–283.

Schwartz, M. F., Saffran, E. M., & Marin, O. S. M. (1980) The word order problem in agrammatism. I: Comprehension. *Brain and Language, 10*, 249–262.

Sechenov, I. M. (1891) *Fiziologia nervnykh tsentrov.* (Physiology of the nervous centres.) 2nd edition 1952. Moscow: Izd. Akad. Med. Nauk. (Russian).

Sechenov, I. M. (1962) *Selected physiological and psychological works.* English translation by S. Belsky. Moscow: Foreign Language Publishing House.

Seron, X. (1979) *Aphasie et neuropsychologie: approches thérapeutiques.* Brussels: Mardaga.

Seron, X., Deloche, G., Moulard, G., & Rousselle, M. (1980) A computer based therapy for the treatment of aphasic subjects with writing disorders. *Journal of Speech and Hearing Disorders, 45*, 45–58.

Seron, X., Deloche, G., Bastard, V., Chassin, G., & Hermand, N. (1979) Word finding difficulties and learning transfer in aphasic patients. *Cortex, 15*, 149–155.

Shallice, T. (1979) The case study approach in neuropsychological research. *Journal of Clinical Neuropsychology, 1*, 183–211.

Shallice, T. (1987) Impairments in semantic processing: multiple dissociations. In M. Coltheart, R. Job, & G. Sartori (Eds)., *The cognitive neuropsychology of language.* London: Lawrence Erlbaum Associates Ltd.

Shallice, T., & Butterworth, B. L. (1977) Short term memory impairment and spontaneous speech. *Neuropsychologia, 15*, 729–735.

Shallice, T., & Warrington, E. K. (1977) Auditory-verbal short term memory and conduction aphasia. *Brain and Language, 4*, 479–491.

Shallice, T., & Warrington, E. K. (1980) Single and multiple component central dyslexic syndromes. In M. Coltheart, K. E. Patterson, & J. C. Marshall (Eds.), *Deep dyslexia..* London: Routledge & Kegan Paul.

Sharpey, W. (1879) The re-education of the adult brain. *Brain, 2*, 1–9.

Sheehan, V. M. (1946) Rehabilitation of aphasics in an army hospital. *Journal of Speech and Hearing Disorders, 11*, 149–157.

Shewan, C. M. (1976) Facilitating sentence formulation: a case study. *Journal of Communication Disorders, 9*, 191–197.

Shewan, C. M. (1986) The history and efficacy of aphasia treatment. In R. Chapey (Ed.), *Language intervention strategies in adult aphasia.* 2nd edition. Baltimore: Williams & Wilkins.

Shewan, C. M., & Bandur, D. L. (1986) *Treatment of aphasia: a language-oriented approach.* London: Taylor & Francis.

Shewan, C. M., & Kertesz, A. (1984) Effects of speech and language treatment on recovery from aphasia. *Brain and Language, 23*, 272–299.

Sidman, M. (1971) The behavioural analysis of aphasia. *Journal of Psychiatric Research, 8*, 413–422.

Sidman, M., Stoddard, L. T., Mohr, J. P., & Leicester, J. (1971) Behavioural studies of aphasia: methods of investigation and analysis. *Neuropsychologia, 9*, 119–140.

Singer, H. D., & Low, A. A. (1933) The brain in a case of motor aphasia in which improvement occurred with training. *Archives of Neurology and Psychiatry, 29,* 162–165.

Skelly, M. (1979) *Amerind gestural code based on universal American Indian hand talk.* New York: Elsevier North-Holland.

Skelly, M., Schinsky, L., Smith, R., & Fust, R. (1974) American Indian Sign (Amerind) as a facilitator of verbalisation for the oral-verbal apraxic. *Journal of Speech and Hearing Disorders, 39*, 445–456.

Skinner, B. F. (1938) *The behaviour of organisms.* New York: Appleton-Century-Crofts.

Skinner, B. F. (1957) *Verbal behaviour.* New York: Appleton-Century-Crofts.

Skinner, C., Wirz, S., Thompson, I., & Davidson, J. (1984) *Edinburgh Functional Communication Profile: an observation procedure for the evaluation of disordered communication in elderly patients.* Winslow, Buckinghamshire: Winslow Press.

Smith, A. (1972) *Diagnosis, intelligence and rehabilitation of chronic aphasia: final report.* Ann Arbor, Michigan: University of Michigan.

Smith, M. D. (1974) Operant conditioning of syntax in aphasia. *Neuropsychologia, 12*, 403–405.

Somerville, J. G. (1974) Rebuilding the stroke patient's life. *Nursing Mirror, 139*, 57–58.

Soury, J. (1899) *Le système nerveux central: structure et fonctions: histoire critique des théories et des doctrines.* Paris: Carré et Naud.

Sparks, R. (1978) Parastandardised examination guidelines for adult aphasia. *British Journal of Disorders of Communication, 13*, 135–146.

Sparks, R., & Holland, A. (1976) Method: melodic intonation therapy for aphasia. *Journal of Speech and Hearing Disorders, 41*, 287–297.

Sparks, R., Helm, N., & Albert, M. (1974) Aphasia rehabilitation resulting from melodic intonation therapy. *Cortex, 10*, 303–316.

Spreen, O., & Benton, A. (1969) *Neurosensory centre comprehensive examination for aphasia.* Victoria, British Columbia: Department of Psychology, University of Victoria.

Springer, L., & Weniger, D. (1980) Aphasietherapie aus logopädischlinguistischer Sicht. In G. Bohme (Ed.), *Therapie der Sprach-, Sprech- und Stimmstoerungen.* Stuttgart: Fischer.

Steinthal, H. (1871) *Einleitung in die Psychologie und Sprachwissenschaft.* Berlin: Harrwitz & Gossmann.

Stoicheff, M. L. (1960) Motivating instructions and language performance of dysphasic subjects. *Journal of Speech and Hearing Research, 3*, 75–85.

Taylor, M. L. (1965) A measure of functional communication in aphasia. *Archives of Physical Medicine and Rehabilitation, 46*, 101–107.

Taylor, M. L., & Marks, M. (1955) *Manual and workbook.* New York: Institute for Physical Medicine and Rehabilitation.

Thompson, C. K., McReynolds, L. V., & Vance, C. E. (1982) Generative use of locatives in multiword utterances in agrammatism: a matrix-training approach. In R. H. Brookshire (Ed.), *Clinical Aphasiology Conference Proceedings 1982*. Minneapolis: BRK.

Thorndike, E. L. (1927) *The teacher's word book*. New York: Teachers' College, Columbia University.

Tikovsky, R. S., & Reynolds, G. L. (1962) Preliminary study: non-verbal learning and aphasia. *Journal of Speech and Hearing Research, 5*, 133–143.

Tikovsky, R. S., & Reynolds, G. L. (1963) Further studies of non-verbal learning and aphasia. *Journal of Speech and Hearing Research, 6*, 329–337.

Tissot, R., Mounin, G., & Lhermitte, F. (1973) *L'agrammatisme: étude neurolinguistique*. Brussels: Dessart.

Tompkins, C. A., Marshall, R. C., & Phillips, D. S. (1980) Aphasic patients in a rehabilitation program: scheduling speech and language services. *Archives of Physical Medicine and Rehabilitation, 61*, 252–254.

Tonkonogii, I. M. (1968) *Insult i afaziya*. (Cerebral insult and aphasia.) Leningrad: Izd. Meditsina. (Russian).

Tonkonogii, I. M. (1973) *Vredenie v klinicheskuyu neiropsikhologiyu*. (Introduction to clinical neuropsychology.) Leningrad: Izd. Meditsina. (Russian).

Trousseau, A. (1861) *Clinique Médicale de l'Hôtel-Dieu de Paris*. Volume II. 6th edition. Paris: Baillière 1882.

Trousseau, A. (1864) De l'aphasie, maladie décrite récemment sous le nom impropre d'aphémie. *Gazette des Hôpitaux, 37*, 13–14, 25–26, 37–39, 49–50.

Trubetzkoy, N. S. (1939) Grundzüge der Phonologie. *Travaux du Cercle Linguistique de Prague, 7*.

Tsvetskova, L. S., & Glozman, Z. M. (1975) 1. A neurolinguistic analysis of expressive agrammatism in different forms of aphasia. 2. On one type of agrammatism in aphasia. *Linguistics, 154/155*, 77–90.

Tsvetkova, L. S. (1980) Some ways of optimisation of aphasics' rehabilitation. *International Journal of Rehabilitation Research, 3*, 183–190.

Ulatowska, H. K., & Richardson, S. M. (1974) A longitudinal study of an adult with aphasia: considerations for research and therapy. *Brain and Language, 1*, 151–166.

Ustvedt, H. J. (1937) Ueber die Untersuchung der musikalen Funktionen bei Patienten mit Gehirnleiden besonders die Patienten mit Aphasia. *Acta Medica Scandanavica (Supplement), 86*, 1–7.

Vallar, G., & Baddeley, A. D. (1984) Phonological short term store, phonological processing and sentence comprehension: a neuropsychological case study. *Cognitive Neuropsychology, 1*, 121–142.

Vargha, M., & Gereb, G. (1959) *Aphasie-Therapie*. Jena: Fischer Verlag.

Vignolo, L. A. (1964) Evolution of aphasia and language rehabilitation: a restrospective exploratory study. *Cortex, 1*, 344–367.

Vinarskaya, E. N. (1971) *Klinicheskie problemy afazii: neirolingvisticheskii analiz*. (Clinical problems of aphasia: neurolinguistic analysis.) Moscow: Izd. Meditsina. (Russian)

Voinescu, I. (1971) Syntactic complexity in aphasics. *Revue Roumaine de Neurologie, 8*, 69–80.

Voinescu, I., Dobrata, I., & Gheorgita, N. (1971) Psychotherapeutic aspects of rehabilitation in aphasia. *Revue Roumaine de Neurologie, 9*, 387–401.

von Monakow, C. (1914) *Die Lokalisation im Grosshirn und die Abbau der Funktion durch kortikale Herde*. Wiesbaden: Bergmann.

Vygotsky, L. S. (1962) *Thought and language*. Translated by E. Hanfmann, & G. Vakar. Cambridge, Massachussetts: MIT Press. (First Russian edition, 1934.)

Wade, D. T., Hewer, R. L., Skilbeck, C. E., & David, R. M. (1985) *Stroke: a critical approach to diagnosis, treatment, management*. London: Chapman & Hall.

Wales, R., & Kinsella, G. (1981) Syntactic effects in sentence completion by Broca's aphasics. *Brain and Language, 13*, 301–307.

Wapner, W., & Gardner, H. (1979) A note on patterns of comprehension and recovery in global aphasia. *Journal of Speech and Hearing Research, 22*, 765–772.

Watamori, T. S., & Sasanuma, S. (1976) The recovery process of a bilingual aphasic. *Journal of Communication Disorders, 9*, 157–176.

Watamori T. S., & Sasanuma, S. (1978) The recovery processes of two English–Japanese bilingual aphasics. *Brain and Language, 6*, 127–140.

Watson, J. B. (1914) *Behaviour: an introduction to comparative psychology.* New York: Holt.

Weidner, W. E., & Lasky, E. Z. (1976) The interaction of rate and complexity of stimulus on the performance of adult aphasic subjects. *Brain and Language, 3*, 34–40.

Weigl, E. (1961) The phenomenon of temporary deblocking in aphasia. *Zeitschrift für Phonetik, Sprachwissenschaft und Kommunikationsforschung, 14*, 337–364.

Weigl, E. (1970) A neuropsychological contribution to the problem of semantics. In M. Bierwisch & K. E. Heidolph (Eds.), *Progress in linguistics.* The Hague: Mouton.

Weigl, E. (1979) Neurolinguistische Untersuchungen zum semantischen Gedächtnis. In M. Bierwisch (Ed.), *Psychologische Effeckte sprächlicher Strukturkomponenten.* Berlin: Akademie Verlag.

Weigl, E. (1980) *Neuropsychology and neurolinguistics: selected papers.* The Hague: Mouton.

Weigl, E., & Bierwisch, M. (1970) Neuropsychology and linguistics: topics of common research. *Foundations of Language, 6*, 1–18.

Weigl, E., & Kreindler, A. (1960) Beitrage zur Auffassung gewisser aphasische Störungen als Blockierungserscheinungen. *Archiv für Psychiatrie und Zeitschrift für die gesamte Neurologie, 200*, 306–323.

Weisenburg, T. H., & McBride, K. E. (1935) *Aphasia: a clinical and psychological study.* New York: The Commonwealth Fund.

Weniger, D., Huber, W., Stachowiak, F-J., & Poeck, K. (1980) Treatment of aphasia on a linguistic basis. In M. T. Sarno & O. Höök (Eds.), *Aphasia: assessment and treatment.* Stockholm: Almquist, & Wiksell.

Wepman, J. M. (1951) *Recovery from aphasia.* New York: Ronald.

Wepman, J. M. (1953) A conceptual model for the processes involved in recovery from aphasia. *Journal of Speech and Hearing Disorders, 18*, 4–13.

Wepman, J. M. (1958a) Aphasia and the "whole-person" concept. *American Archives of Rehabilitation and Therapy, 6*, 1–7.

Wepman, J. M. (1958b) The relationship between self-correction and recovery from aphasia. *Journal of Speech and Hearing Disorders, 23*, 302–305.

Wepman, J. M. (1972) Aphasia therapy: a new look. *Journal of Speech and Hearing Disorders, 37*, 203–214.

Wernicke, C. (1874) *Der aphasischer Symptomenkomplex: eine psychologische Studie auf anatomischer Basis.* Breslau: Cohn & Weigert. Translated by G. H. Eggert (1977) in *Wernick's works on aphasia: a sourcebook and review.* The Hague: Mouton.

Wernicke, C. (1906) Der aphasicher Symptomenkomplex. *Die deutsche Klinik am Eingänge des 20 Jahrhunderts, 6*, 487. Translated by G. H. Eggert (1977) in *Wernicke's works on aphasia: a sourcebook and review.* The Hague: Mouton.

Wertz, R. T., Lapointe, L. L., & Rosenbek, J. C. (1984) *Apraxia of speech in adults.* Orlando, Florida: Grune & Stratton.

Wertz, R. T., Collins, M. J., Weiss, D. G., & 12 others (1981) Veterans administration cooperative study on aphasia: a comparison of individual and group treatment. *Journal of Speech and Hearing Research, 24*, 580–594.

Wertz, R. T., Weiss, D. G., Aten, J. L., & 13 others (1986) Comparison of clinic, home and deferred language treatment for aphasia. *Archives of Neurology, 43*, 653–658.

Whitaker, H. A. (1971) *On the representation of language in the human brain.* Edmonton: Linguistic Research.

Wiegel-Crump, C. A. (1976) Agrammatism and aphasia. In Y. Lebrun & R. Hoops (Eds.), *Recovery in aphasics.* Amsterdam: Swets & Zeitlinger.

Wiegel-Crump, C., & Koenigsknecht, R. A. (1973) Tapping the lexical store of the adult aphasic: analysis of the improvement made in word retrieval skills. *Cortex, 9*, 411–418.

Willcox, M. J., Davis, G. A., & Leonard, L. B. (1978) Aphasics' comprehension of contextually conveyed meaning. *Brain and Language, 6*, 362–377.

Willmes, K., & Poeck, K. (1984) Ergebnisse einer multizentrischen untersuchung über die spontanprognose von aphasien vaskulärer ätiologie. *Nervenartzt, 55*, 62–71.

Wyllie, J. (1894) *The disorders of speech.* Edinburgh: Oliver & Boyd.

Young, R. M. (1970) *Mind, brain and adaptation in the nineteenth century.* Oxford: Clarendon.

Zangwill, O. L. (1947) Psychology, speech therapy and rehabilitation. *Speech, 11*, 4–8.

Subject Index

Author Index